The Later Cantos of
EZRA POUND

The gondola bearing the coffin of Ezra Pound across the Venice lagoon to the tranquil island cemetery of San Michele.

(Courtesy, Wide World Photos)

The Later Cantos of
EZRA POUND

by James J. Wilhelm

WALKER AND COMPANY
New York

For
WILSON RANDOLPH GATHINGS
*in the grand line
of John of Roanoke
and Mr. Jefferson*

The Later Cantos of
EZRA POUND

Contents

Acknowledgments

Grateful acknowledgment is made to New Directions Publishing Corporation of New York City and to Faber & Faber of London to quote from the works of Ezra Pound. Full details of these editions are given in the Bibliography at the end of the book. In quotations from *The Cantos*, I use the 1972 New Directions edition and the 1976 Faber edition, which now has the same pagination as the American; the Faber edition, however, lacks Canto 120 (see note 15 to Introduction).

A portion of the fourth chapter appeared in *Paideuma*, vol. 2, no. 2, under the title "Two Heavens of Light and Love," and Chapter Twelve was published in *Paideuma*, vol. 2, no. 3, both in a somewhat different form; these are reprinted here with the permission of the National Poetry Foundation and the University of Maine Press. Chapter Five appeared in *Twentieth Century Literature*, vol. 20, no. 2, under the title "The Dragon and the Duel: A Defense of Pound's Canto 88," and is reprinted here in an emended form with the permission of Hofstra University Press.

In the text, I follow Pound exactly, using *sic* for only the most obvious of his errors. I have taken the liberty of transliterating all Greek into the Latin alphabet, since many readers are unfamiliar with the Greek alphabet and therefore unable to pronounce the *sounds*, which are extremely important. I include glosses in the right margins for words that I consider troublesome, as well as some explanatory notes. I transcribe Pound's Greek almost exactly as he wrote it, noting egregious errors and making a few minor emendations.

My own work on Pound can be dated back to my undergraduate years at Yale University in the fifties, when I studied with Norman Holmes Pearson and worked in the Yale Collection of American Literature under Donald Gallup. However, I did not really develop my interest until I began teaching medieval literature at Rutgers University, where I had the good fortune to have Siegfried de Rachewiltz, Pound's grandson, in my classes, and the further good luck to be visited by Mary de Rachewiltz in my Provençal seminars. The renewed interest in Pound in the 1960s was especially evident at Rutgers, where I have had many stimulating conversations with such colleagues as George Kearns, Andrew Welsh, Nathaniel Tarn, Wendy Stallard Flory, and Steven Helmling.

Like others interested in Pound, I owe an enormous debt to Carroll F. Terrell, who has advanced all of our knowledge by founding *Paideuma,* an indispensable tool not just for Pound, but for modern poetry in general. As for the preparation of this book, I am indebted to Dale Demy for performing a myriad of useful tasks and to Dong-Sheng Yang for drawing most of the Chinese characters. I must also acknowledge the constant help, financial and otherwise, from Fred Main and the Rutgers Research Council. Joan Hart and Gerrit Lansing lent constant encouragement with their enthusiasm. In addition, I must thank Daniel Karp for his firm and steady critical assistance; Nancy J. Clements for her copy-editing skills; Fran Palminteri and George Vornlocker for their technical and creative contributions to the production of this book; Andrea Curley for her managerial expertise in coordinating the many phases that made this work a physical reality; and my good friend and editor, Wilson Randolph Gathings, whose courage in promoting quality in publications is matched only by his intelligence and wit.

Foreword

At a time when most of the difficult works of the major artists of this century have been fully explicated, Pound's *Cantos* remain to a large extent unexplored. There have been more than enough books recently on Pound's lyric poetry, and some books have touched on the earlier parts of *The Cantos* rather fully, but the later, more complex, sections of the poem, which demand much from the reader, have not been adequately examined. This book is a step toward filling that lack.

The work is not intended, in any sense, to be a complete guide. I touch on the major areas, but the field is too vast to be covered by any one person. Therefore, I restrict myself to what I know the best or like the most. There are three specific areas of the Later Cantos that I do not approach, largely because they have already been dealt with in excellent articles in *Paideuma* magazine; these are the Chinese *History Classic* cantos (85 and 86), analyzed by Thomas Grieve in vol. 4, nos. 2-3, pp. 361-479; the Coke, or English law, cantos (107-09), explicated at length by David Gordon in the same volume, pp. 223-99; and the Alexander del Mar canto (97), covered by Daniel Pearlman in vol. 1, no. 2, pp. 161-80, and supplemented by Steven Helmling in vol. 5, no. 1, pp. 53-57. A reader who is seeking a complete gloss will have to consult the pages of *Paideuma* magazine or the new, enlarged glossary being compiled for future publication by the University of California Press (I am handling the Italian and Provençal entries for this revision of the *Annotated Index*). When finished, that work will be invaluable for defining foreign words and strange references (as, no doubt, this book will also be).

The time has come to supplement our appreciation of Pound as a poet with an examination of Pound as a general thinker—a man who tried to write "the tale of the tribe," to create a poetry that could deal with law or economics as much as with aesthetic images. By handling ideas, Pound dares us to evaluate his success or failure in intellectual as well as aesthetic terms. Of course, this is painful to many people, who would prefer to see him as Mallarmé. By reducing Pound to a lyric poet, one gets rid of difficult subjects like law and economics, as well as embarrassments like a rather naive infatuation with Benito Mussolini or a vitriolic condemnation of usurers that tended at times to include all Jews. Yet Pound would be the last one to want us to excuse him too easily, to take the easy road out by writing him off as an intellectual dilettante. Whatever his weaknesses—and he had his human share—his synoptic view of "Kulchur," modeled after the German anthropologist Frobenius, has a definite relevance for the modern world. He can present universals, as structuralism does, but without the blurring effect, the abolition of the particular. Also, as one surveys the economic muddles in the Occidental world, one appreciates the fact that Pound was keenly aware that something was wrong with the system—whether this defect was a willful fraudulence by a syndicated few or merely the plain old greed of the many. Even as he saw his own worst prophecies coming true, Pound never smirked; he felt that it was not too late for an ethical revival or a return to the wording of the American Constitution and the spirit of the Magna Charta.

The Later Cantos, however, are the work of an old man who has passed through his dark night of the soul and has paid for the excesses of his youth. They correspond loosely with Dante's *Paradiso*, especially in their moments of illumination and feeling of spiritual hilarity. They bring to a close Pound's interest in subjects that were constant in his life: Confucius and Oriental culture, Neoplatonism and a nature-loving Christianity, John Adams and other Founding Fathers, Renaissance art and medieval architecture, Western law, and the sound principles of economics exemplified in the Byzantium and England of the Middle Ages. These remain the solid blocks on which any society can rebuild.

Pound, in short, never gave up his search for the Earthly Paradise, which haunts men even today, when many other artists have surrendered to vulgarity or violence. Even in the darkest moments of his life—in the American detention camp at Pisa or during his incarceration in St. Elizabeths at Washington—Pound never surrendered totally to despair. More than his friends Joyce, Yeats, and Eliot, he constantly toiled for a vision of perfection here on earth, refusing to divorce spiritual beauty and harmony from the here and now.

It has been common in recent reviews of books about Pound to criticize the authors for not being more objectively critical in their approaches, for accepting Pound's work too eagerly in its entirety. I am well aware that the same criticism could be leveled at this book, and must say a few things in defense. First, for years Pound was bitterly assailed for his political views and accused of willful obscurantism in a way that almost defied anyone to approach his work. Thus a critic who makes that approach has to adopt an essentially accepting attitude from the start. Second, the time is ripe for showing that there *are* beauty and coherence within *The Cantos.*

On the other side, however, I can assure the "critical" Pound readers that I am fully aware of certain imperfections. Some of the Later Cantos are too dense, and some are vague in stretches; some places are even dull—but what is more obvious than what is difficult or boring? The reader scarcely needs to be told that something is hard or dull. At all costs I wish to avoid the ciceronic, aesthetic-sampling approach of those who want to show us a pretty passage here, a difficult one there, and who do nothing but indulge in willful subjectivism. Either we accept *The Cantos* as a fit object for study or we do not; if our decision is positive, we can then proceed to the task.

J. J. W.
30 October 1976
New York City

Introduction
The Man Behind the Later Cantos

On November 1, 1972, two days after his eighty-seventh birthday, Ezra Pound, one of the most influential and controversial American poets of the twentieth century, died in his beloved city of self-exile, Venice. Pound was a founder of the imagist school of poetry and the author of *The Cantos*, one of the longest poems written in this century. He had deeply and directly influenced the careers of numerous other writers, including T.S. Eliot, James Joyce, Ernest Hemingway, E.E. Cummings, and Marianne Moore.

Yet, despite this enormous influence and his own significant achievements, Pound's funeral was a lonely event. The handful of mourners in attendance included his lover and housekeeper, Olga Rudge, and their daughter, Mary de Rachewiltz. The poet's estranged wife, Dorothy, was ill in London. Their son, Omar, was detained. Pound had outlived most of his close friends, and the wintry cold may have kept away the few who survived. Clearly, though, the absence of these family members and friends did not fully explain the strange silence with which Pound's death was greeted.

This desolate scene was made especially poignant by the contrast it presented to the funeral of another great artist—the musician Igor Stravinsky—who had died in Venice the year before. His death brought official tributes from all the major capitals of the world. Flocks of mourners attended his funeral, including Pound himself.[1] Stravinsky was in many ways to modern music what Pound was to poetry: a great innovator and an inspiration to others. But, unlike Pound, Stravinsky had led a very placid, unpolitical

1

life. He had maintained a steady silence about affairs that he felt were of no concern to him.

Pound, on the other hand, had seldom been uncommitted about anything. From his youth, when he was dismissed from a teaching job at Wabash College in Indiana because of his "Latin Quarter type" behavior, to his life among the true artists of London and Paris, Pound had always struck people as daring, exciting, brash, and perhaps more choleric than was healthy.[2] The letters of William Butler Yeats, for example, refer to Pound's eccentricities in equal terms with his brilliance.[3] But the dashing poet of Pound's youth is not the man behind the Later Cantos (85 to 120). That man is a silent, introspective figure given to periods of humility and self-disparagement at the same time that he was penning some of the finest lines of his career.

What caused this dramatic change? Ezra Pound's life can be viewed in terms of a tragic rhythm consisting of purpose, passion, and perception. From the time he visited his father, Homer, who was working at the United States Mint in Philadelphia, Pound was fascinated by money. He believed that one could not adequately understand history without understanding economics, and since he had in the back of his mind the idea of writing a poem dealing with world history, he was vitally concerned with monetary matters.[4] Then, too, his life as an expatriate from Academe and America forced him to assume numerous hack jobs in writing, and this work increased his sense of the social injustices perpetrated by capitalistic countries. When Mussolini rose to power in the 1920s, Pound was drawn inexorably to Italy, a retarded country that was beginning to enjoy a renascence. Like many other intellectuals of the period, he felt that Mussolini's brand of fascism was a compromise between the anarchy of capitalism and the oppressiveness of communism.[5] And, rightly or wrongly, he gave his whole energy to the new movement.

When Italy drifted into World War II, Pound did not leave his adopted country, although he was still an American citizen. This act might have been precarious enough, but the poet compounded it by making broadcasts over Radio Rome, which could be picked up as far away as the United States. Despite his careful attempt to preface these speeches, which were unabashedly pro-Italian, with the words that he was acting entirely on his own behalf as an

American citizen with no tie to the Italian government, his actions could be (and were) interpreted as giving comfort to an enemy power in time of war—a treasonable act punishable by death.

When Italy fell to the Americans in 1945, Pound was arrested and thrust summarily into the Disciplinary Training Center at Pisa. There the sixty-year-old man was forced to survive in a gorilla cage, with only the barest protection from the elements. Yet here, under the most debilitating circumstances, Pound carved some of the finest lines of his *Pisan Cantos:*

What thou lovest well remains,
                    the rest is dross
What thou lov'st well shall not be reft from thee . . .
The ant's a centaur in his dragon world.
Pull down thy vanity, it is not man
Made courage, or made order, or made grace,
    Pull down thy vanity, I say pull down.   (81/520-21)

The only books he had were a text of Confucius (which he took with him), the Bible (which was given to him), and a cheap anthology of English poetry (which he found in a latrine). Yet with these, and with his own incredible energy and memory, he created beautiful poetry:

            nothing matters but the quality
of the affection—
in the end—that has carved the trace in the mind   (76/457)

In November of 1945, Pound was whisked away by air to Washington to stand trial. There, after an agonizing period when he was close to total physical and mental exhaustion, he was deemed unfit to be tried and was sent to the federally controlled insane asylum called St. Elizabeths Hospital, which is located in the southwestern part of the District of Columbia.[6] If the detention camp at Pisa served as a purgatorial experience for Pound, the asylum, curiously enough, seemed to blossom into a magic enclosure, redeemed from grostesquerie by the sheer power of the poet's mind and charm. People flocked there—the young, the old, the talented, the curious—all to converse with the master. The poet Charles Olson was merely one of the many to join the Poundian tradition.[7]

There, with a view of the United States Capitol, Pound wrote the *Rock-Drill* section of his poem, Cantos 85 to 95, which contain some precious moments of escape from his desperate situation. The lesson of humility learned in Pisa did not escape the incarcerated poet, who turned increasingly inward for fulfillment, following the words of the Egyptian Khaty, who said, "A man's paradise is his good nature'" (93/623). The ranting propagandist of the thirties yielded gradually to a figure who could say matter of factly yet poignantly: "Even you were happy last Wednesday" (92/621).

Despite this new stage of controlled awareness, Pound was plagued by the feeling that he had failed in his mission, and with this self-imposed guilt came a passion of regret:

Le Paradis n'est pas artificiel   [Paradise is not artificial]
                    but is jagged,
For a flash,
            for an hour.
Then agony,
            then an hour,
                        then agony,
Hilary stumbles, but the Divine Mind is abundant
            unceasing
                improvisatore   [improviser, spontaneous]
                                                                          (92/620)

For, although he had abandoned a lost political cause, Pound could never quite relinquish his fervent desire to build a true Utopia: "The wrong way about it: despair" (89/598).

The *Rock-Drill* section of the poem begins with the Confucian *History Classic (Shu King)*, which insists, like the Earlier Cantos, that proper moral values can be learned from the past. Pound continued his pursuit of ethical standards in American history by moving onward from Jefferson and Adams to the Age of Jackson (Cantos 88, 89). And, along with a continuing faith in the retributive force of nature (Cantos 90-92), the poet found a constant reinforcement and consolation in the teachings of the great Italian poet Dante Alighieri (Canto 93). For, as Pound adjusted his vision to his depressed condition, he came increasingly to appreciate the central message of Dante's *Convivio* (Banquet): that the true basis for political action must be a love for the people, and that men and societies that do not exist with love are doomed to extinction. The heart of everything that the Italian and his circle of poets believed is presented in the Later Cantos, and is aligned with Confucian and Neoplatonic thought in Pound's continuing pursuit of a dream of perfection.

During the next thirteen years, the poet's cause was argued more or less constantly by Harry Meacham and a variety of writers, including Hemingway, Cummings, Eliot, Moore, a more reluctant Robert Frost, and an always energetic Archibald MacLeish.[8] Finally in April of 1958 Pound was freed from trial— though not cleared of guilt—and was remanded into the custody of his wife. Dorothy and he returned almost immediately to Italy by ship, and went to live in the paradisal surrounding of Brunnenburg Castle, which belonged to his daughter Mary, who had married an Egyptologist—Prince Boris de Rachewiltz.

But life in Italy was not what it had been in the thirties in the seacoast town of Rapallo. The poet felt isolated in the mountainous Tyrol, with its rigorous winter weather, and he was much disturbed by the constant bickering inside the castle between his female friends and relatives. Finally one day he quoted Mary a line from a Greek tragedy that can be translated "Shall we to all our ills add cowardice?"[9] His sentiments are expressed in the Later Cantos: "If love be not in the house there is nothing" (116/796). Pound went to Rome to stay with friends, and eventually joined his longtime lover, Olga Rudge, living with her sometimes in her house in Sant'Ambrogio above Rapallo and sometimes in Venice, where he had gone on leaving the United States in 1908.

This is the period of the writing of *Thrones* (Cantos 96 to 109, published in 1959) and *Drafts and Fragments* (Canto 110 to the end, published in 1969). This last phase of Pound's career marks still another step in his passage from youthful frenzy to quiet acceptance. *Thrones* opens with an evocation of the magic city of Byzantium and ends with an act of love for her people by Queen Elizabeth I of England. This section of the poem deals with peaceful, ordered societies living under the equitable, sane laws of the Byzantines, the Lombards, the Chinese, and the English. In fact, Pound focuses on the Magna Charta, which he considers the forerunner of the American Constitution and—along with the teachings of Confucius—another bedrock upon which an ideal society

can still be raised. There is little polemic in this stretch of the
poem; there is much serious meditative study; and there is always
the awareness that Pound's ideal city, like Coleridge's Xanadu or
Yeats's Byzantium, is just a dream.

Outside the poem, the poet became strangely silent in a deep
and immovable way. Some of the silence was caused by old age,
some by self-doubt, some by constant inner contemplation. There
was the suggestion that his conversation now was either with those
to come or those who had gone:

> In love with Khaty
> > now dead for 5000 years.   (110/779)

The last parts of the poem, the *Drafts and Fragments,* are like the
unfinished bravura sonatas of a grand master who has moved from
melodic certainty through staccato crises to disordered but comprehensible measures of acceptance in a steady diminuendo:

> Only sequoias are slow enough.
> > BinBin "is beauty."   [Laurence Binyon]
> "Slowness is beauty."   (87/572)

Pound was now the kind of old-man scarecrow that Yeats had
described in his Byzantium poems, but he was still capable of
voicing moments of triumphant affirmation, despite his personal
sadness and what he considered the deplorable state of world
politics:

> A blown husk that is finished
> > but the light sings eternal
> a pale flare over marshes
> > where the salt hay whispers to tide's change.   (115/794)

Gone was the fascist fervor; gone the ferocious desire to free the
English language of Victorian frills; gone the mission to save the
human race from greedy manipulators. The poet was practicing
the lesson learned at Pisa:

    the sage
delighteth in water
    the humane man has amity with the hills   (83/529)

In an interview of Pound written by Michael Reck in the company of Allen Ginsberg, one can study the interesting encounter of the untalkative, self-effacing elderly poet with the exuberant, brash young man of the future. Ginsberg was full of extravagant but sincere praise for Pound, saying, "You have shown us the way . . . The more I read your poetry, the more I am convinced it is the best of its time."[10] Pound replied with a humility that can only come from age and suffering: "Any good I've done has been spoiled by bad intentions . . . But the worst mistake I made was that stupid, suburban prejudice of anti-Semitism."

Ginsberg's reply is noteworthy for its magnanimity: "It's lovely to hear you say that . . . because anyone with any sense can see it as a humour, in that sense part of the drama, a model of your consciousness. Anti-Semitism is your fuck-up, like not liking Buddhists, but it's part of the model and the great accomplishment was to make a working model of your mind. Nobody cares if it's Ezra Pound's mind but it's a mind like everybody's mind . . . Prospero threw away *his* magic staff at the end of the play."

These remarks may be the most cogent to date about a work that, from the start, was meant to tell "the tale of the tribe,"[11] and that, according to Archibald MacLeish, is the "nearest thing we have...to a moral history of our tragic age."[12] The encounter of the Buddhistic, liberal young poet with the Confucian, conservative master has to be one of the most dramatic literary meetings of the century, ranking in importance with Pound's introductions to Yeats and to Eliot in the London of pre-World War I days. Here, prejudices and animosities fade; what matters is the love operating between two vital forces who keep humane communications alive: "To be men not destroyers" (117/802).

C. David Heymann's account of Pound's later years, in *Ezra Pound: The Last Rower,* is filled with anecdotes about the poet, and with superb photographs of the solitary figure—clad in dramatic black cape and hat with cane—strolling the streets of his beloved city of water.[13] On the one hand, one can see a figure who has been defeated:

That I lost my center
                fighting the world.   (117/802)

Yet, on the other hand, Pound was in some ways unbowed. Despite certain moments of depression and regret, he could think of his masterwork, and that would do the speaking for him: "The production IS the beloved" (104/742).

And so, as the gondola carried him to the little island of San Michele, where Protestants are buried in Venice, Ezra Pound was ready to meet the elements for the last time. As he himself put it in the closing words of *The Cantos:*[14]

I have tried to write Paradise

Do not move
    Let the wind speak
            that is paradise.

Let the Gods forgive what I
        have made
Let those I love try to forgive
        what I have made.

Chapter One
The Central Ideogram
of the Cantos

From the time that he was presented with the work of Ernest Fenollosa, Ezra Pound was fascinated with the Chinese writing system. He believed, along with Fenollosa, that the Chinese written character is indeed an ideogram, a pictorial form of an idea. For example, the *jen*[2] character for "man" seems to show a pair of legs, and the *i*[1] for "one" is a single horizontal line; therefore, the concept of one man's importance in Confucianism is expressed in this way:[1]

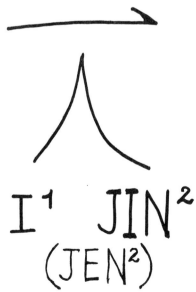

Other characters are more complex. The *tan,*[4] or "dawn," character can be said to show the sun above a horizon, whereas an abstract concept like "faith" (*hsin*[4]) can be analyzed as an individual or a spear standing beside a mouth (a word), with four lines of control above it:[2]

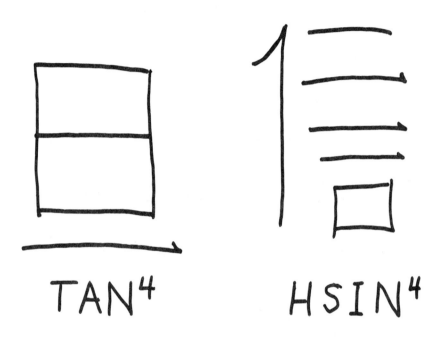

TAN⁴   HSIN⁴

Pound accordingly chose to express his own poetic ideas in imagistic clusters rather than in logical or episodic chains. Therefore, *The Cantos* must be examined with an eye toward identifying the ideogrammic pattern that underlies the entire structure.

It is also necessary to establish some basic tenets that Pound himself has made clear about his work. With Dante in the back of his mind, the modern poet sought to classify the experiences of the human race in approximately three major divisions. Rejecting the Heaven, Purgatory, and Hell of the medieval world as fixed places, Pound preferred instead to speak of states of mind, and he used Richard of St. Victor as his primary source. According to Pound, Richard had spoken of these intellectual modes as follows: 1) cogitation, the mind whirling around an object, in an almost hellish, frenzied pattern; 2) meditation, the mind in concert with an object in purgatorial concentration; and 3) contemplation, the mind in paradisal calm in a state of oneness with an object.[3] *The Cantos* themselves are not rigidly divided into these three groupings because Pound did not believe in their permanence. He conceived of the mind always as an ever-changing, ever-revolving thing (here the force of Ovid's *Metamorphoses* is felt). Nevertheless, there is a discernible difference between the Early Cantos (1-30), the Middle Cantos (31-71), and the Later Cantos. In part, the moves in Pound's life, from London to Paris to Mussolini's Italy to an American detention camp to a madhouse in Washington and back to Italy, help to account for these variations.

Another triad that concerned Pound is mentioned in his *Letters* (p. 239): the permanent (gods), the recurrent (ideals), and the ephemeral or transitory (matter). Essentially, this is a trinity that one can find from Plato through Richard, and in the Neoplatonics who figure prominently in the modern epic. When we place this triad next to Dante's scheme and the one established above, we have the following pattern:

Hell	ephemeral	cogitation
Purgatory	recurrent	meditation
Heaven	permanent	contemplation

Since many of the cantos, especially the early ones, move in a rapidly swirling, changing pattern that suggests hellish disorder, the reader is, in effect, seeking poles of an ideogram in order to hold on to something. Out of the flux, certain basic elements must return. According to the diagram, this repetition of images and themes will point the way to what is stable or fixed.

The first canto is an induction to the work. It establishes the first of Pound's many masks: as Odysseus, the voyager into the past, who seeks the ghosts of yesteryear in order to garner knowledge. Indeed, this is the basic theme of the whole work, and has been explored many times.[4] Essentially, Odysseus' journey for knowledge is a linear, or horizontal, analogue that supplies a scheme for development, whereas Dante's three-part system supplies the variations on the main theme. These two interact with Confucius, whose slowly unraveling thought presents *what* is learned. All three are interwoven in a musical sense, providing orderly points within a free form.

The contrast between chaos and order is obvious in Cantos 2 and 3, but in Canto 4 certain basic figures are brought into sharp relief. There is mention of a troubadour (Peire Vidal), his unnamed woman, a church roof in Poitiers, three streams out of Ovid, and two Japanese places with religious connotations (Isé and Taka-sago). In addition to this already rich detail, one can see that Pound is relating south French troubadours to characters from Greek myth. The bewildered reader may well throw his hands up into the air and ask what is to be made of all this. The answer is: the poem is just beginning, and patience is in order. Already one should see that Pound is focusing upon certain geographical locales that he considers important: southern France (Provence), Italy, Greece, and the Orient. These four areas supply the primary centers for action, with America added later, and with Byzantium brought in toward the end of the poem as the midpoint between East and West.

In Canto 4, one also enters a Roman marriage rite, turns to a conversation that seems either Japanese or Chinese, and en-counters another Greek myth, the marriage of the beautiful Danaë with Zeus in a romantic city, Ecbatan. The canto then skips to some Japanese rocks, returns to southern France (with echoes of Greece in the background), and closes in a surrealist blaze with the mention of two rivers (Garonne in France and Adige in Italy), five Italian or French artists (Cabestan, Vidal, Stefano da Verona, Guido Cavalcanti, and Polhonac), and another woman who under-went a marriage with God, the Virgin Mary. At the beginning of Canto 2, Pound mentions the "eyes of Picasso," and that allusion is important, for Pound's interweaving of planes is similar to the great artist's. By laying one form upon another, Pound forces the reader to see their similarity: is Danaë's marrying Zeus signifi-cantly different from Mary's union with God? Is a beautiful reli-gious shrine on a Japanese lake different from a marriage proces-sion to a shiny cathedral of southern France or a basilica by an Italian river? Though varying his specifics, Pound insists upon the perpetuity of the general form. Thus, one can see archetypes developing out of what at first seemed chaos.

Canto 4 thus provides the work with its primary figurative poles, which will remain to the very end: men of achievement (as opposed to nobodies); beautiful women, suitable as brides for heroes or gods; ideal towns and cities; temples with gods; and images from nature, primarily the mountain and the river. Already one can see that the human and the divine tend to merge. The canto opens with the word "Palace," the home of a king, and goes on to mention a church and a sacred mountain. The human marriage of Aurunculeia, taken from the poetry of Catullus, blends with the marriage of Danaë. When one sees that it is difficult to separate the metaphysical from the physical, one realizes that this is precisely Pound's purpose—and it will intensify as the work progresses.

After a violent Canto 5, Canto 6 is a quiet interlude. Here some male figures cited earlier are presented more fully. The canto opens with the mention of Odysseus and closes with Theseus. Between these two Greek heroes, noted equally for bold achievement and for romantic derring-do, are the troubadours: first, William IX of Aquitaine, with two lines of his scurrilous verse; Arnaut Daniel, with a few words that he toyed with in a sestina; Bernart de Ventadour, mentioned with the Lady of Ventadour, whom he supposedly loved, and with a line from his verse; and finally, Sordello, who eloped with the married Cunizza da Romano, with four lines of his verses cited:

"Winter and Summer I sing of her grace,
As the rose is fair, so fair is her face,
Both Summer and Winter I sing of her,
The snow makyth me to remember her."[5]

In each case, these men are flawed by their sexual desires; but in each case, too, they have created something—their undying songs.

William's granddaughter, Eleanor of Aquitaine, is used as a transitional figure and becomes almost an emblem of the beautiful woman as a temptress. It is no surprise that she is linked in the following canto with that other prime seducer, Helen of Troy, both through reputation and similarity of name (see Chapter Two). But despite all this destructive sexual activity, the canto does not descend into mere brutality. Pound does not castigate people for their sexual activity, especially when they leave something beautiful behind, their work. Thus, one can see that the road to purgation, in Pound's eyes, lies through commitment to something, to action, to productivity. It is significant that the Greek word for poet, *poietes*, is based on the verb meaning "to make"; similarly, the Provençal word for troubadour derives from a verb meaning "to find, to invent." In this canto Pound holds up the

poets for scrutiny, and later he honors legislators such as Adams
and Jefferson as men of significant action. In short, constructive
acts are the things that redeem people from the chaos around
them.

This idea is distilled perfectly in the so-called Malatesta
Cantos, 8 to 11. Here the deeds of a great Italian nobleman, Sigismundo Malatesta, are focused upon. Sigismundo was a well-
rounded man like Odysseus and Duke William IX of Aquitaine.
He was a soldier, a patron of poets and artists, and an intellectual
who was vitally interested in the new ideas coming in from Greece
in the fifteenth century. Perhaps most importantly to Pound,
Sigismundo was the builder of the Temple of Rimini, a magnificent
early Renaissance building that was styled like a Greek temple and
contained many art treasures, such as the elephants supporting the
tomb of his wife, Isotta, for whom the church was built.

Sigismundo thus brings together all the elements that have
been drifting in the previous cantos. His wife, who was immor-
talized by his great act of love, takes her position in the picture,
along with the temple itself, the city of Rimini, and whatever gods
Sigismundo believed in. What are the gods of *The Cantos?*
Essentially *all* gods, none excepted. Sigismundo himself patron-
ized the Neoplatonic philosopher from Greece, Gemisthus
Plethon, who emphasized the water element, which was associated with the old god Neptune-Poseidon. The presence of some
water-babies in the sculpture inside the Christian Temple underscores the point. If one is working toward archetype, all gods will
eventually merge into a divine ideal.

The first true presentation of the divine, but still within a
human and social context, occurs in Canto 13. Here Kung or
Confucius appears, walking by a temple and a river. From this
paradisal scene come some simple words that have a ring of eternal
truth.

>   If a man have not order within him
> He can not spread order about him;
> And if a man have not order within him
> His family will not act with due order;
>   And if the prince have not order within him
> He can not put order in his dominions.
> And Kung gave the words 'order'

and 'brotherly deference'
And said nothing of the 'life after death.'

Kung is a step beyond Sigismundo into the ideal.

One might summarize the basic positions of the three heroic figures mentioned to this point as follows: the low point for establishing a cultural ideogram would be that of Duke William (also called Guillem or Guillaume of Poitou by Pound), for William's poetry is often obscene, and his life, which was marked by adultery and blasphemy, led to at least one excommunication.[6] Sigismundo represents a purgatorial norm; he was a man who was dedicated to beauty and to truth, but he was also mired deeply in the chaotic politics of the Italy of his day. Confucius is a bridge to the gods, for this man of wisdom far exceeds the limitations of most human beings; even in life, he walks in an almost paradisal calm.

To crystallize the basic images or poles of *positive* action developed in the first thirteen cantos, one might construct a graph. The relationships, which hold for the entire length of the poem, include the following basic elements of a hexagram:

Woman		Secular place	
•		•	
Beauty		City, palace	
DARKNESS	Moon	Sun	LIGHT
Man		Gods	
Product		Sacred place	
•		•	
Laws, art		Hill, temple, river	

Here is a visual representation of everything said before. The man is flanked on one side by his woman and on the other by the work of his hands and mind. Both man and woman are closely allied to their native ambience, and the secular place, when redeemed by creativity, becomes a sacred one. Both the man-made city and divinely made nature lead directly to the gods. Light and dark imagery naturally enforce this central picture, for if one draws a line from the Man to the Gods, it will trace the horizontal journey that Odysseus must make to Athena and Ithaca, that Pound must make to his final enlightenment in the Later Cantos.

The two important things to stress are that this graph is neither fixed nor unique. Any one of the six points of the hexagram can be replaced: Venice and Ferrara take the place of Rimini in the remaining Early Cantos, just as John Adams and Thomas Jefferson stand in later for Sigismundo. The second thing is that this one graph does not rule out the possibility of other graphs being superimposed: one could, for example, have inferior ideograms accompanying it. The Ferrara of the Estes, especially after Niccoló, fell into disunion and disintegration; the Florence of the Medici never, in Pound's eyes, quite gains the stature of the Venice under the artist-patronizing doges.

Also, one must remember that if a woman like Cunizza takes her place with Sordello in a rather wild syndrome of love and sexual activity, she may refine herself later, as in Canto 29, when she frees her serfs, or in the *Pisan Cantos*, where she becomes an emblem of beauty. People can change in *The Cantos*. Unlike Dante, whose Christian judgment was rigid and unyielding, Pound admits constant development in a way that is meaningful in terms of the human personality. Pound himself changes his mind drastically about people and places. Talleyrand, whom he first distrusted, he finally came to admire. London, a hell-city in Canto 14, is presented as a paradisal city under its great early Tudor rulers in Cantos 107 to 109.

In the Middle Cantos, the free-wheeling techniques of the Early Cantos are abandoned for a more methodical approach. The reader is introduced to the early America of Thomas Jefferson and John Adams, watches them at work shaping the government of the United States, and explores in depth their attitudes toward life and their fellow men. There is little variation here, and the technique is not imagistic. It is, in the main, purely rhetorical, based on snippets from letters, thoughts, and poems. Similarly, in the passages describing the creation of the Bank of Siena or in the Chinese Cantos, which tell the history of that country largely in terms of Confucian emperors, the poetic technique is narrative and discursive, rather than lyrical and imagistic. As a result, one experiences orderly calm rather than lively activity; the countryside is fixed, vast, and unchanging in a broad sense; ideas can be approached by study.

After Canto 71, time and history brought about a sudden, dramatic change in Pound's life and, with it, a great change in the poem. After the downfall of Mussolini and the collapse of Italy, man and his products were no longer the things that interested the poet most. Instead, he became concerned with finding his place with the redemptive forces of nature, in entering the "process," as he called it. This process includes the workings of the wind, the clouds, the sun, the moon, the stars, and even the ants and the wasps that lay about him in the open fields of Italy. The original ideogram already established is not replaced; it is at times supplemented, and at times compressed.

Throughout the *Pisan Cantos*, Pound mentions temples, rivers, mountains, and cities, and he adds a vast list of the names of the artists whom he had known in Paris and London, along with their attractive women friends. But the original hexagram, in a sense, becomes more compact at the very same time that it is elaborated upon. Intead of a hexagram, one now has a rectangle or a square. The number four suddenly assumes great significance in the *Pisan Cantos:*

4 giants at the 4 corners (74/429)
4 times was the city rebuilded, Hooo Fasa (430)
4 times to the song of Gassir (442)
4 gates, the 4 towers (77/465)

The camp at Pisa, like most military installations, was shaped in a general rectangular form. The four lights at the corners glared mercilessly in a way that made this rectangularity absolutely inescapable. Four is traditionally the number of solidity and confinement, suitable not only for prisons, but for forts and citadels. Most of the old Roman towns that Pound admired (Ravenna, Verona, Pavia) were hexagonal or rectangular. If one examines the walls and gates of the city of Peking, one finds this interesting distribution:

ALTAR OF EARTH
•

•   •

ALTAR OF MOON   ALTAR OF SUN

•

TEMPLE OF HEAVEN

The Chinese created their model city by making these four points their primary gates or poles. They felt that they were thus honoring the major forces of life. Naturally, these four poles are also important to Pound.[7] In fact, one could adapt this design to suit Pound's basic ideogram by merely adding some words from the earlier hexagram:

These relationships are of paramount importance in the *Pisan Cantos*, where the presence of the clouds (Father Heaven) is felt upon the hills (Mother Earth), and the poet digs down into the soil for what he calls a *connubium terrae*, or marriage with the earth:

lie into earth to the breast bone, to the left shoulder. . .
        to the height of ten inches or over
man, earth: two halves of the tally
but I will come out of this knowing no one
neither they me
        connubium terrae   (82/526)

This realignment with the four basic elements is what ultimately saves the poet, for as Pound insists: "When the mind swings by a grass-blade/an ant's forefoot shall save you" (Canto 83/533). This ability to group things into units and to see the essential core of the whole is a vital part of the vision of the true poet.

After the nightmare of Pisa, even the madhouse at Washington came as a relief. Here Pound continued the process of refining his thought to its essentials. At the start of the *Rock-Drill Cantos* (85/545), Pound uses the Chinese character *tuan*[1], which means "foundation," noting that there are four of them in all of nature—an idea that is repeated in 89/601. Essentially, Pound is referring to the four basic Confucian virtues, which underlie moral conduct, as he makes clear in 99/701: "There are Four Books and the 5 relations." In Canto 99/711, he says:

But the four TUAN
>> are from nature
> jen, i, li, chih[8]
Not from descriptions in the school house;
They are the scholar's job,
>> the gentleman's and the officer's.

In a wider sense the concept is also geographic or geometric, with a religious dimension:

Then knelt with the sphere of crystal
That she should touch with her hands,
>> Coeli Regina,   [Queen of Heaven]
The four altars at the four coigns of that place . . .   (92/619)

Either the sun-altar fortress atop Montségur, where the last of the Albigensians was massacred, or the classically conceived Maison Carrée (from *quadratum*, four-sided) in Nîmes contains this basic principle or organization. The strongest statement occurs in 91/616:

and if honour and pleasure will not be ruled
> yet the mind come to that High City . . .
> and the whole creation concerned with "FOUR"

This process of imagistic distillation and the formation of vast, positive ideograms continues through the Later Cantos to the end of the poem, where the poet embraces the winds of Paradise. In the two chapters that follow—especially the next one, in which the images of woman and gold are fixed upon and traced both as constants and variables—the reader will see this consistent "ground bass" in the work. However many men, women, cities, temples, mountains, and acts of great achievement one sees—and the reader of *The Cantos* sees many—one also sees the persistent, recurring norm that enables one to judge them and to form an ideogram of beauty and order. For over the many diverse names, one feels the force of a central archetype working inexorably toward formation of the One: indeed, what are the Many, after all, but the proliferations and productions of the One? Blurred and contradictory shadows eventually lead to incandescent centers. Intuitions and suppositions lead to ideas. In his old age, Pound passed beyond the deceptive differences that seem to inhere in matter, and was close to the secret heart of things.

Chapter Two
The Three Changing Phases
of Woman and Gold

One of the greatest barriers to a full appreciation of Pound's *Cantos* is an unwillingness on the part of many readers to accept the fact that the work is built upon a dynamic principle of change. The concept in Ovid's *Metamorphoses* that the world is constantly in a state of mutation is central to the epic, and this concept of constant change is in turn linked to the triadic division that underlies the poem: the ephemeral (hell), the recurrent (purgatory), and the eternal (paradise). The continual development of forms can be seen clearly if one fixes one's attention on two basic thematic archetypal images of the poem: woman and gold. Why these two subjects in particular? Aside from their eternal fascination for men—both objects of avarice, the dominant vice of mankind— they are inextricably linked together, even though, for purposes of analysis, it is necessary to speak of them separately.

The first of the Early Cantos (1-30) offers three women who fit the triadic organization outlined in the previous chapter: Circe, a hellish temptress who is herself benevolent when she sends Odysseus to the Underworld to gain the knowledge that will lead to his salvation; Anticleia, Odysseus' mother, a representative of the home and order; and Aphrodite, the goddess of love who is a dominant figure in the heavenly constellation of the Poundian poem. From the start, then, the reader sees the range of womanliness from an ambivalent type, who can change a man into a swine, to types who can redeem socially, such as the mother, or metaphysically, such as the goddess.

Gold is also mentioned conspicuously in the first canto:

> with the golden crown, Aphrodite,
> Cypri munimenta sortita est,[1] mirthful, orichalchi, with golden
> Girdles and breast bands, thou with dark eyelids
> Bearing the golden bough of Argicida . . .   (1/5)

The canto thus rises steadily from the dark deprivation in Circe's house to knowledge gained from the dead (the prophet Tiresias carries a "golden wand"). It ends with the promise of the "golden bough," the traditional symbol of entrance into an Underworld for purposes of enlightenment. The gold in Canto 1 is primarily that of illumination and regal splendor, both things that are paradisal in their effect, and both are clearly linked to the divine; but in the mentions of Aphrodite's golden raiment, there is also the clear suggestion of the baubles of the temptress, like the Circe who opens the work. So in this single canto occur three manifestations of woman, with the suggestion that all three are variations of the one.

The notion of the female force as something ungodly and even destructive recurs in Canto 2, with a brief portrayal of that archetypal destroyer, Helen of Troy. Pound uses various Greek words to describe her, punning on her name: *helenaus* (destroyer of ships) and *heleptolis* (destroyer of cities). Then, instead of the name Helen, he uses Eleanor. One might guess Eleanor of Aquitaine, and this identification is confirmed in Cantos 6 and 7. Pound is forcing the reader to see the Greek and the south French woman as one. They are both seductive forces with "naked beauty" and "tropic skin" (7/26), objects which may lure men to their destruction. Helen of Troy caused the Trojan War, and Eleanor's marriage to Henry II of England after her divorce from Louis VII of France led to that interminable series of wars that plagued the two countries. The Greek verb *helein* (destroy) is a part of their names and also one side of their characters, although just one side.

The reader can see three levels of womanhood established in Canto 3. Near the start one finds oneself in the house of a fertility goddess, Kore or Proserpina, and then outside among the bright Tuscan gods in nature. But this heavenly calm does not last, for in the second strophe emerges that adventuresome rascal, The Cid, riding to Burgos, where he is greeted and warned by a nine-year-old girl. This charming picture, dear to the readers of romantic epic, changes swiftly as The Cid deceives two pawnbrokers and is found "Breaking his way to Valencia." This violent action culminates with the mention of "Ignez da Castro murdered." Without pressing very deeply, one can see that the rhythm falls from the heavenly order of nature into man-made chaos, and that three females pinpoint the descent: the goddess, the little girl, and the murdered Portuguese lady—a range that extends from religion to romanticism to brutal realism.

The destructive potential of women occurs again in Canto 6, in which Pound emphasizes the sexual excesses of the troubadours (see Chapter Three). Here one finds swashbuckling men and potentially dangerous women in an atmosphere of wildness. Yet, as was seen in Chapter One, the hellish note does not dominate, for the lines of the poets linger in the mind of the reader and have a redemptive value. The troubadours here are more the makers of poems than the seducers of women, and the ladies are raised up a step by being the sources of much of their inspiration.

Women, in fact, fare rather well in the distinctly hellish passages of the Early Cantos. Pound exempts them largely from the "real" Hell of Cantos 12 and 14-16, where men are the worst perpetrators of social injustice. Pound's famous tirades against usury obviously are not going to be directed to women, since women, even today, are usually not powerful in the ranks of financiers, bankers, munitions-makers, and industrialists—although time may change that situation. Pound's obsession with money crimes as the worst sins against man and nature spares him from any suspicion of antifeminism.

Furthermore, as made clear in the Introduction, Pound was never a Puritan. He himself had been the victim of "blue-nose" morality at Wabash College, and he was not about to point a finger at other people's sexual activities. In Canto 39, he presents a convincing case for sexuality as natural and necessary, and, even though the canto contains at least one passage that may remind one of Henry Miller, it is written with much more taste:

When I lay in the ingle of Circe
I heard a song of that kind.
    Fat panther lay by me

Girls talked there of fucking, beasts talked there of eating,
All heavy with sleep, fucked girls and fat leopards,
Lions loggy with Circe's tisane,
Girls leery with Circe's tisane   (193)

Pound runs the risk of downgrading woman only in the sense that
he is an heir to Christian Neoplatonism, and thinkers in this tradition sometimes equate woman with matter, as in Canto 20/91:

> Jungle:
> Glaze green and red feathers, jungle,
> Basis of renewal, renewals;
> Rising over the soul, green virid, of the jungle,
> Lozenge of the pavement, clear shapes,
> Broken, disrupted, body eternal . . .
> Glazed grape, and the crimson,
> HO BIOS,   [life]
>   cosi Elena vedi   [so see Helen]

There is no doubt here that the destructive Helen (Elena in
Pound's adaptation of Dante's Italian phrase from *Inferno* 5.64)
blurs into a confused, chaotic world that is distinctly feminine at
base. Yet, what redeems the scene are the words "body eternal"
and "renewals." Mother Earth in her archetypal role restores as
much as she devours.

A similar passage occurs in Canto 29/144:

Wein, Weib, TAN AOIDAN   [Wine, Woman, Song]
Chiefest of these the second, the female
Is an element, the female
Is a chaos
An octopus
A biological process

Here the woman-matter parallel is fully spelled out, but the lines
go on to mention two verses of Sordello's poetry and speak of "Our
mulberry leaf, woman, TAN AOIDAN." It would be difficult to say
that Pound is doing anything worse here than what Joyce did with
Molly Bloom: that is, he is making archetypal woman the basis
upon which all else grows, just as the finest Neoplatonics, such as

Scotus Erigena, delighted in matter as the base of the universe, and did not run to condemn it.

If Pound tends to see woman as a "biological process," he also notes that "Matter is the lightest of all things" (143). Perhaps he uses this idea of Plotinus to make his definition of matter coincide with Richard of St. Victor's notion of cogitation (the lowest form of thought) as a whirring, moving, chafing activity that is disruptive and chaotic. This concept is in keeping with his notion of the infernal, and it may also explain why he likes to concentrate on drifters like Cunizza da Romano or women with hellfire in them— Parisina d'Este and Lucrezia Borgia. But for every incestuous destroyer like Parisina, Pound balances with an Isotta, the wife of Sigismundo Malatesta, for whom the Italian nobleman built the beautiful Temple of Rimini. And although Cunizza was a hellcat in her youth, one learns in Canto 29/142 that she redeemed herself with a great act of kindness when she freed her slaves in the house of the Cavalcantis in Florence in 1265:

Free go they all as by full manumission
All serfs of Eccelin my father da Romano
Save those who were with Alberic at Castra San Zeno
And let them go also
The devils of hell in their body.

Cunizza is depicted first as a loose woman who runs away with the troubadour Sordello, but later Pound stresses her purgatorial activities and qualities, her kindness and compassion, which enable her to change from slut to saint. Dante finally put her in his third heaven; but in Dante's *Paradiso*, she is *just* a saint because Christian judgment sees the soul as a fixed entity. In Pound's *Cantos*, her being ranges over the three degrees of human conduct from the lowest to the highest. In the *Pisan Cantos*, Pound sees Cunizza's face with the faces of other beautiful women and with goddesses. Her apotheosis is thus completed.

If Pound sees woman as truly infernal in any lasting sense, it is only woman as whore. Most women, Pound believes, are victims of the games of men, political pawns such as Helen and Eleanor. The worst females are the prostitutes mentioned obliquely in Cantos 19/88 and 22/105-6, or perhaps those stiff, wooden, un-sensual American-Puritan women of Canto 28/135, women who have a "ligneous solidness" that is not a part of the easy, flowing activity that Pound most admires. The prostitute, who lives and loves for gold, is cursed by Pound, although the woman who lives for love is not. In general, the Early Cantos are typified by a lack of solidity, of something to hold onto. Everything fades away, as the light does around the brilliant gold mosaics in the tomb of the Roman empress Galla Placidia in Ravenna: "In the gloom, the gold gathers the light against it" (11/51).

Human beings and objects become much more solid and identifiable in the Middle Cantos (31-84), which serve as Pound's intellectual Purgatory. Here people are engaged in tasks: Jefferson and Adams in the building of America, the Tuscan people in the founding of the Bank of Siena, the Chinese emperors in the ruling of China. The central cantos continue the work of Sigismundo and the Medicis and the Estes in the first thirty cantos, and in them woman is placed next to man, as in the famous gold mosaics in San Vitale, Ravenna, where Theodora faces her husband, Justinian. Thus, Abigail Adams is mentioned quite undramatically with John (62/344 ff.), the mother of Emperor Yong Tching is given her due (61/339 ff.), and faithful Chinese wives abound in Canto 54. The most important woman is Maria Maddalena, the mother of Duke Ferdinand II of Tuscany, one of the prime movers in the estab-lishment of the bank at Siena that was based on the distribution of nature's bounty for all, rather than upon the personal greed of a select few. Pound emphasizes her femininity in this great act, calling her "M. Magdalene the She Guardian" of her young son (42/214), with the last word from Latin "tutrices" (43/215). In several cases where Maria's name occurs, the Virgin Mary is also mentioned, for Pound wants to create the distinct impression that a great act of social love has a divine aura about it.

Of course, there are bad women, too: Peggy Eaton, who scan-dalized Washington at the time of President Jackson (34/169), the Chinese empresses who hired their relatives (56/302), the women who tried to gain control of their men ("brat was run by his missus," 55/299), and the prostitutes (71/420). Pound stresses the fact that the Bank of Siena (Monte dei Paschi) made it possible for the town whores to reform and to strike their names off the city rolls as streetwalkers: 43/219. In the main, he emphasizes the dignity of women when he repeats the mullings of John Adams: "why exclude women from franchise?" (70/411).

But if the general status of women improves in the Middle Cantos, with just a few relinkings of the feminine with the material forces of life (largely in Cantos 39 and 47), the role of gold assumes much greater importance. In these cantos, economics begins to emerge more clearly as one of the organizing principles of Pound's view of history. People who misuse gold become more obviously the villains of the epic. In their direst form, the misusers include the usurers, the great international frauds who tamper with the value of money or monopolize it, as in the famous Usury Canto, 45, or even more clearly in 46/234:

Aurum est commune sepulchrum. Usura, commune sepulchrum.
helandros   kai heleptolis   kai helarxe.
Hic Geryon est. Hic hyperusura.

These words, like an epitaph written in mixed Latin and Greek, can be translated as follows:

Gold is a common sepulchre. Usury, a common sepulchre.
Man-destroying   and city-destroying   and rule-destroying
Here is Geryon.   Here is hyperusury.

The *hel-* words, which were earlier applied to Helen and Eleanor, are now applied to the real culprits: the men who manipulate woman and gold for their own private ends.

Pound hit hard on a selfish handling of coin in 52/257:

Thus we lived on through sanctions, through Stalin
          Litvinof, gold brokers made profit
rocked the exchange against gold

In fact, he clearly contrasts this ill-gotten gold with the brilliant gold of the Church of La Daurade (the Gilded) in Toulouse, where the Italian poet Guido Cavalcanti met the beautiful girl Mandetta:

          Between KUNG and ELEUSIS
Under the Golden Roof, la Dorata

In this canto occur two seminal lines: "Life and death are now equal/Strife is between light and darkness." Here, at what might have been the midpoint of the poem (Pound was never sure about the exact length), one begins to leave the pits of darkness behind and to enter the corridors of light. Even though the image is not underlined, the gold of the sun emerges as an obvious metaphor. Canto 51 opens with the Neoplatonic analogy of God with the sun, using Guido Guinizelli's famous *Al cor gentil repara sempre amore* (Love always repairs to the noble heart) as its source. Perhaps the most beautiful occurrence comes in Canto 55/292:

> In the city of Tching-tcheou are women like clouds
> of heaven,
Silk, gold, piled mountain high.

With lines like these, the reader knows that he is on the road to Heaven.

But Pound does not want to rush there, in the manner of T. S. Eliot. He wants to examine history carefully, showing that those who steeped themselves in gold, such as the debased heirs of the Estes in Ferrara, who used gold forks (aureis furculis: 26/122), did not create anything lasting. Pound stresses the fact that "gold is inedible" (56/303), and that the benevolent ruler provides bread. He is anticipating what he later emphasized from the work of the statistician Alexander del Mar: that gold is merely a measure of value, not necessarily a valuable commodity per se.[3] Similarly, Pound rails out against the alchemists, who tried to pervert nature by converting perfectly good minerals into magic elixirs, as if the very possession of gold were a salvation in itself. The hoarding tendency Pound views as the basest drive in the human animal. Gold-vultures, or gold-lice as he calls them, cannot exist without a host to feed off (one can't forever create money *ex nihilo*, the way banks do, without clients to loan it to), and yet they almost unconsciously destroy the organism upon which their survival depends.

The *Pisan Cantos* form an important interlude in Pound's poem. As the poet was placed in the detention camp at Pisa, he realized that he would have to align himself with nature in order to survive. In so doing, he directed his appeal largely to the feminine forces: the pagan goddesses (Venus-Aphrodite, Demeter, Proser-

pina), the Chinese figure of mercy Kuanon (Kuan-Yin), Christian
saints (Perpetua, Agatha, Anastasia), beautiful women from Renaissance and nineteenth-century painting, and women from
actual life (H.D. or Hilda Doolittle, Anne Blunt, and others).
Naturally, men also appear here, but in the main it was the soft,
compassionate spirit of women nurtured in memory that helped
the poet to survive.

In expressing this attitude toward the feminine, Pound had to
reshape his earlier words about matter, the Madame Hyle of
Canto 30. Instead of presenting woman as a biological process or
the mansion of darkness that man's reason must penetrate and
illuminate, Pound sees her as an integral part of the beautiful
natural landscape around him. He calls the nameless hills around
Pisa the breasts of Tellus or Helen, or he uses a composite name:[4]

Mist covers the breasts of Tellus-Helena and drifts up the Arno
came night and with night the tempest   (77/473)

This redemption of the feminine is completed in the poet's "marriage with Earth," which was already mentioned in the previous
chapter:

How drawn, O GEA TERRA,   [Mother Earth]
        what draws as thou drawest
                till one sink into thee by an arm's width
embracing thee. Drawest,
        truly thou drawest.
Wisdom lies next thee,
        simply, past metaphor.   (82/526)

Another transformation of the feminine occurs with relationship to
the moon. Pound frequently sees his women in triads, and in one
of the most common groups, he links Cunizza with a barefoot girl
(la scalza), who says, "Io son' la Luna" (74/438), "I am the moon";
there is also a little sister who danced on a sax-pence ("sorella,/
che ballava sobr'un zecchin'": 77/475). This grouping brings the
little girl and the historic woman into conjunction with the lunar
force. Thus, the range of femininity extends from the mythic to the
physical to the cosmic. When one reads the seminal line "Cythera,
in the moon's barge whither?" (80/510) and soon after learns that

the rosy-fingered Dawn is "in the moon barge," one sees all these forces coalescing. Woman is love, is the moon, is universal compassion. Her darkness is that of the night, but this can be soothing, especially after the brutal glare of the lights of the detention camp.

As noted in Chapter One, Pound effects some even stranger mythic transformations in these Later Cantos.[5] First, he clearly shows that his idea of Paradise is, at its base, social and earthly by titling his two major sections *Rock-Drill* and *Thrones*. Canto 85 begins with the mention of two queens, Elizabeth I and Cleopatra. They are cited not for their beauty, but for their devotion to work and thought:

That Queen Bess translated Ovid,
        Cleopatra wrote of the currency.

Cleopatra is mentioned again in 86/565 with the Hapsburg empress Maria Theresa. From the start, then, women are presented equally with men as excellent rulers. Theodora is mentioned side by side with Justinian I in 91/611, and the *Mémoires* of Madame de Rémusat dominate Canto 101. Pound voices a slight antifeminism only in Cantos 98 and 99, where he is following the words of the *Sacred Edict* of the Chinese emperor, K'ang Hsi; but these passages are muted, and he emphasizes that "there be no slovenly sloppiness/ between goodman & wife" (99/705).

The equality theme is stated even more strongly in terms of the gods who hover over the kingly thrones. The hero of justice is Athena (*Athana*), the asexual goddess (87/571):

Was not unanimous
        Athana broke tie,
That is 6 jurors against 6 jurors
           needed *Athana*.

She is cited again in Canto 89/601. Other feminine spirits appear frequently in the Later Cantos, and they continue to merge together: Isis and Kuanon in 90/606, St. Ursula with Ysolt and Piccarda Donati (of Dante's *Paradiso* 3) in 93/628, and Fortuna or Fortune with Luna (86/566)—all with the suggestion of the moon somewhere in the design.

Then, a further transformation takes place as the women begin to merge with their male counterparts:

Beatific spirits welding together
         as in one ash-tree in Ygdrasail.
            Baucis, Philemon.   (90/605)

Sometimes the assimilation brings the solar force in touch with the lunar, as when Kuanon is mentioned as wearing "the sun and moon on her shoulders" (101/726). The earlier linking of the female with the moon is taken a step further as the Egyptian male sun god, Ra, is fused with the male god of evil, Set, and the composite figure is spoken of as if it were feminine:[6]

The Princess Ra-Set has climbed
         to the great knees of stone . . .   (91/611)

This figure is then linked to Helen of Troy and Queen Elizabeth (through Francis Drake) as riders in the moon-barge that is pictured as a hieroglyph on page 612:

Helenaus That Drake saw the armada
            & sea caves
Ra-Set over crystal
               moving

In fact, Pound is effecting poetically here what he knew, years before, that Scotus Erigena had done philosophically in Book 5 of his *On the Division of Nature:* he is abolishing sexual differences.[7] Even in Canto 91, which can be called the Queen's Canto, in part because of the strange name Reina (variant of Regina or "Queen") with which it opens, this marriage of male and female in a chaste, mystical world of light and shadow is beautifully hymned:

Merlin's fader may no man know
Merlin's moder is made a nun . . .
        all that she knew was a spirit bright,
A movement that moved in cloth of gold
        into her chamber.
"By the white dragon, under a stone
        Merlin's fader is known to none."

Lay me by Aurelie, at the east end of Stonehenge[8]
  where lie my kindred
Over harm
Over hate
   overflooding, light over light . . .
the light flowing, whelming the stars.
   In the barge of Ra-Set
On river of crystal   (613)

On the highest mystical plane, as Scotus Erigena had affirmed, woman is not differentiated from man. There is no sexuality in the upper spheres of contemplation, just as there is no temporal difference between night and day. Both sun and moon have their purposes: "Our science is from the watching of shadows" (85/543). Even the Underworld entered in Canto 1 is redeemed in the Later Cantos as two members fly upward in a shower of light: "out of Erebus, the delivered,/ Tyro, Alcmene, free now, ascending" (90/608). As Scotus had written and prayed, Hell has finally been abolished by being understood, and Heaven has become universal.

  In Canto 106/755, Pound remarks that Selena, an alternate name for Moon in Greek, has risen as a queen to Heaven. This statement alone is somewhat extraordinary, but it is eclipsed in the previous canto, when reason, which is frequently thought of as male, is aligned with the moon: Ratio . . . luna (105/747). This is then followed by the strongest statement of the purity of woman in *The Cantos*, and it is attributed to one of Pound's favorite medieval philosophers, St. Anselm, who will be discussed further in Chapter Twelve:

"Ugly? a bore,
   Pretty, a whore!"
     brother Anselm is pessimistic,
digestion weak,
   but had a clear line on the Trinity, and
By sheer grammar: Essentia
    feminine
     Immaculata   (750)

Essence is immaculate! No matter how much Pound may be reading into Anselm—he merely implies that the feminine gender of the word "Essentia" determines the femininity—this is surely one of the strongest cases for redeemed femininity from the pen of a man.[9] These lines show the heritage of years of devotion to the finest elements of Christian thought.

Perhaps the whole vindication of woman can be seen best in the Chinese character that opens and acts as a presiding emblem for the Later Cantos, *ling²* (Canto 85/543). This character is analyzed in Canto 104/740 as "The small breasts snow-soft over tripod." *Ling²* means "sensibility, tradition" or "ghost, soul." It has been analyzed in descending fashion as the rain radical over three mouths which are in turn propped up by two feet.[10] But Pound, instead, sees the mouths as breasts, like the hills in the *Pisan Cantos*, which in turn are supported by tripods (accoutrements both of monarchs and of wizards). Then he immediately shifts his interpretation and takes a more accepted one: "under the cloud/ the three voices." Pound is telling us that sensibility or a knowledge of the traditions of the past is, in Confucian terms, an absolute essential for good government or the ideal life; it is a sentient, feminine force, and is observable all around us in the beating heart of nature (some people see the two bottom elements in the *ling²* character as dancing feet).

If woman is aptheosized in the Later Cantos, gold also finds its way to Heaven. For gold is presented primarily in two ways: as material, in the form of money, and as a color or symbol with a hieratic value. In those cantos where economics predominates, the first point of view prevails. Thus, Canto 96, which treats the history of the Lombards and gives the rules for governing Byzantium, abounds with mentions of gold objects or the work of goldsmiths. Pound's point here, lifted in part from the work of Alexander del Mar, is that it is a government's job to superintend the minting and proper distribution of gold.[11] This duty cannot be allowed to fall into the hands of private enterprise, as it did under Charles II of England and thereafter. Even when talking about money, Del Mar titles his chapter "The Sacred Character of Gold."

Canto 97 opens with a consideration of the just ratio between silver and gold in coining, but as the poetry progresses, it leaves behind the marvelous names of coins that Pound the nominalist-at-base adores—the dinars and scats and mithcals and tussujs and

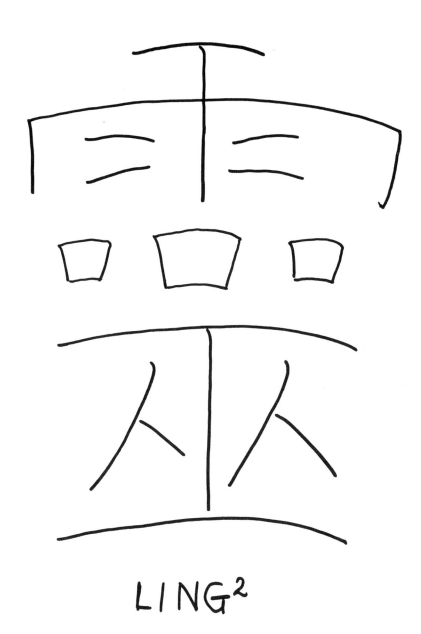

LING²

baugs and vadmals—and rises on the wings of Pound-the-idealist's vision into the "russet-gold" lacquer of the sunlight (675). For Pound is both a realist and an idealist, dreaming of perfection but concerned with the here and now. Similarly, his vision of woman embraces both her mysterious capacity to destroy as well as her power to redeem: "And in every woman, somewhere in the snarl is a tenderness" (113/789).

Pound's encompassing vision is nowhere better exemplified than in Canto 109, where, after considering one of the kind acts from the Statues of the 31st year of the great Elizabeth I of England, he ties in his economic idea that justice is achieved only by a control of the gold of the realm.[12] The gold, the love (amor), and the Great Queen are like a resplendent mosaic in verse:

```
For every new cottage        4 acres
                 Stat de 31 Eliz.
                         Angliae amor                    [love of England]
And false stone not to be set in true gold
to the king onely to put value
                and to make price of the quantity
```

On this note of acceptance—of England, which he had formerly despised, and woman, whom he had occasionally denigrated—the elderly Pound wrote a close to the formally ordered *Cantos*, demonstrating a vision and a balance that point to a world outside of time.

Chapter Three

The Troubadours As Guides to Poetry and Paradise

The South French troubadours—their lives, their poetry, their native places, and their women—appear prominently throughout *The Cantos*. The influence of these poets of the Middle Ages on Ezra Pound has long been recognized.[1] From the time when he studied with Professor William P. Shepard at Hamilton College and with various teachers at the University of Pennsylvania, Ezra Pound was fascinated by the poetic creators of Provence. He revealed this influence first in the preliminary chapters of his first book of criticism, *The Spirit of Romance*, which was published in 1910. He also revealed it in his early lyric poems, when he adapted the voice of Bertran de Born in his "Sestina: Altaforte" in an attempt to invigorate the dull, worn-out rhythms and diction of Victorian and Edwardian poetry:

Damn it all! all this our South stinks peace.
You whoreson dog, Papiols, come! Let's to music!
I have no life save when the swords clash.
But ah! when I see the standards gold, vair, purple, opposing
And the broad fields beneath them turn crimson,
Then howl I my heart nigh mad with rejoicing.[2]

In the critical writing of his early years, Pound also mentioned the troubadours, but with a certain restrained deference: "It is mainly for the sake of the melopoeia [melody-making] that one investigates troubadour poetry."[3] Later, however, Pound, in his masterwork, made the troubadours serve a far broader purpose than merely to create interesting sounds and melodic patterns. In fact, in Pound's epic the troubadours are given even greater importance than they are by those many critics who claim that they invented a new style of loving called "courtly love." Pound would claim that they rediscovered the joy of love under the ascetic, mystical tidal wave of the Middle Ages, and, even more importantly, that, after centuries of Gregorian chant, they captured the thrill in song of the lyric I.

In the explosive, ever-changing world of the Early Cantos (1-30), the troubadours play a major role. Obviously, Pound was attracted to them not only for their poetic accomplishments but also because of the strange beauty of their lives. The biographies of the South French poets are revealed in a variety of *vidas*, or life-stories, appended to the poems in the songbooks that come down from a variety of sources. Although modern scholars tend to discredit these life-stories totally, Pound is not always interested in mere historical fact; he is also concerned with that point where myth meets known history.

The life-stories say, for example, that the troubadour Peire Vidal dressed himself like a wolf in order to creep into the castle where he could woo Loba (whose name means Wolf-Girl), and that he was attacked mercilessly by her dogs and almost killed. Pound compares this story in Canto 4 with the tragic death of the Greek Actaeon, who was torn apart by dogs when he refused to acknowledge the true power of the god Dionysus. Pound also mentions the murder of the troubadour Cabestan by a jealous husband, who served the poet's heart to his wife, since he thought that Cabestan had been courting her in his poems. Pound contrasts this hideous tale with the dreadful murder of the little boy Itys by his mother, Philomela, when she learned that her husband, Tereus, had raped her sister Procne. The flight of Philomela and Procne, as nightingale and swallow, away from the hawklike Tereus is compared with Cabestan's mistress tossing herself off a balcony in the South French town of Rodez (which is likened in sound values to the Greek island of Rhodes):

And she went toward the window,
                    the slim white stone bar
Making a double arch;
Firm even fingers held to the firm pale stone;

Swung for a moment,
                    and the wind out of Rhodez
Caught in the full of her sleeve.
                    . . . the swallows crying:
'Tis. 'Tis. Ytis!
                    Actaeon . . .   (4/13)

In Canto 5, Pound recounts how Pieire de Maensac's love affair
with the wife of Bernart de Tierci caused a war at "Troy in Au-
vergnat" (Troyes in the Auvergne). By mentioning the name
Menelaus, he shows that he is drawing a parallel with the far more
famous war at Troy in Asia Minor, caused by Paris' abduction of
Helen from her Greek husband (Canto 5/18). As noted in Chapter
Two, Helen of Troy is linked constantly with Eleanor of Aquitaine,
and her adventuresome grandfather is the first troubadour, Duke
William IX of Aquitaine (whom Pound calls Guillaume-Guillem of
Poitiers-Poitou); he is coupled with Odysseus in Canto 6. By the
end of that canto, the amorous escapades of Eleanor, Bernart de
Ventadour, Sordello, and Cairels of Sarlat are brought together in
a vast ideogram that is directly related to that original swashbuckling seducer, Theseus of Athens. Clearly, Pound is fascinated
by the misadventures of such poets as the self-defrocked monk
Poicebot, who is knighted by Savairic Mauleon, so that he can
marry a certain woman (Canto 5/18). When Poicebot decides to
journey into Spain, his wife runs away with an English soldier, and
eventually winds up in a bordello. On his return from Spain,
Poicebot happens to stumble upon her there, and after enjoying a
night of her charms again, he leads her off to a nunnery, and then
abandons his song:

Poicebot, now on North road from Spain
(Sea-change, a grey in the water)
            And in small house by town's edge
Found a woman, changed and familiar face;
Hard night, and parting at morning.

In his essay "Troubadours—Their Sorts and Conditions," Pound
recounted in some detail these stories, presumably from his own
editing of manuscripts.[4] He was drawn not only to the poetry of the
troubadours and to their lives, but even to their native haunts. He

frequently took walking trips in southern France before and after
World War I, with T.S. Eliot and others as companions. In the
Early Cantos, where he linked them with the Greeks, Pound
could see a mythic grandeur in the poets' lives. Sordello, for
example, he viewed as an almost archetypal romantic scoundrel,
an incorrigible but lovable seducer of women. As noted in the
previous chapter, Pound was intrigued by Sordello's affair with:

> . . . the Lady Cunizza
> That was first given Richard St Boniface
> And Sordello subtracted her from that husband
> And lay with her in Tarviso
> Till he was driven out of Tarviso
> And she left with a soldier named Bonius   (29/142)

Yet also in Canto 16, one gets an indication of the fact that the
man's life can admit another rather different judgment. There, as
Pound is exiting from the London Hell of Cantos 14 and 15, he encounters the naked, screaming poet William Blake, the anti-papal
troubadour Peire Cardinal, who has his neck bent foward, Dante
looking at Hell in his mirror, and Sordello gazing at the same
infernal scene on his shield.

Pound is suggesting here that Peire, Sordello, and the others
are kinsmen. They are all men who look at the hellish reality of
existence and refuse to comment upon it with a false optimism.
Pound is thinking in the back of his mind of Sordello's famous
dirge written on the death of his lord, Blacatz of Aups. In it the
poet summons the reigning rulers of Europe to come and devour
the dead man's heart because they have no real "heart" of their
own.[5] Suddenly, instead of being a mere seducer of women,
Sordello assumes the dignity of a Jeremiah, prophesying doom.
He continues in this grander role in Canto 32, where, thanks to
some reminiscences from Dante's *Purgatorio 6*, he is cast as the
overseer of the Vale of Princes, condemning the rulers of Europe
at the time of John Adams and Thomas Jefferson.[6] Here is a
straightening out of the man's crooked past. Here is a movement
away from the tortured turns and twists of cogitation into the
studied calm of meditation, which is the dominant thought-pattern
of the Middle Cantos. It is clear that, at this moment, one sees a

purgatorial Sordello who is very much at home in this moral surrounding. Dante, of course, put Sordello into his Purgatory once and for all.

But, "Hang it all, Robert Browning" and Dante Alighieri, there is still a third Sordello: the paradisal one. He occurs as early as Canto 29/144, where two lines of his Provençal verse are quoted; these may be translated:

Alas! what shall my eyes do
since they don't see the one whom I desire?[7]

Here a few brief lines of poetry are salvaged out of the prevailing chaos of a man's life. Here, too, the commanding beauty of a woman is abstracted from the "biological process" of which she is an important part. Here, in effect, is a snatch of heavenly calm in the midst of disorder.

Sordello's real apotheosis into the ranks of the contemplative occurs in the much-quoted Canto 36, which is dominated by a translation of Guido Cavalcanti's *Donna mi prega* (A lady asks me). After the translation, Pound suddenly links the name of Scotus Erigena with a snippet from Sordello's life: his being awarded some lands in southern Italy by Charles "the Mangy" of Anjou. The canto then goes on to end with a line from the troubadour's verse, which might be translated: "When I think deeply into my rich thoughts."[8] Why this juxtaposition of Cavalcanti, Erigena, Manicheans, and Sordels? They are all eccentrics who in some way opposed the workings of the Church. Scotus Erigena did not believe in Heaven or Hell as substantial places. In his poetically written *On the Division of Nature,* Scotus spoke of life as a kind of Hindu exhalation and return, a fall into matter and a dancing back to its inscrutable source, which is a God whose ineffable nature exceeds any easy monistic appraisals.[9] He was foolishly condemned in the early 1200s for being a Manichean or Albigensian dualist, but he was far closer to being a pantheist.

The most important figure of this canto is, of course, Guido Cavalcanti. Guido's *Donna mi prega* is an explanation of love as a physical and psychic event; in the poem he uses psychological and physiological terms that can be traced to Albertus Magnus or Averroes and the Arabs as his prime sources.[10] Dante put Guido's father, Cavalcante, in his *Inferno* 10 among the heretics, and there is every indication that Guido would have wound up there too. But what is his achievement? Why is his poem given so much space? Because, unlike many other men of his age, Guido spoke of life in hard, realistic terms, accentuating the beauty of sex and refusing to take recourse to any "comic" metaphysical tone. Love in his poem inextricably links sex with compassion; it is the most important thing that a man may experience, but it is limited, for, like the body, the passion will flicker and die.

Cavalcanti thus becomes a spokesman for Sordello and his fellow troubadours, who burned in passion incandescently, and who, more often than not, came to sudden, tragic ends. By the ideogrammic yoking, Sordello is raised to the heights of philosophy, especially through the line: "Sacrum, sacrum, inluminatio coitu" (Sacred, sacred, the illumination in the sexual act). Pound sees the troubadours and Cavalcanti as men who kept the life-force alive when established thought was subtly working to stifle romance and to shroud the sexual act with darkness and guilt. Cavalcanti and the troubadours are proud, birdlike hymners of the beauty of love and the honesty of the natural life. It is no accident that most of Canto 75 consists of the *Chant des Oiseaux* (Song of the Birds) of the Frenchman Clement Jannequin, in a modern musical setting by Gerhart Munch. Jannequin was a Renaissance link in the chain of those who kept the cry of the bird alive, who perpetuated the instinctive *Getriebe* that the troubadours had first voiced in the post-Dark Ages world.

The mention of birds leads to Bernart de Ventadour and his famous lark poem, *Can vei la lauzeta mover* (When I see the lark moving).[11] The title line is first cited in Canto 6, in the midst of a recount of Bernart's alleged adulterous affair with the wife of his patron Ebles (Pound's Ebles) of Ventadour. The last line of the section, "who sheds such light in the air," sounds more like a translation of Guido Cavalcanti's *che fa di clarità l' aer tremare, a* line beloved by Pound,[12] than of Bernart's work, but, as has been seen, Pound constantly forces the reader to "put things together."

The next use of Bernart occurs in 20/89, with an oblique citation of one of his poems in the second and third lines of the canto; the original Provençal is translated into English much later in 92/619:

"And if I see her not,
no sight is worth the beauty of my thought."[13]

Canto 20 opens with a montage of lyric love expression, combining bits of Greek, Italian, Provençal, and Latin. The canto goes on to relate the story of Pound's journey to Freiburg, Germany, to see Emil Lévy, the author of the *Petit dictionnaire provençal-français* (Little Provençal-French Dictionary). Pound made the journey with some strips of copy of a manuscript of Arnaut Daniel's that he had uncovered in the Ambrosian Library in Milan. He was puzzled by the curious Provençal word *noigandres*. Always an academician at heart, he was determined to consult the foremost authority on the subject:

And I went to old Lévy, and it was by then 6:30
in the evening, and he trailed half way across Freiburg
before dinner, to see the two strips of copy . . .
Not that I could sing him the music.
And he said: Now is there anything I can tell you?"
And I said: I dunno, sir, or
"Yes, Doctor, what do they mean by *noigandres*?"
And he said: Noigandres! NOIgandres!
"You know for seex mon's of my life
"Effery night when I go to bett, I say to myself:
"Noigandres, eh, *noigandres*,
"Now what the DEFFIL can that mean!"[14]   (20/89)

Eventually, Pound broke the word up into the units *d'enoi gandres* (refuge or haven from trouble or pain), but the phrase has always remained a puzzler. The point of the passage is that Arnaut is a smith of words, and Pound, as a critic, is an apprentice of the smith, just like the lexicographer and philologist Lévy. All three toil together in purgatorial splendor.

Throughout *The Cantos*, Arnaut, more than any other troubadour, is Pound's Logos man, probably because the modern poet had devoted so many years to translating his medieval predecessor. Pound tinkers with words like *ongla* (nail) and *oncle* (uncle) from a Daniel sestina in Canto 6.[15] Arnaut's suggestive word *remir* (either "look" or "contemplation" according to Lévy),

which describes a nude woman standing by candlelight, is cited by
Pound in Canto 7/26, and more dramatically in 20/90:

Air moving under the boughs,
The cedars there in the sun,
Hay new cut on hill slope,
And the water there in the cut
Between the two lower meadows; sound,
The sound, as I have said, a nightingale
Too far off to be heard.
And the light falls, *remir*,
from her breast to thighs.[16]

Arnaut also accords with Bernart in his adoration of nature, as in
29/145:

So Arnaut turned there
Above him the wave pattern cut in the stone.[17]

Bernart and his lark are balanced with Arnaut and the waves which
were carved into the walls of the castle at Excideuil, a castle that
was actually connected with Guiraut de Bornelh, whom Pound
ignores as an inferior poet. The waves come back in 80/510 and
107/758. Thus Arnaut is truly a purgatorial figure, a worker who
struggles upward in his hewing of the Word. His undulating wave
and Bernart's soaring lark also point the way to Heaven.

But before arriving there, one encounters Pound's dark night
of the soul in the *Pisan Cantos*. After the downfall of Mussolini and
Pound's arrest by the American Army, the poet suddenly had to
re-evaluate his life in a personal way. Dropping pedantry, he
began to identify with people fictional and real in a closer way than
ever before. Some of his old techniques remain, as in the citations
of Bernart in Canto 74 and in his use of Arnaut's word *consiros*
(thoughtful, worried) in 83/529, taken from Daniel's speech in
Dante's *Purgatorio* 26.143. But in the main, the troubadours as
love-makers and wordmongers yield to the more stirring figure of
Bertran de Born, the manly poet whom Pound had admired in his
youth, and who now came to the detention camp at Pisa to lend the
aged prisoner a hand.

Bertran had been cited bookishly earlier: his phrase *y cavals*

armatz (and armed horses) from *Be.m platz lo gais temps de pascor*
(I like the gay time of spring) was mentioned in 7/24; and in
80/509, it recurs with a citation of Bertran's magnificent castle,
Altaforte (Hautefort).[18] But the Bertran of military strife is not the
one that Pound primarily recalled. Instead, with no texts to aid
him, he summoned up the tragic voice of Bertran's dirge *Si tuit li
dol e.lh plor e.lh marrimen,* which was written on the death of
Prince Henry, the son of Henry II of England and Eleanor:[19]

If all the grief and sorrow, the strife,
The suffering, the pains, the many ills
That men heard tell of in this woeful life
Assembled, they would count as nil
Compared to the death of the young English King,
Who leaves behind youth and worth in tears
In this dark world beset with shadowy fears,
Lacking all joy, abounding in doleful spite.

Pound thinks back to a journey that he took years ago into the
English countryside, and the violence of English history (and his
own past) breaks over him:

That would have been Salisbury plain, and I have not thought of
    the Lady Anne for this twelve years
        Nor of Le Portel
How tiny the panelled room where they stabbed him
      In her lap, almost, La Stuarda
    Si tuit li dolh ehl planh el marrimen
      for the leopards and broom plants   (80/515)

Again at the beginning of Canto 84, as Pound hears of the death of
the poet J.P. Angold in the war, he summons Bertran's opening
line for another brief threnody.

    In the Later Cantos, where contemplation and the motifs of
Heaven abound, Pound saw the troubadours as companions of the
Neoplatonics, who kept a love of nature alive in the metaphysically
inclined Middle Ages. Birds abound in the Later Cantos, and the
beat of the village dance can be heard in the cry from Raimbaut de
Vaqueiras' *Kalenda Maja* (113/788), "Kalends of May."[20]

    The lyrical Canto 91 opens with two versions of the fourth line of Bernart's *Can vei la lauzeta mover*, along with musical accompaniment in nondurational measure.[21] Here Pound seems to be doing with music what he did with Arnaut's word *noigandres:* teasing it, testing it, trying to find the right phrasing. The poetic line *ab lo dolchor qu'al cor mi vai* (with the sweetness that comes to my heart) varies from Carl Appel's reading with an *ab* (with) substituted for *per* (through), with an incorrect *lo* for *la*, and with *li* (to him, the bird) changed to *mi* (to me, Pound). In the line Pound takes on the persona of the bird that is going to begin a flight. In fact, the entire canto can be read as a winging to the third heaven, the "terzo ciel" that closes it. Bernart's words and music impel the vision; when Bernart arrives at Dante's Italian words at the close, the reader sees the troubadour having arrived in the Italian's Heaven.

A similar assimilation occurs in Canto 93, which abounds with citations from Dante's *Convivio*. On page 624, part of the fourth stanza of Bernart's *Tant ai mo cor ple de joya* (I have a heart so full of joy) is dropped into a paradisal setting by the brook of Castalia, where the lines accord perfectly with the ambience:

First petals   and then cool rain
                         sward Castalia again
                              Peitz trai pena d'amor
                              Que Tristans l 'amador
                              Qu'a suffri mainta dolor
                                   Per Iseutz la bionda
First petals
                         and then cool rain
By sward Castalia again

The four lines of Provençal verse can be translated:

I undergo worse pain of love
Than Tristan the great lover,
Who suffered such great anguish
For Isolde the blonde.[22]

But all is not bliss in the Later Cantos, and here the satiric troubadours come into play. The bitter Peire Cardinal is cited in an antiwar context in 97/677, and Bertran's cry to warring barons to put their lands up on mortgage before making war *(Baros metetz en gatge)* is cited with wild abandon by Pound, who wants to underscore the economic nature of combat in Cantos 85/548 and 105/749.[23] The city of Poitiers, where the troubadour tradition was born, is named in connection with the martyrdom of Jacques de Molay in 87/573, and he in turn is linked with those Albigensians who died so bravely at Montségur in 87/574 and 92/619.

Yet what lingers longest in the mind after reading the Later Cantos are the magnificent passages in which the troubadours blend into the natural setting of their native southern France, which Pound knew so well: the ruined parapets of Ventadour, the brambles overgrowing Excideuil, the precipitous canyon beside Ussel, the rounded ledge where Hautefort proudly faces the sun, the willows drooping into the rivers south of Poitiers, the wild crags around Foix and Comminges, the arch at Orange, the temple at Nîmes, the moats of Périgueux, the battlements of Carcassonne, the sun-filtered parks of Toulouse, the poplar-lined, roller-coaster roads from Tulle to Brive and Cahors. Although Pound flirted with the Arabic-origin theory of composition in his early years, he finally came to see the poets fully at home in their true habitat, with the music school of Limoges on one side and the Platonizing school of Chartres to the north.

In a final fragment on page 802, Pound assembles one last ideogrammic tribute to the troubadours. He puts two lines from Bernart de Ventadour's lark poem alongside a natural setting of larks rising from a field at Allègre.[24] This rise and fall is mirrored in the "bankruptcy" *(faillite)* of François Bernouard, who failed in his grand quest to print handsome editions of important books.[25] In a similar way, Bernart's lark failed in his noble attempt to climb to the heavens, and Pound himself feared that he had failed to find a suitable conclusion for his own work. All these "fallers," or failures, trail off in a brilliant blaze of glory that imitates the rise and fall of the roads of Provence and Périgord:

La faillite de François Bernouard, Paris
or a field of larks at Allègre,
    "es laissa cader"   [and lets himself fall]
so high toward the sun and then falling,
    "de joi sas alas"   [with joy his wings]
to set here the roads of France.

Chapter Four
Dante As a Cohering Voice in the Later Cantos

Although the Later Cantos are not unified in a strictly logical or narrative manner, they do hold together in a number of ways. First, there is the central ideogram discussed in Chapter One that lends coherence; second, there is the recurrence of basic image clusters, such as those treated in Chapter Two; and third, there are the repetitions of certain voices, or "personae," as Pound liked to call them, with their particular "messages." The following chapters will deal separately with these messages (banking in Five; nature worship in Six; civilizing art in Eight; city rule in Nine) or with particular voices (Apollonius of Tyana in Seven; Leo the Wise in Nine; Confucius in Ten; Madame de Rémusat in Eleven; and Anselm in Twelve).

Perhaps the most important of the cohering voices is that of Dante Alighieri, one of Pound's favorite personae.[1] It would be foolish to say that the Later Cantos form an exact parallel to Dante's *Paradiso*, but there is a strong heavenly cast to much of the rhetoric. There are also many clues in *Rock-Drill* and *Thrones*, the two major parts of the Later Cantos, that Pound is attempting to soar to celestial heights. For example, one can cite the lines "to enter the presence at sunrise/ up out of hell, from the labyrinth" (Canto 93/632), which indicate a sudden turning upward from the contorted context of the Early Cantos. The beautiful dawn scene of *Purgatorio* 1.115-17, with "the gentle rustle of the sea," is recalled in Canto 92/620: "And from far/ il tremolar della marina."[2] Similarly, the line "Alighieri, a rag over his eyes" in Canto 100/718 seems to present a reaction to the blinding light (Chinese characters *pai² jih⁴*, "white light") which precedes it. This is the blinding light of the Empyrean. Furthermore, Pound himself frequently spoke in special terms of this last part of the work, as in a letter to George Santayana, written on December 8, 1939: "I have also got to the end of a job or part of a job (money in history) and for personal ends have got to tackle philosophy or my 'paradise.'"[3]

A distinction must be made between the visions of Heaven presented by Dante and Pound. Dante treated his Paradise as an ethereal, abstract place, having nothing to do with the traditional Elysian Fields or with a Utopian city. Pound would not settle for this cosmological setting. (In Chapter One, the city was shown to be an important part of the basic ideogram of the work.) Pound's Paradise is, at its base, a terrestrial one, and far more urban than pastoral. He absolutely refused to see the city as Hell, even though he traded London and Paris for the rather small city of Rapallo as his own dwelling place.

Since his philosophical training was heavily influenced by the Neoplatonists, Pound did not, however, want to limit his concept of the ideal to a social context. After the late 1930s, when he was finishing his basic work on economics, he turned with renewed interest to mystical works, even to the spiritualism of William Butler Yeats which had previously troubled him gravely. He rediscovered men like John Heydon, the forgotten seventeenth-century occultist, and delved into little-read works like Philostratus' *Life of Apollonius of Tyana*—that brilliant account of the life of a Hellenic Messiah. It is hard to imagine Pound spending much time on Apollonius in the 1920s and 1930s, for he would have seen too much of the Buddhist in the unheralded wise man.

After the purgative effect of the Pisan detention camp, the madhouse of St. Elizabeths seems to have almost magically transformed itself into a kind of monastery. Pound had many friends to take him books, and he finally had access to what had always been lacking in Rapallo, the magnificent reserve of scholarly material in the Library of Congress. As a result, his homecoming was not as bitter as it might have been. Out of the hellish atmosphere of the asylum, Pound was able to achieve high states of mind far removed from the chaos around him, even though they did not last long: "but the mind as Ixion, unstill, ever turning" (Canto 113/790).

Pound fully believed that the continuum of the mind will never admit long periods of any one of the three states of mind that Dante had carved into his canticles. This conviction may well answer the criticism of the anti-Poundians who complain that there is no continuity in the Later Cantos, that 85 and 86, which depend heavily on the *Shu King*, or *History Classic*, are placed at random next to 87 and 88, where the American history of the Age of Jackson predominates, without any clearly marked correlation between the two units. The negativists will hold that the social nature of most of *Rock-Drill* and *Thrones* does not blend well with the mystical elements. How can we go from the technical language of the *Code of Justinian* to snippets from the *Life of Apollonius*, or how can we relate the Del Mar lecture on economics, which forms the underlying structure of Canto 97, to the imposing religious opening of Canto 98? Pound's answer might on the one hand be: don't ask for continuity from an author who does not prize it or even believe in it. On the other hand, one must broach the problem about the welding of Aristotelian and Neoplatonic elements in Pound's philosophy, for the trouble lies here.

Undoubtedly, the arrangement of the Later Cantos indicates that Pound does not feel that a problem of unity exists. He implies that a rock-drill is necessary for the erection of thrones, thrones that are both the seats of kings (and thus social in nature), but also "something God can sit on/ without having it sqush" (Canto 88/581). Pound would ask: why separate your physics from your metaphysics? Why can't the two be related? In fact, his admiration for Confucius and Mencius lies precisely in the fact that he feels that their philosophy is intimately bound up with the handling of religious rites. There is no meta-physics, strictly speaking, in their world-views, for nature is presented as an undifferentiated continuum. Pound actually goes so far as to suggest that the same holds true for a great deal of the best Occidental thought:

meta ta physika
    metah, not so extraneous, possibly not so extraneous
most "*metas*" seem to be in with.   (97/680)

Canto 98 is a good illustration of the way in which Pound builds on the so-called *Sacred Edict*, or *Sheng U*, of Emperor K'ang Hsi in

order to establish ground rules for the construction of an ideal
society (see Chapter Ten). During the course of the canto, Pound
lists all sixteen of the points which the edict covered, usually in
paraphrase and sometimes obliquely. The canto ends with the
mention of six rites for a festival, thus linking the religious
ceremony, which is tied in with nature, to the social proclamation.
The process is continued in Canto 99, where the religious rites and
the "blue grass" of the natural scene blend with a further spelling
out of the sixteen points; it contains the line: "To trace out and to
bind together" (725). Doubtlessly, Pound is using the justifiable
etymology which analyzes the Latin word *religio* as a composite of *re-* (again, together) and *ligo* (bind). Religion is the
instrument for binding all things together, including those of
ostensibly lower orders. To invert the idea, a social paradise is a
necessary prelude for a lasting psychic one. If one is thinking in
terms of perfection, he must bind nature, society, and the
individual psyche into an ideogrammic relationship where whatever is said of the one must relate to the other. As Pound himself
says at the close of the canto:

The fu jen receives heaven, earth, middle   [blessed man]
                        and grows.

The design of the Later Cantos becomes apparent to anyone who
reads them with a sincere attempt to give them their due. Granted
they are full of many apparently arbitrary details, and the language
in them is sometimes clipped; still, one can see that this section
shows the hand of a master. The last part of the work shows a
development of many of the ideas that Pound had introduced
earlier. The Kung of Canto 13 merges with Mencius fully as the
voice of human reason in the sphere of social conduct. Cantos 85
and 86 reinforce the lesson of the earlier Chinese Cantos: that
justice and peace were attained only in dynasties that followed
Confucian precepts. Cantos 88 and 89 continue the work of the
Jefferson and Adams Cantos, presenting the administrations of
Jackson and Van Buren largely as seen through the pages of
Thomas Hart Benton's *Thirty Years' View*. These cantos are all of
the true rock-drill type, for they deal with the forging of a paradise
as a political entity.

Canto 90, by contrast, presents the heaven of pure contemplation, the place of beautiful women, ocular apprehension, prayer, and love. One might say that the balanced state of mind in Canto 90, in Pound's view, can exist only upon the foundation of the preceding parts of the work. Similarly, in Canto 94 the Messiah of love, Apollonius, rises out of the ordered world of the Roman Empire. Unlike Christ, whom Pound constantly criticized for being unpolitical, Apollonius was concerned with the Empire's effect on Greece. He lectured Vespasian and thus helped to prepare the way for the overthrow of Nero. It is no wonder, then, that next to some lovely paraphrases of Philostratus' Greek, which describe Apollonius riding up the Nile River in his barge or communicating with seals, tigers, and leopards, Pound presents the rock-like legal language upon which the Roman and Byzantine Empires were founded.

The influence of the economist Alexander del Mar is quite apparent in the *Thrones* section of the poem, where Pound discovers Byzantium. Del Mar claimed in his *History of Monetary Systems* that the Byzantine Empire's standard silver-gold ratio of 12 to 1 and its equitable rates of interest sustained the impressive millennial sweep of its empire. He thus supplied economic grounds for asserting the might and the majesty of an empire that Pound had admired for other reasons: Neoplatonism, which may rightfully be regarded as one of the primary heritages of the Byzantine Empire, and Byzantine or Romanesque art and architecture. After reading Del Mar, Pound had the final period to place between his America of Adams and the Greco-Roman past. The Italian Renaissance thus becomes largely ignored in the Later Cantos; instead, Byzantium moves in as the heir to the greatness of Greece and Rome and the direct progenitor of what is most salvageable for the present. Not curiously, Dante is seen as the Roman or Western product of the Byzantine development. Instead of regarding Dante as a pre-Renaissance realist and kinsman of Aquinas, Pound views him as a member of that fraternity of Neoplatonic nature disciples who preached love in the Apollonian tradition, with a strong dash of Aristotelian logic in his social thinking and classical precision in his words.

While Pound is bringing his Ancient-Medieval-Modern phases of history into focus, he is also doing something else that he has done before in his poem: linking the Greek (now the Byzantine Greek) with the Chinese, for Pound feels that these two cultures furnish the cornerstones for what is permanent in human endeavor, standing against the ravages of the Mongols, Moguls, Tartars, Cazars, Avars, Gepids, and the many tribes that roll off the pages of *Thrones.*

Pound scatters his Chinese characters throughout Canto 96, which presents the early history of the Lombards (admirable lawgivers under Rothar and his successors), the history of Byzantine rulers after Constantine, and finally the *Edict of the Eparch,* a decree issued by Leo the Wise (ruled 886-912). For example, Pound offers a direct correlation of the Greek words in the edict with some Chinese that runs in the right column on page 659. The edict itself lays down the laws for merchants and tradesmen in clear, concise language. Pound admires the precision so much that he is constantly commenting on individual words in a way that makes the word of the lord seem almost the logos itself. The canto that follows gives Del Mar's yoking of the Chinese and Byzantine systems as prime samples of achievement. In Cantos 98 and 99, a fusion occurs, for here Pound pulls K'ang Hsi's *Sacred Edict* into alignment with the decree of Leo the Wise. He thus accomplishes poetically what Del Mar does discursively.

But of all the sources available to Pound, Dante is perhaps the most important in his unifying effect. To fully appreciate the Italian, the reader must focus on the modern writer's handling of philosophy. In so doing, one must move to the *Convivio,* that much-neglected philosophical work that Dante himself abandoned, a work that appealed greatly to Pound during his incarceration in St. Elizabeths.[4] In his handbook, Francis Fergusson spells out the importance of the *Convivio* in the subtitle of his third chapter: "Dante's Cult of Reason, 1293-1308."[5] More than any other twentieth-century critic, Fergusson was keenly aware of the relationship between Dante and the Greek philosopher, as when he makes the seminal equation: "For Dante, *amor* = the movement of the spirit toward what it perceives as pleasant or good = 'action' (in Aristotle's terms)" (p. 50). Pound repeatedly expresses this movement as the *directio voluntatis* or the "direction of the will"; he in effect makes the *voluntas* or will almost equal *voluptas* or desire. The Latin term beloved by Pound is fully applicable to the volitionist tendencies of the *Convivio* as a whole. In Canto 87/572, Pound puts the Latin phrase under the Chinese character *chih*[4], which means "aim, intention," and later he expands his application:

Justice, directio voluntatis,
    or contemplatio as Richardus defined it in Benjamin Major.   (576)

Acts of cognition, acts of implementing virtue, and acts of love are all interrelated in Pound's mind. Most Dantistas will acknowledge that the same holds true for the Italian. Without love there can be no justice, and without love there can be no true knowledge, as is stated in Canto 77/467:

Their aims as one
directio voluntatis, as lord over the heart
    the two sages united

Another Chinese character called *chih*[4], which is defined on page 476 as "direction of one's will," appears to the right.

    Many medievalists would align Dante with St. Thomas Aquinas, but Pound rejects this coupling. He sees Dante working in a tradition that has its roots in Aristotle, but one that proliferates through those Neoplatonics who resisted hypermysticism on the one hand and an arid Scholasticism on the other; it was a tradition that retained some sense of love and a respect for nature, as Pound insists in 85/546:

Dante, out of St Victor (Richardus),
    Erigena with greek tags in his verses.

In Canto 87/570, Pound employs the tripartite Neoplatonic stages of cognition:

"Cogitatio, meditatio, contemplatio."
    Wrote Richardus, and Dante read him.

The love element is present in almost all the Neoplatonics, from Plotinus through St. Francis of Assisi, and is especially strong in Richard of St. Victor.

To return to the *Convivio*, which adds rational philosophic commentaries to poems of the heart, one can spell out at least three major statements of the work:

1. Love is presented as the perfect operation of the human organism.
2. What is said of individuals is fully applicable to societies.
3. Nobility is the name of the virtue that emanates from love; it cannot be attained by blood ties or money.

Point 1 is established in several places in the *Convivio*, but nowhere more eloquently than in the First Canzone, where Love is called the "true lord" (*segnor verace,* line 51), and in the commentary that follows. Pound seizes on this idea in Canto 93/626, which might almost be called the Dante Canto:

> That love is the "form" of philosophy,
> is its shape (è forma di Filosofia)
> and that men are naturally friendly
> at any rate from his (Dant's) point of view
> tho' he puts knowledge higher than I should
> and, elsewhere: "her" beltà,   [beauty]
>   cioè   moralitade,   [that is, morality]
> rains flakes of fire,"
>   but is not speaking of knowledge.

This is a general amalgam of several Dantesque passages, most notably the entire commentary in *Convivio,* Book 3, where Lady Philosophy is taken as the woman loved by the poet and in turn bestowing love upon him; the statement that "Love is the form of Philosophy" is made at 3.13.10. The rain of fire occurs in the canzone before the commentary in line 63: *Sua bieltà piove fiammelle di foco* (Her beauty rains down flakes of fire). The idea "that men are naturally friendly" is stated in *Convivio* 1.1: *ciascuno uomo a ciascuno uomo naturalmente è amico.* This concept is compressed in the general phase *compagnevole animale,* which means "companionable, friendly animal" or also "social animal," as is clear when Dante mentions Aristotle as his source in *Convivio* 4.4: *E però dice lo Filosofo che l'uomo natural- mente è compagnevole animale* (And thus the Philosopher says that man is naturally a friendly animal). Pound places the Italian phrase on page 626 of Canto 93, beside the hieroglyph that he associates with the Egyptian Kati (Khaty). It occurs again in Canto 95/643:

"Not political," Dante says, a
            "compagnevole animale"

Pound does not want us to interpret Aristotle's *politike* as "political"; a few lines later he connects the Greek word with the verb *poleuo*, "to plow," thereby underscoring the pastoral qualities of the connotation, as against the smoke-filled rooms of cities.

As one can see from the discussion, point 1 above leads quite naturally to point 3, for a man in love will radiate not only the emotion, the physical *virtus*, but also the moral virtue that proceeds from it. As Pound says on page 626 in Canto 93: " 'onestade risplende.' Dio, la prima bontade" (Honor or honesty shines. God, the first goodness).[6] These fragments occur in the *Convivio's* Third Canzone, from line 121 onward:

The soul which is adorned by this goodness
never holds it concealed in her,
for from the principle which is wedded to her body,
she manifests it to her death.
Obedient, gentle, and modest
she is in her first age,
and her person is adorned with beauty . . .

L'anima cui adorna esta bontate
non la si tiene ascosa,
ché dal principio ch'al corpo si sposa
la mostra infin la morte.
Ubidente, soave e vergognosa
e ne la prima etate,
e sua persona adorna di bieltate ...

The major ideas are picked up in the commentary that follows in 4.25.11 ff., and in 3.15.11 as follows:

Whereby one should know that morality is the beauty of philosophy;
for just as bodily beauty results from the members being rightfully
placed, so the beauty of wisdom, which is the body of philosophy . . .
results from the ordering of the moral virtues, which make this
pleasure felt sensibly. And so I say that her beauty—that is,
morality—rains down flakes of fire.

Dove è da sapere che la moralitade è bellezza de la filosofia; chè
così come la bellezza del corpo resulta da le membra in quanto sono
debitamente ordinate, così la bellezza de la sapienza, che è corpo di Filosofia . . .
resulta da l'ordine de le virtudi morali, che fanno
quella piacere sensibilmente. E però dico che sua biltà,
cioè moralitade, piove fiammelle di foco . . .

Pound draws the social implications from this passage in Canto 93/627:

> and mentions distributive justice, Dante does, in Convivio
>> Four, eleven
> "cui adorna esta bontade". . . .

Indeed *Convivio* 4.11.6 does contain the phrase *distributiva giustizia*, and the social ramifications of the words, which spring from the psychology of the individual, are never forgotten.

Both the Second and the Third Canzoni of the *Convivio* seem to have blended in Pound's mind, and indeed the fusion is not incorrect, for what is said of the good operation of a soul in love can be said equally well of a loving society, as was noted in point 2 above. It is a Neoplatonic tenet that there is never a dearth of love from loving, for love is not a material object like a pie, and therefore it is not diminished as it is distributed. Love is increased through distribution, like all things spiritual, including light, or the bread of angels, the *panis angelicus* of Canto 93/623, which Dante promises to distribute among his readers in *Convivio* 1.1. We can all share the feast of wisdom, where the bounty is ever flowing. But the spiritual quality for Pound must also be pragmatic, for his metaphysic is never entirely divorced from his concerns for politics or for ethics, any more than it is in Dante. That is why Pound puts the name of the good Egyptian nobleman Antef next to the Dantesque quotation on page 623; it underscores the social application of the metaphysical rule, for Antef distributed bread as well as love among his people, and

> . . . T'ang opened the copper mine
> (distributive function of money). (88/580)

Pound uses "bread" in the social-communal sense, as well as in the religious-communal, but without any Christian application: the wheat is produced through hard work and attention to the soil, not by any miracles.

The doctrine of love as the never-ending "bread of the spiritual life" is beautifully stated by Vergil (how Reason apprehends!) in a longish passage in *Purgatorio* 15.46 ff. It is repeated in an abbreviated form in *Paradiso* 5.105, with the cry "Look! here is one who will increase our loves!" (*"Ecco chi crescerà li nostri amori"*), which is uttered by every one of the souls who approach Dante in the sphere of Mercury. Pound picks up the line in Cantos 89/590 and 116/796, using it perhaps to the fullest advantage in 93/631:

E "chi crescerà" they would be individuals.
      Swedenborg said "of societies"
                  by attraction.

Emanuel Swedenborg is used to expand the concept outward—a typical centrifugal movement in Pound's poetry.

The importance of man's social nature is spelled out again and again in *The Cantos* and in the *Convivio*. Dante remarks in 4.27.3: "as Aristotle says, man is a social or political animal" (*sì come Aristotile dice, l'uomo è animale civile*). In *Paradiso* 8, Charles Martel, who died in 1294 but knew Dante well enough to cite the opening line of the First Canzone of the *Convivio* upon meeting him, is discoursing with the pilgrim about a variety of topics, one of them being the apparent disparity between the talents of people, a disparity that does not correspond with the absolutely equitable way in which the heavens revolve. He says abruptly (line 115):

      "But tell me—would it be worse
for man on earth, if he wasn't a citizen?"

      *"Or di: sarebbe il peggio
per l'omo in terra, se non fosse cive?"*

Dante has to reply: yes. Charles goes on to explain the disparity by saying that we mortals are too far removed from Perfect Intelligence to operate with perfection. This is, in a sense, another statement of the Fortuna theme, that everything under the moon is imperfect.

But given this inequitable social base, man must strive for justice, even though at times the attainment of it seems impossible. Dante uses the ancient Roman Cato almost as a symbol for the concept in *Purgatorio* 1.42, where he speaks about the man "moving his honest feathers" like some proud bird: *movendo quelle oneste piume*. Pound, who was much concerned with the workings of justice during his confinement at St. Elizabeths, mentions Cato in Canto 86/565 and "Honest feathers" in Canto 96/664. He gives us a tiny capsule of the birth of philosophy through Pythagoras in Canto 93/626:

> In the time of Numa Pompilius
>   che Pitagora si chiamò.
> "non sempre" (in the 3rd of Convivio)
> or as above stated "jagged"
>   l'amor che ti fa bella[7]

These elliptical allusions depend first upon *Convivio* 3.11.3:

> . . . almost at the time of Numa Pompilius, second king of the
> Romans, there lived a very noble philosopher, who was
> called Pythagoras (*che si chiamò Pittagora*).

The verse establishes the foundation of philosophy concurrently with a strong kingship that paved the way for the Roman Empire. Pound (and Dante?) suggests that there is a correlation between the two. Pound's "non sempre" (not always) appears in *Convivio* 3.13.3:

> I say therefore that people who are in love here,
> that is: in this life, feel [intelligence] in their
> thought, not always, but when Love makes his peace felt.

> *Dico adunque che la gente che s'innamora 'qui,' cioè*
> *in questa vita, la sente nel suo pensiero, non sempre,*
> *ma quando Amore fa de la sua pace sentire.*

Philosophy is connected with the emotions here, and the notion that tranquility is a paradisal state of mind achieved through love and the intellect is clearly expressed, although, as Pound notes

HSIEN³

again, the duration is "jagged." Philosophy thus becomes a
sentient thing, as Cavalcanti had presented it. Pound further
makes Dante subscribe to his own belief that heaven is a condition
of mind; as the Egyptian Kati says at the opening of Canto 93: "A
man's paradise is his good nature."

The regenerative power of intellectual love, leading to a "new
life," was Dante's central theme in the *Vita Nuova*. Love redeems,
as well as sustains. This idea is also central to Pound's thought, as
he shows in Canto 93/630, when he writes the words "nuova vita"
under the Chinese character *hsien*[3], which means "show, appear"
as a verb and "glorious, manifest" as an adjective. Next come the
Italian words "e ti fiammeggio" (and I flame, glow for you), which
is what Beatrice says in *Paradiso* 5.1 as she illuminates the mind of
her lover and enlightens his eyes. Pound constantly relates this
concept of renovation to the Confucian idea of renewal through
learning and action, as in Canto 93/629, where the words harken

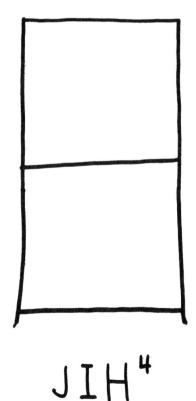

JIH[4]

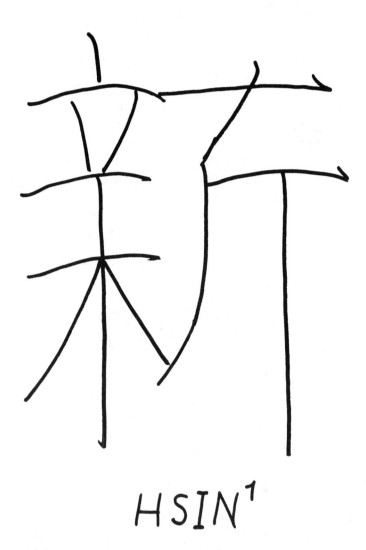

HSIN¹

back to Canto 53/264: "Tching prayed on the mountain and/ wrote
MAKE IT NEW/ on his bath tub." The *hsin¹ jih¹* characters appear
to the right, with a punctuation mark inadvertently added by
Pound's wife, Dorothy.[8] On page 629 they are related to the eyes
and knowledge, with a stress on the empirical nature of learning
and upon spiritual radiance. Since the character *hsin¹* consists of an
axe clearing out weeds, it can be further related to Dante's use of
novelle piante (new plants) to replace the old in *Purgatorio* 33. 143.

We thus see Dante and Confucius blending in matters imagistic as well as conceptual.

The eyes and light, in fact, dominate Canto 93, just as they permeate the *Paradiso*. Pound almost seems to see the entire personality in terms of light, as in Canto 107/756:

Light, cubic
            by volume
so that Dante's view is quite natural;
            (Tenth, Paradiso, nel Sole)[9]

Or again on page 762, where the Dante-Confucius (Kung) correspondence is spelled out, in company with a Neoplatonic philosopher, an English lawgiver, and an America-Swiss scientist:

So that Dante's view is quite natural:
            this light
                        as a river
            in Kung; in Ocellus, Coke, Agassiz
                        rhei, the flowing
                        this persistent awareness

The Greek word *rhei* means "flows," as in *panta rhei* (all things flow), and serves to connect the light and the river.

The Later Cantos are bathed in words of love, just as they are resplendent with light—the two going naturally together. The *terzo cielo* (third heaven) mentioned in Canto 91/617 is, properly speaking, the locus for the entire last third of the poem. [10] For Love as the great dictator (Dante's *ch'e' ditta dentro*[11] of *Purgatorio* 24.54) is cited in Canto 85/552, and the warm, flowing movement of the Later Cantos of the *Paradiso* is captured in lines such as these from Canto 91/611:

Light *compenetrans* of the spirits
The Princess Ra-Set has climbed
            to the great knees of stone,
She enters protection,
            the great cloud is about her,
She has entered the protection of crystal
                        convien che si mova
                        la mente, amando
                        XXVI, 34

Here Pound sees the whole universal turning as an act of love, pre-
cisely as Dante did, with the outer stretches of the protective
Crystalline Heavens mentioned. The Italian lines, taken from
Paradiso 26.34-35, mean "It is right that the mind should move
itself by loving." At this point, the words seem as much Pound's as
Dante's.

One can see as one proceeds through the Later Cantos how
Pound, in fact, becomes Dante, who in turn takes on much of the
form of the great sage of China. All three personalities by the end
of *The Cantos* are inextricably interwoven. The sage delights in
water, in tranquility, in joy. And in Canto 100/716, Pound again
cites Dante's *Paradiso* 18.42 in a context of social joy and grace
abounding:

Barley, rice, cotton, tax-free
                    with hilaritas.
Letizia, Dante, Canto 18   a religion   [Joy]
Virtù enters.   [Virtue]
            Buona da sè volontà.   [Will is good by itself]
Lume non è, se non dal sereno   [No light if not from the serene]
            stone to stone, as a river descending
the sound a gemmed light,
form is from the lute's neck.[12]

Pound uses the Florentine in a way that brings the admirer of
Dante as much surprise as delight. For example, one of the most
formidable passages in the *Comedy* occurs in *Paradiso* 24.65 ff.,
where Dante is defining faith for St. Peter in order to enter the
gates of Heaven:

"Faith is the substance of things hoped for,
and the proof of things not apparent,
and this I take to be its quiddity."

"*fede è sustanza di cose sperate*
e argomento de le non parventi;
e questa pare a me sua quiditate."

One can read this passage a hundred times in the Italian and see
only an arid Scholastic definition here. But when one sees Pound's

adaptation of the puzzling word *quiditate*, as in Canto 89/600, he pauses and considers:

Wright spoke to mind not to passions and
    he it was brought in Polk.
        Quiditas, remarked D. Alighieri.

Suddenly, we are forced to rethink Dante, to see that the "faith" he is talking about is a very dynamic thing that depends upon ideals, not upon actualization; the proposition is firmly volitionist and active: faith is something that one must constantly create. The concept springs to life with renewed vigor, and this vigor can be translated by Pound into poetry of the highest order:

"A spirit in cloth of gold"
    so Merlin's moder said,
or did not say,
    left the quidity
        but remembered
& from fire to crystal
    via the body of light,
        the gold wings assemble   (91/615)

Faith is substantial, is a part of the what-ness of the perfectly realized human creature. Only in the last moments of ascension to the purely spiritual can it be put aside, or not so much put aside as truly transcended.

    In Washington the Italian master almost seemed to step down out of his books and lend a hand to the man who more than any other over the last seven hundred years had heeded his every word and had tried to "make him new." The figure of the Italian sage—whether the benign Dante of Botticelli or the magic Dante of the medievalists—was certainly the kind of man whom Pound envisaged during those troubled days. The Dante of fire and brimstone and tirades on usury never disappeared; he merely yielded to the more tranquil figure, who stands in the great tradition of Apollonius of Tyana and Confucius. It was this persona that Pound himself finally adopted, and it is this spirit that pervades the Later Cantos.

Chapter Five

The Battle Against the Unholy Marriage of Banking and Politics

Of all Pound's Later Cantos, the most dramatic may well be Canto 88. It falls roughly into three parts: a duel between John Randolph of Roanoke and Henry Clay; a long meditative stretch; and the crucial encounter between the forces of Thomas Hart Benton and Andrew Jackson against Nicholas Biddle and the Second National Bank of the United States.

In every epic there is a villain. Sometimes it is human, such as Blazes Boylan in Joyce's *Ulysses*, and sometimes it is bestial, such as Polyphemus in the *Odyssey*. More often than not, the bestial acts like a human being (one thinks of Grendel's mother in *Beowulf*) or the human acts like a beast (as the Heirs of Carrion beat and disgrace the daughters of The Cid in *El Cid*). In Canto 88 there is a comparable situation. The true beast is the Bank, which Andrew Jackson constantly called a "hydra of corruption." This monster had been fought in its earlier form by John Adams and Thomas Jefferson; in its second appearance, it was resisted by Benton and friends.

But the National Bank is not the only source of villainy in *The Cantos*—far from it. Evil is symbolized in the central figure of Geryon, adapted from Dante's *Divine Comedy*. This is a money-devouring beast with the tricks and turns of the shyster. It has many spawn, ranging from the grain-hoggers of the Roman Empire through the coin-debasers of the Byzantine period, and finally, in the worst form, to the High Financiers who asserted their power at the time of the founding of the Dutch East Indies Company. They extend to the present day with the shadowy "gnomes of Zurich," the stock-market riggers, cartel operators, sovereign-state monpolists, and—to use one of Pound's coinings—the international *Usurocrats,* who play speculative games with dollars, pounds, yen, and marks, thus triggering depressions, inflations, and revolutions.

In his brilliant autobiography, *Thirty Years' View,* Thomas Hart Benton, a Congressman from Missouri, tells how he faced the evil directly.[1] An eloquent spokesman of the old school, with a flair for rhetoric and a keen concern for the needs of the people, he attacked the Bank with the courage of a Beowulf. Benton was a more polished version of Andrew Jackson, with whom he sided often against Daniel Webster, Henry Clay, John Calhoun, and Nicholas Biddle. But the canto does not present Benton immediately. It is Pound's intention to withhold certain facts until the last minute, for what is dismissed as fast as what is too easily grasped? Instead, Pound focuses on the duel between John Randolph (self-styled "of Roanoke") and Henry Clay, the most famous duel in American annals after that of Burr and Hamilton. Why this particular event? An examination of the poetry tells all.

Randolph of Roanoke was a brilliant, aristocratic, eccentric, fiery orator, a cousin of Thomas Jefferson: "As a political entertainer he had no rival in his day and has had no adequate successor since."[2] He hailed from Charlotte County, Virginia, where he delivered some of his greatest speeches, as well as in Congress, where he appeared attired in English riding gear, flourishing a whip. He dazzled audiences with his epigrammatic wit and his caustic tongue at a time when many politicians were unspeakably drab. Yet, like most men of genius, he sometimes went too far. In attacking President John Quincy Adams and his Secretary of State, Henry Clay, for trying to entangle America in Caribbean politics, Randolph said that "a letter from General Salazar, the Mexican Minister at Washington . . . bore the ear-mark of having been manufactured or forged by the Secretary of State, and denounced the administration as a corrupt coalition between the puritan and blackleg"—with Adams the former and Clay the latter.

These harsh words were immediately picked up by Clay, who "gave the absolute challenge, and received the absolute acceptance" for fighting a duel. The canto opens at this point on April 1, 1826, when Benton is being asked by Randolph to be his second, but he has to refuse, because he is related to Mrs. Clay. Randolph, therefore, chooses Colonel Josiah Tattnall of Georgia as his second and Clay takes General Jesup (not "Tatnall" and "Jessup," as Pound spells them). The events are presented by Pound rather hazily—intentionally so—for even if one reads the prose account by Benton, he sees here a pathetic series of misunderstandings that could lead to a real tragedy (Aaron Burr's killing of Alexander Hamilton). The interplay is really like a minor war, in which one side moves a little too far in one direction, forcing the other to take a reverse action in a way that both deplore. As Pound notes, Randolph was acting in "defiance of Adams, not Clay," and Clay was not the least bit anxious to confront his dynamic opponent in a duel. The entire incident had mushroomed out of a mere suggestion that Clay might have tampered with certain documents to lead public opinion in a certain direction, but ultimately Clay interpreted Randolph's "bitter philippic" as charging him "with having forged or manufactured a paper connected with the Panama mission." And so the duel, which was totally lamentable, seemed inevitable.

Pound stays close to Benton's concise, excellent prose throughout the opening lines of the canto. His first verse is virtually identical with the opening words of Benton's Chapter 26, and except for some occasional crypticizing in the narration, the poetry skims over Benton's surface, presenting the facts, but obscuring them slightly with a certain mist. Insofar as there was any palpable motivation for the duel beyond Clay's defense of his name, it was countered by Randolph's curious decision that he would allow himself to be shot at above the bridge in Little Falls, Virginia, but that he would not shoot back. He thus wanted to give Clay a chance to defend his name, but also to protect his own contention that whatever is said in a public forum is not privately answerable. Also, his failure to shoot would leave him with no guilt for having violated the statutes of prohibition against duels in the state of Virginia. Pound admires the hauteur of Randolph. He also approves heartily of the man's separation of his private life and personal conduct—a separation that Pound himself found lacking in America, where he had lost a teaching job on charges of sexual license.

On the night before the duel, Benton visited Clay's residence, and talked with the man, his wife, and his children. Then in

Georgetown he called on Randolph, who was making out his will, leaving some coins to his good friend, Nathaniel Macon. Having sent his cousin and godson John Randolph Bryan away from the scene, Randolph confided in Benton that he would not harm Clay's children by shooting their father. He then sent his black serving-man, Johnny, to the local branch of the National Bank to get some gold pieces, since he wanted to leave his friends some memorial coins in the event that he was killed. A comic episode ensues when Johnny returns, saying that no coins are available. Randolph, venting his legendary fury, swept up on his horse and galloped down Pennsylvania Avenue, where he

> . . . asked for the state of his account, was shown it, and found to be some four thousand dollars in his favor. He asked for it. The teller took up packages of bills, and civilly asked in what sized notes he would have it. "I want money," said Mr. Randolph, putting emphasis on the word; and at that time it required a bold man to intimate that United States bank notes were not money. The teller, beginning to understand him, and willing to make sure, said, inquiringly, "You want silver?" "I want my money!" was the reply. Then the teller, lifting boxes to the counter, said politely: "Have you a cart, Mr. Randolph, to put it in?" "That is my business, sir," said he.[3]

The anecdote does at least two things: it further reduces the seriousness of an already questionable duel; and it emphasizes Randolph's lofty, condescending attitude toward the American banking system, which was issuing notes wildly, without anything solid behind them. Benton and Randolph were both "hard-money" men who were against a too-easy issuance of currency; Pound was less severe on this point, although he leads one to believe that in early nineteenth-century America, with its abundant stores of silver and gold, this policy was perhaps preferable.

As we move on to the actual encounter, Pound mentions that Randolph's stepfather brought out an edition of Blackstone's *Commentaries,* an indispensable item for lawyers of the day. Pound thus views Randolph in a great historical tradition of political action and law.[4] We are then introduced to the dueling area in a forest, which contains a depression, or "basin" (Pound uses the

word "basis"; the final letter is blacked out of most editions of
Benton through faulty type), and suddenly—just when we expect
the heart of the action—the whole event seems to trail away. What
happened? Who won? Pound does not tell us. If the reader wants
to know, he has to go to Benton (which is part of Pound's purpose:
driving people to seldom-read but extremely important sources).
The answer is: nobody won. Both men misshot one time; Clay had
a second shot, ripped a hole in the coat of Randolph, who leapt forward, saying, "I do not fire at you, Mr. Clay." He extended his
hand, asking for a brand-new coat. "I am glad the debt is no
greater," replied Clay. In short, the entire event was abortive, and
"The joy of all was extreme."

Pound sighs: "Bellum perenne," perennial war, and later in
the canto he repeats in Latin: "I sing perennial war." But in this
case, there is a pleasant outcome. As Benton comments, this was
the "last high-toned duel that I have witnessed." And so the
episode ends. What follows are some sad dates in the history of
banking: the creation of Paterson's Bank of England, which began
the whole process of creating currency "out of nothing," and a
mention of the year 1878, when paper notes in America were
issued endlessly, in part controlled by foreign money interests.[5]

What is one to make of the duel? Why is it given such a prominent role? The conflict between the hard-money-minded, anti-
Banking Randolph and his opponent, Clay, sets the stage for the
major confrontation between Jackson and Biddle. Old Andy
wanted wealth "in the pants of the people," as Pound was fond of
quoting: Biddle did not. Randolph stands in the great line of
Americans who fought for their principles: nonentanglement in
the politics of others, antislavery, hard money as opposed to loose
paper currency that could be endlessly printed at the whim of a
few individuals in charge of a "national" bank that was really operating like a private trust. Randolph's virtues may be summed up in
Pound's unforgettable line: "Without honour men sink into
servitude."

In the meditative, associative stretch that follows, Randolph is
aligned with a host of others: the Chinese emperor T'ang, who
distributed money to the people by opening the copper mines; the
Roman Emperor Antoninus, who loaned money on behalf of the
state; the Chinese philosopher Mencius, who stressed that every

man had a role in contributing to the general welfare; St. Ambrose, who cried out against "hoggers of harvest" in his attacks on usurers; Carlo Delcroix, a Mussolini advisor who constantly inveighed against the actions of the greedy; and finally two of Pound's great heroes: "Master" John Adams, who told Americans that "Every bank of discount is downright corruption" (Canto 71/416), and Major C.H. Douglas, who first put Pound onto his economic quests in London in the pre-World War I period.

Alternating with these men who attack banks and any private hoarding of the bounty of nature, the heritage of all, are the men who stress beauty: the pantheistic philosopher Scotus Erigena (and his patron, Charles the Bald, Carolus Calvus); the nature-loving Italian Baccin, who liked to plant trees; the American poet E.E. Cummings; the Catholic priest Henri Jacques, who liked to talk with the Japanese nature spirits atop Mount Rokku; and the French novelist Anatole France, who showed in his allegorical novel *Penguin Island* that states can run autonomously, without meddling in each other's economic systems, as Russia and China have demonstrated even to this day. With the opening of Japan to world trade by Commodore Perry—an act that was once hailed, but is now surrounded by certain doubts—we switch to the third and final part of the canto, the fateful battle between pro-Bank and anti-Bank forces.

Once again Pound does not rush into his subject. He considers a variety of acts and attitudes that are drawn from volume 1 of Benton's work about events during the administrations of John Quincy Adams and Andy Jackson. We begin with the exclusion of all foreign coins except the Spanish after 1819, an act that Benton

> . . . denounced . . . as a fraud . . . upon the people of the States. The States had surrendered their power over the coinage to Congress; they made the surrender in language which clearly implied that their currency of foreign coins was to be continued to them; yet that currency is suppressed; a currency of intrinsic value, for which they paid interest to nobody, is suppressed; and a currency without intrinsic value, a currency of paper subject to every fluctuation, and for the supply of which corporate bodies receive interest, is substituted in its place.[6]

Benton notes that "Since the law took effect the United States had only been a thoroughfare for foreign coins to pass through." Their exclusion shows that private individuals were gaining control of the currency.[7] Pound stresses this passage because it clearly states that the States or Congress—not a Federal Reserve System— should control the money flow.

These ominous words are followed by a haunting obituary notice: "OBEUNT 1826, July 4." Thomas Jefferson and John Adams, whom Pound respects as the true founders of the nation, both died on that very same day "exactly fifty years after . . . that Declaration of Independence."[8] Then a series of short statements appears, that can be tabulated as follows: land should go to settlers, not for the building of military establishments; a tariff is needed to protect certain American goods from British competition; Monsieur de Tocqueville's acid attacks on Jackson and the American democracy are sharply reprimanded as the work of a pretentious and inaccurate outsider; Nathaniel Macon, the close friend of Randolph, who fought at the battle of Guilford during the Revolutionary War, retires; renewal of the charter of the National Bank "has failed in the great end of establishing a uniform and sound currency"; "war upon the British salt tax . . . finished it in 1822"; Jackson opposes the centralization principle in the building of the Maysville Road, leaving such construction up to the individual states.[9] Here, in rapid-fire order, a list of facts is thrown at the reader. Is it possible to digest them all now? Probably not. This is not Pound's intention. His ideogrammic method consists in throwing out bait, teasing the appetite with certain seemingly disconnected facts, and then tying them together later.

After "uncontrovertable [sic] paper," we have four lines that form a unit. Benton contrasts England, which was "a prey to all the evils of unconvertible paper" with the United States, which "possess gold mines, now yielding half a million per annum, with every prospect of equalling those of Peru. . . . We have what is superior to mines, namely, the exports which command the money of the world."[10] This is a statement of Pound's basic belief that the riches of any nation are its resources in terms of the abundance of nature. Even today, the United States' power to export or to produce for itself (or to develop new goods to replace those which it lacks in sufficient richness, such as oil) is so strong that it could probably subsist alone, whereas few other nations could. Again, Pound and Benton favor tangible goods and cold hard cash to bank notes, which can vary according to the manipulations of a few powerful, greedy men.

After the mention of Biddle, there is another extended section in which American dependence on England is shown.[11] England floods the States with indigo, which was once an American staple, but has now declined; the Jacksonians want a duty placed on its import, but Clay and his friends water down the proposal until it is ineffective. Two things are happening: the South, with its productivity hampered, is falling prey to Northern bankers, and the whole country is falling back into economic bondage to England. Benton states that "federal legislation has worked this ruin." Pound notes that this endless taking of the North from the South will eventually lead to disaster: "The Civil War rooted in tariff" (Canto 89/596). This is another basic Poundian belief: that behind all significant actions in history there are economic explanations that are as important (if not more so) than the ideological ones (the Civil War was fought to free the slaves).

The line "Freemen do not look upward for bounties" returns to the good old Yankee principle of giving land to the people so that they can *earn* their livings, not exist in semiservitude as tenant farmers (today we would draw analogues with welfare rolls). This noble and practical ideal was stated by George McDuffie in the House of Representatives: "He is not in fact a freeman who habitually looks to the government for pecuniary bounties."[12] Instead, freeholds are for the people at large. Benton cites examples of nations ancient and modern which gave land away, including the following grand proclamation: "Mirza Mahomed Saul, Ambassador to England, in the name and by the authority of Abbas Mirza, King of Persia, offers to those who shall emigrate to Persia, gratuitous grants of land, good for the production of wheat, barley, rice, cotton, and fruits, free from taxes or contributions of any kind . . . London, July 8th, 1823."[13] Aside from the general principle involved, Pound is showing the brilliant depth of historical knowledge shown by American Congressmen in this period.

The next nine lines concern the election of Andrew Jackson. He is voted in by "having received 178 electoral votes to 83 received by Mr. Adams" (Pound's eye catches the 83, and wrongly adds it to Jackson's figure). Benton notes that "There was no jealousy . . . in the North at that time against the South."[14] He then runs down Jackson's achievements: he found a jungle of "Stay laws, stop laws, replevin laws," and cleared them away; he caused "Protective tariffs . . . national bank left to expire . . . public lands redeemed . . . public debt paid off." Benton then defends his hero against the charges of De Tocqueville, who ridiculed Jackson's part in the "insignificant" Battle of New Orleans. Benton corrects the wrong date cited by the Frenchman, as well as some of the facts, and remarks, "This may pass for American history, in Europe . . ."[15] but indicates that Americans themselves will do better.

The next six lines, beginning with the battle of Guilford, describe in bravura detail the highlights of the life of Nathaniel Macon, whose retirement from public life in 1828 is drawn from pages 114 to 118 of Benton's work. This is one of the most endearing chapters, presenting a Plutarch-like picture of a statesman whom Benton calls an American Cincinnatus, a man who hoed and plowed until he was sixty. The Greek words ("He untiringly vexes the imperishable Earth") provide a quality like that found in the verses of Hesiod, who extolled the virtuous, strong man of the soil, as did Jefferson also: "Those who labor in the earth are the chosen people of God . . ." (*Notes on Virginia*). Educated in part at Princeton, Macon was "rich enough" . . . to receive all guests in his house from the President to the day laborer." He was a tireless friend of the difficult John Randolph, whom he defended once with a knife in a theater in Philadelphia, "when menaced by some naval and military officers for words spoken in debate, and deemed offensive to their professions." In his opposition with General Greene against General Cornwallis, he turned the tide of the Revolution against the British at Guilford, and opened the way for the ultimate victory of Washington at Yorktown. In short, Macon was that stolid type of man who built the United States. Before he died, he asked—in typical Chinese fashion—to be buried on a hillside, so as to conserve the usable land for agriculture (Canto 89/590).

Next comes an excerpt from the inaugural speech of Jackson on March 4, 1829. In fuller words than Pound offers, Jackson says that he aims at "extinguishment of national debt—the unnecessary duration of which is incompatible with real independence; and because it will counteract that tendency to public and private profligacy which a profuse expenditure of money by the government is but too apt to engender."[16] This attitude stands in such pronounced contrast with those held by Presidents from Roosevelt to Ford that the modern reader must pause to wonder at it. Pound then mentions the honor roll of the men confirmed in Jackson's cabinet: Martin Van Buren, Secretary of State; James Hamilton, who held the job temporarily until Van Buren could assume the duties; Samuel D. Ingham of Pennsylvania, Secretary of the Treasury; John M. Berrien of Georgia, Attorney General; and William T. Barry of Kentucky, Postmaster General.

Jackson stresses that the role of a navy is not that of an "instrument of power" but that of an "instrument of defence."[17] He opened up trade with the West Indies that had been allowed to languish because of British harassment. He promoted further expansion on the American continent, especially in the Northwest Territory, according to the Ordinance of 1787, drawn up by Nathan Dane of Massachusetts, in which servitude was strictly forbidden.[18] There is a second mention of the British repeal of the salt tax and Jackson's opposition to the federal building of a state road; and then we have the encounter that brings this canto to a close: Benton against the Bank.

The section in *Thirty Years' View* that deals with this major incident extends from pages 187 to 205, and forms a unified whole. Pound's poetry plays over the surface, extracting significant details, until the taking of the vote, which is given in an abbreviated form as 20 Yeas and 23 Nays. Benton's speech and Pound's poetic handling of it correspond closely. Pound moves from Benton's statement, "I knew it was not sufficient to pull down; we must build up also," through his enumeration of the twelve major flaws of the Bank. Throughout, Benton sees the Bank of England behind the American Bank, causing intervention into American affairs. He uses the following Britons as his models for rhetoric and logic: Henry Parnell, Joseph Hume, Edward Ellice, and William Pult[e]ney, all of whom he calls "practical, sensible, upright business men." Benton states his primary interest as having a "hard money government, as that of France has been since the time of *assignats* and *mandats*."[19] He does not want a bank modeled on England's, which creates money *ex nihilo,* out of nothing, on sheer whim.

Benton lists his three main grievances against Biddle's creation:

1. It is "too great and powerful to be tolerated in a government of free and equal laws."

2. It is "pernicious to the government and the people."

3. It favors "exclusive privileges, and anti-republican monopoly."

Under Point 2, he lists six subsections that Pound inserts in fragmentary form: "the bank tends to subjugate government"; "It tends to collusions";"it tends to create public DEBT." Figures are cited to support this last point. The Bank also "tends to beget and prolong useless wars"; "aggravate inequalities"; "make and break fortunes."[20]

Under Point 3 above, Benton indulges in a long list of sins committed by the beast, beginning with its tendency to "carry on [the] trade of banking upon the revenue [and credit], and in the name, of the United States," and ending with its insistence on having a monopoly. The only point that Pound plays down here is that the Bank deals in pawns that it can recall. As a result of this masterly analysis of fact and this model for rhetoric, delivered before the Congress in 1831, the Second Bank of the United States was started on its downhill course. Webster & Co. carried the day temporarily with their twenty-three votes against Benton's proposals, but the public had been aroused.

Pound next moves to the year 1832 and pages 220-21 of Benton's work, when the Bank was under fire for having issued a "kind of currency [that] was . . . invented by a Scotch banker of Aberdeen who issued notes payable in London, always of small denominations, that nobody should take them to London for redemption." This vicious paper currency, payable only in Philadelphia, leads Benton to launch his second major assault. He made "an application for leave to bring in a joint resolution declaring it to be illegal [to issue such currency], and ordering it to be suppressed," a resolution that "declares against the legality of these orders, AS A CURRENCY." Benton then draws up a series of questions, of which Pound prints the first four in order, then skips to the sixth (does the Bank have Treasury supervision?) and then to the fourteenth, which dealt with the "right to sue."

Pound then jumps to page 237, where an investigation launched against the corrupt workings of the Bank lists seven violations and fifteen abuses. As recounted in Benton, Mr. J. M. Clayton of Georgia read off this list of sins from a strip of paper rolled around his finger, so that other members could not see that the handwriting was Benton's. Then the canto ends swiftly with the four suits of playing cards (a heart, a diamond, a club, and a spade turned upside down) running down the left side of the page, while on the right are these words: "And/ fifty/ 2/ weeks/ in/ 4/ seasons."

The reader might well ask first: did Benton succeed? then, did the beast really die? Pound does not offer an answer. One must go to Benton for a chronicle of the demise. It took a presidential veto and direct action by Andrew Jackson to kill the Bank. When in 1837 Jackson removed the deposits from the large bank to smaller banks, Clay mustered the strength to have the President censured by Congress—an act that was later expunged from the record; or as Pound says:

And as to expunging?
    that is perhaps prose,
        you can find it in Benton.   (89/603)

Why does Pound end the canto with playing cards and the cryptic comment? He seems to be saying that the hundred-headed monster never really dies. Even if Jackson and friends did succeed in killing the Bank, a national system of monetary control in the hands of nonelected private individuals with close connections to Wall Street (and each other) did emerge with the Federal Reserve System, which is totally beyond Congressional control, as the Director in 1976, Arthur Burns, was fond of whimsically reminding. National debt increased at a staggering rate, as the Government is actually forced to buy money from the system to put it into circulation, since it does not control the issuance directly. Politicians with brothers and friends who are bankers frequently run up enormous debt-increasing bills (malls in suburbia, doles for the poor, more state highways than the United States landscape can possibly absorb), while the friends and brothers gather in the annual interest.

The playing cards symbolize luck, chance, the Fortuna motif, running side by side with a statement of order; fifty-two weeks in four seasons. In one sense, order was accomplished: Benton and Jackson must be honored for their rhetoric and the immediate results; but in another sense they (or posterity) failed. Eva Hesse has stated that Pound "saw the playing cards printed on the skirt of one of his visitors to St. Elizabeths. He interpreted it as an evil omen that the printer placed the Ace of Spades upside down."[21] In a sense, the order-disorder motif stated here reflects the same rhythm in history. Neither the villains nor the heroes really ever die; they constantly return in new forms: "I sing of perennial war."

An evaluation of Pound's uses of history can now be made. Some people might question the very fact that history *can* be adapted to poetry, but Pound challenged that notion from the start, since he always defined an epic, such as *The Cantos*, as a poem containing history. A second more penetrating objection might be a calling into question of Pound's sources. How does the poet know that he is right? What is wrong with the American banking system and its allegiance to politics? In short, how can anyone know the truth?

Pound's answer is, first of all, that there are certain things that are objectively good and others that are objectively bad. In order to get to the truth in history, we must seek out the best sources available. In terms of American history, that would be the written work of John Adams, Thomas Jefferson, John Quincy Adams, Andrew Jackson, Thomas Hart Benton, and Martin Van Buren. Pound was fortunate in that when he had examined these sources, he found that these men's concepts of banking, government, and morality accorded fully with his own. They were all solidly on the side of the people against selfish vested interests. On the other side—which is so weak that almost no one asserts its strength *in an open way*—we find Hamilton, Biddle, Clay, Calhoun, and Webster. Pound thus follows the greatest Founding Fathers and their political descendants. He stands firmly in the great tradition not only of those who *made* the history but also those who wrote about it, as can be seen in his use of Benton's work. Pound interposes himself only to correlate, to connect, to argue over certain points.

Pressing more deeply, suppose that Benton and the favored Founding Fathers (and Pound) are wrong: suppose that private manipulation of public funds is a good thing—can the past ever really be known in an absolute sense? Emerson's pessimism about the very existence of history comes to mind, balanced by his faith in biography. We may know men, but can we authoritatively understand that chain of events that they create? There is no sure answer to this question. Andrew Jackson's killing of the Bank was certainly a personal triumph, but is the totality of the Jacksonian spirit (government removal from local affairs) necessarily good? In terms of men themselves, is anyone all sinner or all saint? Here is where biography parts company with history, where the novelist-creator replaces the logical thinker.

The true guide to history lies in the emotional re-creation of the past. Pound's assessment of the chain of actions leading to the destruction of the Bank is not as important as his presentation of the personalities involved: the erratic but honest Randolph, the courageous Benton, the unpretentious Jackson, the Roman-spirited Macon. Pound conveys the courage of the American spirit, fighting despotism within and control from without. This is a *poetic* use of historical material, and it is not quite the same in its claim as a textbook; the textbook insists that it is true, the poem hopes that it is. Working with the heart and the tools of a poet, Pound can make the past live more vividly than can the leaden-prosed historian (Benton excluded, of course). The poet is not afraid of slanting and error because he works freely and frankly with the emotions.

And now a last look at the shaping of this canto: 1) an abortive duel; 2) a meditative stretch; 3) three swipes at the head of a beast without a *coup de grace*. Pound is not forcing the reader into a heavy-handed acceptance of anything. Clay is hardly a villain, and Biddle is little more than a name, and that seldom mentioned. The description of events is often as murky as the air around Grendel's meer. Similarly, in the last portion of the canto, we do not have the satisfaction of seeing the beast beheaded. We are led from a confrontation of what *seems* good to a confrontation with what *seems* evil, but no victory is presented as an actual fact. What we see as evil never dies; the worm Geryon moves inexplicably on. We can close our eyes to this actuality totally and say that everything is beautiful in its own way and that no absolute statement can be made about anything. But true courage and true genius lie in the attempt to take positive action against that very real but hard-to-apprehend canker that kills societies, whether the attempt is made by a political historian like Benton or a creative poet like Pound. That attempt may be all that ultimately matters. The evil lurks in the silence.

Chapter Six

Canto 90 As Incantation: The Poet As Priest of Nature

Of all Pound's cantos that "sing" the most lyrical is possibly Canto 90. It begins with a sing-song Latin inscription that may be translated: "The human soul is not love, but love proceeds from it, and it does not delight in itself, but in the love which proceeds from it." Many readers will immediately want to know the source. It is, for the record, *How the Holy Spirit Is the Love of the Father and the Son (Quomodo Sanctus Spiritus est amor Patris et Filii)*, contained in volume 196 of the *Latin Patrology*, column 1012. Yet once one learns the source, one knows little more than before, except that Richard of St. Victor, the author of the tract, is a favorite of Pound's.[1] The Later Cantos are not all meant to be read in the same way. Some are meant to be studied closely; others are to be experienced directly. Here, the purpose is not to explicate sources, but to clarify tones. Source-hunting tends to particularize a context, but the true movement of this canto is one of ascent, from the particular to the universal.

If a reader who has already covered the Chinese material in *The Cantos* reads the first few lines, he will immediately see a similarity with the Ninth Rule of the *Sacred Edict* of K'ang Hsi, which deals with a man's manners and character in a way that is related directly to nature (see Chapter Ten). Yet the lines are not identified, and the way that they open into a broader picture of nature might refer to any nature-loving mystic, such as Richard of St. Victor or John Heydon, author of *The Holy Guide*:

"From the colour the nature
      & by the nature the sign!"

Beatific spirits welding together
      as in one ash-tree in Ygdrasail.
            Baucis, Philemon.

The verse moves swiftly to the ash-tree of Norse mythology,
Ygdrasail, which holds the universe together, and we meet two
Ovidian characters, hospitable old Baucis and Philemon, who were
transformed into the single trunk of an ever-living tree as recom-
pense for their kindly acts toward visiting gods. The idea of a
divine tree is thus the binding image for the lines. Ovid's poetic
metamorphoses blend with a mystical attitude toward nature as a
solid continuum stretching from the individual outward, for the
Chinese also conceived of a towering tree-trunk known as *chien-
mu* as the center of the world.[2]
      Ovid continues as a guiding spirit:

Castalia is the name of that fount in the hill's fold,
            the sea below,
                  narrow beach.
Templum aedificans, not yet marble,   [building the temple]
            "Amphion!"

Ovid had sung of the poets' brook of Castalia on Mount Parnassus
in his *Metamorphoses,* and he had also dealt with Amphion's "building the temple" in Thebes by his music (Book 6.176 ff.). Yet the
Latin phrase *Templum aedificans* is not necessarily looking backward to myth; it can also refer to history, for it is used in Canto 8 to
describe the building of the Temple of Rimini by Sigismundo
Malatesta, and it is used later in Canto 96 to describe the construction of the Hagia Sophia by Justinian. In other words, one is
working toward a general, inclusive, archetypal reference. This
can be shown easily by citing similar lines from Canto 89/596:

And in the time of Mr Randolph, Mr Benton, Mr Van Buren
      he, Andy Jackson
            POPULUM AEDIFICAVIT
which might end this canto, and rhyme with
            Sigismundo.

The idea of "building the people" here is merely an extension of
"building the temple." In any case, all the people mentioned are

coming together to form a central concept of the Doer, the Maker. Pound calls this process "rhyming"; it has nothing to do with similar sounds, but everything to do with analogous ideas, as shown in Chapter One.

The temple imagery continues from the Chinese words *San¹ Ku¹*, which refer to imperial officials,[3] to that room in the Hôtel de Ville at Poitiers, once part of the home of Duke William IX of Aquitaine, where a man cannot cast his shadow. The temple, the palace, and the sacred ground are brought together in a context that emphasizes the instinctive drive of a spoken tradition (Sagetrieb or "say-drive" in Pound's German coining) along with a sense of due proportion:

> to the room in Poitiers where one can stand
>   casting no shadow,
> That is Sagetrieb,
>   that is tradition.
> Builders had kept the proportion,
>   did Jacques de Molay
>   know these porportions [sic]?
> and was Erigena ours?

Just as Duke William spun poetry out of a void, and lived in a castle whose relation to the solar forces might be seen as Manichean or at least pagan and anti-Establishment, so Jacques de Molay, the last Grand Master of the secret cult of the Knights Templar, is seen as the possessor of mystic, subterranean secrets, including possibly magic and gnomon-reading, which can be related to Chinese and Manichean sun-rites.[4] In any case, De Molay was accused of all kinds of anti-Christian acts before he was burned at the stake in 1314 in a collusion between King Philip IV of France and Pope Clement V. His open defiance of these Establishment forces makes him in Pound's mind similar to the brilliantly progressive theologian Scotus Erigena, that transplanted Irish "pantheist" who spent a great deal of his life in France, and whose theology contains a vivid affirmation of natural forces. It was rumored that Scotus was murdered—stabbed to death by his students and stuffed into a winecask—under very mysterious circumstances. Duke William, De Molay, and Scotus were all fighters for their individual beliefs, and they were all either murdered or excommunicated.

At this point, the reader may see an undercurrent of violence beneath the smooth and beautiful surface of the canto. Poor, kindly Philemon and Baucis were transformed almost violently into trees; Ovid was exiled to the Black Sea; Amphion killed himself out of grief when he lost his sons. Suddenly, the creation of something beautiful seems not only difficult but dangerous. The solid tradition of saying something, asserting something (Sagetrieb), is an enormously powerful tool that may bring a curse upon the heads of those who use it. It seems to emanate from the sun, and yet it also has a kinship with the shadows and the moon, with the total force of nature: "Moon's barge over milk-blue water." To distinguish the shadows from the light, one must put one's self in a sacrificial position; and be prepared to cry out to the force of love:

Kuthera *deina*   [Powerful Cytherea, Venus]
Kuthera sempiterna   [All-eternal Cytherea]

This cry for mercy is followed by four lines of Latin, which has now become a sub-rosa language, although it was the valid mystical language of Western Europe for centuries. The lines, taken from Richard of St. Victor again, say, first of all, "Where love is, there is the eye."[5] This statement stresses a correlation between seeing and loving that would delight Guido Cavalcanti as much as a Confucian scholar. Pound repeats it as the closing line of the canto. The other three lines may be translated: "Woe to you who cogitate upon the useless./ an image will be found in us resembling the divine."[6] Their appropriateness to the general context is obvious.

However, the reader may well ask: "Why use Latin?" Pound would reply: "Because the statements were made that way originally." He would also add that every tongue has its own particular genius in conveying certain kinds of tones or ideas. The English translation for the lovely phrase *ubi amor, ibi oculus*, does not begin to capture the rhythm and the internal rhyme of the original; nor does it carry with it the authoritative weight of a millennium of precise theology. As Pound always stressed, the English language cannot do everything perfectly. Therefore, especially in a canto where the poet is employing the secret, semi-arcane language of chant, he will take ready recourse to the mysterious. To read this canto properly, one needs a pronunciation guide more than a glossary of facts.

The line "Mother Earth in thy lap" removes the reader from the divine realm and places him in the human. It is linked with the great orator John Randolph of Roanoke, who "loved much," as the Greek words *egapesen poly* declare. John was a strange, mysterious person whose words are only half-preserved in his letters and Congressional speeches.[7] Yet Pound is not thinking so much of his love for the people at large, but for his great act of kindness when "he freed his slaves," as the Latin words *liberavit masnatos* inform us. These words point back to Cantos 6 and 29, where they were applied in part to Cunizza da Romano, the Italian noblewoman who indulged in a similar act of kindness. Cunizza herself is linked often in the *Pisan Cantos* with the moon as shown in Chapter Two.

The canto next presents Castalia in the moonlight, not with the bright sun that usually bathes it. Pound depicts the vacillation of the waves, as opposed to the steady lap of Mother Earth, and the Fortuna theme—so closely connected to the waxing and the waning of the moon—is mentioned with relation to the Perons of Argentina: "Evita, beer-halls, semina motuum." The tempestuous, shifting affairs of Buenos Aires, coupled with a suggestion of the Bierstuben of Munich, are thrown upon the screen of the mind, along with the Latin phrase "seeds of movement," which suggests continual renewal in the midst of continual change.

The idea of loss in the parched grass is quickly replaced by the rain, and the phrase "furious from perception," which is elsewhere linked with Hilter,[8] is attributed to the all-seeing prophetess Sibyl and the "rubble heap." In the rise and fall of his own life, Pound sees himself set against the cosmic forces; and in his own desolation, he sees the destructions of Berlin and Argentina. However, instead of despairing, which is always the wrong way out in Pound's work, the poet prays in language adapted from Dante's prayer in *Paradiso* 1.75, using the phrase *m'elevasti*, which means, "You have raised me." This incantational form of the poetry resembles that of primitive shamans:

                              Sibylla,
from under the rubble heap
                    m'elevasti
from the dulled edge beyond pain,
                    m'elevasti
out of Erebus, the deep-lying
     from the wind under the earth,
                    m'elevasti
from the dulled air and the dust,
                    m'elevasti
by the great flight,
             m'elevasti
                    Isis Kuanon
     from the cusp of the moon,
                    m'elevasti

The lines rise out of despair with the help of natural forces presided over by the great Egyptian goddess Isis and the Chinese-Buddhist goddess of mercy, Kuanon (Kuan-Yin). The forces of love and mercy are needed to combat the relentless movements of time, destruction, fortune, and change.

When the viper and the blue serpent appear, the reader may think that he has fallen backward, but he must learn how to read the signs of things from their colors and their motions. The blue here is that of Heaven, and the "glides" denotes a smooth movement. In three lines that recall Italians fishing by night at Portovenere or Portofino along the Italian Riviera (thus rhyming with the verbal picture created in Canto 17), the reader returns to the depths (de fondo) into which Ezra Pound and his world have fallen. Yet, the soul struggles upward like a mermaid; the thrust is upon ascent, until reader and poet reach the brook on the mountain and the pool of Arethusa. The line "Grove hath its altar" echoes the Roman poet Nemesianus,[9]and again accentuates the sacred quality of the pastoral place. Then the scene shifts rapidly to some Chinese rivers which rush together in much the way that Philemon and Baucis joined in the single tree. Clarity, lightness, fluidity—these are the basic elements of the contemplative Heaven:

                    water jets from the rock
and in the flat pool as Arethusa's

a hush in papyri.
Grove hath its altar
        under elms, in that temple, in silence
a lone nymph by the pool.
        Wei and Han rushing together.
two rivers together
        bright fish and flotsam
torn bough in the flood
        and the waters clear with the flowing

It is fitting that the Neoplatonist Richard of St. Victor should
say next that the bird is to the flight of the mind what the land-
animal is to the body.[10] Nous flows upward; Hyle, or Matter, pulls
down. But suddenly the competing tendencies are held in a
moment of stasis as true creativity begins to assert itself. With
Zeus' help, the word-painter turns into architect. The mere smith
of words starts to build something solid, the way Amphion turned
notes into stone. Pound feels the objective creation taking place at
his hands, as the fauns and sirens of the temple begin to assume
their form:

The architect from the painter,
        the stone under elm
Taking form now,
        the rilievi,   [reliefs]
    the curled stone at the marge
Faunus, sirenes,
    the stone taking form in the air
    ac ferae,   [and wild beasts]
        cervi,   [deer]
        the great cats approaching.

Pound thrusts the reader back into the world of Bacchus-
Dionysus, the Ovidian world of Cantos 2 and 17, where beasts
such as deer, pards, and wild cats sniff their way out of the woods
and walk onto the earth (*epi chthoni*), onto the earthly (*hoi
chthonioi*) fields of praise. This is, without any question, an
Earthly Paradise that is etched in marble relief. It is the world of
Sigismundo's marble freed from its stone, loosed back into flight
seeking ultimate form. Around about are the trees of the sacred
grove, with twittering swallows (*chelidon*) and banners and flutes.

The smoke, purling off the altars, begins its slow ascent into the heavens:

Pardus, leopardi, Bagheera
   drawn hither from the woodland,
woodland *epi chthoni*
     the trees rise
  and there is a wide sward between them
hoi chthonioi myrrh and olibanum on the altar stone
giving perfume,
     and where was nothing
now is furry assemblage
    and in the boughs now are voices
grey wing, black wing, black wing shot with crimson
and the umbrella pines
       as in Palatine,
as in pineta. *chelidon, chelidon*   [pine forest]

At this magic moment, the damned are suddenly freed from Hell. Tyro and Alcmene, who were enslaved in the Infernos of Homer, Vergil, Dante, and Pound, are now allowed to ascend with the dead cavaliers (soft reminiscence of Dante),[11] until the dark has been transformed into light, and Hell has been changed to Heaven. The last one to ascend is Electra, whose name means "amber" (know her by her color and her sign). She rises, even though she carries the weight of Aegisthus' wrongs upon her:

    thick smoke, purple, rising
bright flame now on the altar
    the crystal funnel of air
out of Erebus, the delivered,
    Tyro, Alcmene, free now, ascending
e i cavalieri,   [and the chevaliers]
   ascending,
no shades more,
    lights among them, enkindled,
and the dark shade of courage
      Elektra
bowed still with the wrongs of Aegisthus.

This ascent is like the great vision portrayed by Scotus Erigena in the last book of his *On the Division of Nature:* Odysseus'

return home becomes the spiritual Nostos (Return); Earth evapor-
ates, and all the souls move like sparks in the Dantesque firebrand
upward. Earth goes, tree goes, and only the visionary dream remains. In lines that now loosen the Latin locked in as the epi-
graph for the canto, Pound says:

Not love but that love flows from it
ex animo   [from the soul]
& cannot ergo delight in itself
but only in the love flowing from it.

And finally the canto ends with that unforgettable Latin line that is
proved by the poetry in which it is contained: Where love is, there
is the eye—UBI AMOR IBI OCULUS EST.

The performance is so extraordinary that it defies re-creation.
The finest parts of the Chinese-Greek-Roman sensibilities have
been brought together, as Pound presents the gigantic upward
surge of Universal Soul, which Plotinus, Scotus, Richard, and
Anselm had described in the poverty of philosophical prose.
Surely, this is one of the most charmed moments in world literature, and surely—despite all of Pound's assertions that he had
failed to create his Paradise—one must, as one examines this
canto, say that the poet was too humble. Pound has raised his
temple with the clarity of a Greek stone-cutter or the sure but
sensitive touch of a Chinese watercolor painter. With Amphionlike
music and the insistent, prayerful urges of chant, he has first
created a vivid series of forms, and then freed them for flight. The
miracle has taken place before our eyes: "We have seen what we
have seen."

Chapter Seven
Under the Larches with Apollonius: The Message of a Lost Messiah

The Life of Apollonius of Tyana, written by the Greek Philostratus, who was born about the year 172 after Christ, dominates Canto 94. For centuries both biographer and subject were all but forgotten, for, as Pound remarks:

no full trans/ till 1811,
　　　　remarks F. C. Conybeare, the prelector,
who says it is (sic:) "lightly written"
although no theologian touches it . . . well?
　　　　NO! not even Richardus　　　　　　　　　　　　　　(637)

Despite its underground history, the work is a brilliant re-creation of the life of this Neoplatonic saint of the first century, who vied with Christ in reputation as late as the time of St. Augustine.

　　　　The translator of the Loeb edition of the work, which was used by Pound, was F.C. Conybeare, who was a fellow and prelector at University College, Oxford.[1] His English translation, appearing first in 1912, was preceded by that of E. Berwick in 1811. It has been followed most notably by a very readable rendition in the Penguin Series.[2] Thus, Apollonius is another of Pound's unsung heroes, another who has been blacked out by ignorance or intolerance. One reason is stated succinctly by Conybeare himself: Apollonius' "eminent power over evil spirits or demons, made him a formidable rival in the minds of Pagans to Jesus Christ" (p. xiv). Volume 2 of the Loeb edition contains the attack of

88

the Christian Eusebius upon Apollonius' teachings. Thus, once Christ had conquered, Apollonius was forced into the background.

The neglect of Apollonius is a great pity because he offers an excellent link between ancient philosophers, such as Pythagoras and Plato, and the best Christian and Arabic minds of the Middle Ages. This is precisely where Pound sees him:

> 2 thousand years, desensitization
> After Apollonius, desensitization
>   & a little light from the borders:
>   Erigena,
>   Avicenna, Richardus.
> Hilary looked at an oak leaf   (92/622)

Despite Conybeare's statement that Philostratus' work is "lightly written" (p. vii), the portrait of the seer is beautifully and convincingly drawn. One might compare the total structure with a modern work such as Hesse's *Siddhartha,* for it follows the pattern of a novel, with attention to dramatic confrontations and a diminution of elements that a biographer might relish but that a historian might well ignore.

The *Life* was commissioned by the Roman Empress Julia Domna, the wife of Septimius Severus, whom Pound calls "Daughter of a sun priest in Babylon" (639).[3] Pound spells Apollonius' birthplace "TYana" at this point, emphasizing the Indo-European root for "shine" (TU-DU) that is apparent in such god-names as Dyaus (Sanskritic), Tiw (Germanic), Zeus (Hellenic), and Ju-piter (Latin), as well as in DEUS-DIOS-DIURNUS-DIONYSUS. As the form of the canto indicates, Apollonius takes his place with John Adams, Justinian, Coke, Ocellus, and the other heroes who "build light": *jih⁴ hsin¹.*

Since Pound follows Philostratus' narration largely in its chronological order, it is appropriate to begin a commentary with citations from *The Cantos* on page 635, including a book-by-book summary of the *Life.* Book One concerns Apollonius' youth, his early dedication to the philosophy of Pythagoras, his five years of silent meditation, and his mastery of the languages of men and birds. From the start, Apollonius was a devout worshiper of nature. Pound stresses that he "made peace with the animals" and Conybeare translates: "he would not stain the altars with blood"

(1.1, p. 3; also, 1.20). Apollonius wore his hair long and uncut, and would never clothe himself in animal skins; like the sages of India, he always wore linens.

After Pound inserts a brief passage relating to Justinian's affection for his people and Sargon of Agade's grain distribution, he picks up the thread again. Apollonius' mother bore the Messiah in a meadow, where she had been told in a dream to go (1.5). Swans surrounded her and set up such a clamor that she was forced to give sudden birth; a thunderbolt was also heard, thus stressing the divine nature of the parturition.

After receiving his early training, Apollonius begins his wanderings, which take him over most of the known world. At Nineveh, he acquires a lifelong friend named Damis, who is the first of his many disciples. He then goes to Babylon and meets the king, Vardanes, who asks him what the most stable form of government is. Apollonius replies: "To respect many, and confide in few" (pollous timon pisteuon de oligois; 1.37, pp. 108-09). In lines that Pound does not cite directly, the king asks how to employ his wealth. Apollonius becomes a supporter of distributive justice (like the other members of the canto) by replying: "By spending it . . . for you are a king" (1.38, p. 111).

In Book Two, Apollonius moves on toward his ultimate goal, India, which he regards as the mother of all wisdom, including Pythagoras'. Pound naturally does not stress this aspect, because his attitude toward Hinduism and Buddhism was always one of suspicion. The line "For styrax to Pamphilia," followed by the word "leopards," refers to Chapter 2, p. 121, where Apollonius, passing the Caucasus Mountains, notices that the air is redolent with fragrance. He then sees leopards, and Philostratus tells us that "these animals delight in fragrant odours . . . and traverse the mountains in search of the tear or gum of the Styrax." This is one of the many sections of the work where animals, plants, and human beings are drawn together in a related context that is both scientific and romantic.

Arriving then at Taxila, the largest city in India, Apollonius and Damis marvel at the intelligent elephants and the architectural wonders. They are escorted across the River Indus to the capital of King Phraotes (not Pharaotes, as Pound spells it). Pound equates him with a king from the Chinese Classics when he says:

"Our customs . . . are dictated by moderation . . . and though I
have more than other men, yet I want little, for I regard most
things as belonging to my friends" (2.26, p. 183). Apollonius replies: "Blessed are you then in your treasure . . . if you rate your
friends more highly than gold and silver, for out of them grows up
for you a harvest of blessings." These words "rhyme," as Pound
puts it, with some Chinese characters that state "with money get
nothing with value," thus bringing Confucian lore into direct
comparison with the Greek.[4] The king holds a banquet at which
many animals are served, but only the "loins of tigers; for they decline to eat the other parts of this animal, because they say that, as
soon as it is born, it lifts up its front paws to the rising Sun" (2.28,
p. 189).

In discussing the relationship between drunkenness and
visions, Apollonius says that "we are rapt by the nymphs"
(*nympholeptoi*) "and are bacchantic revellers in sobriety" (*Bakchoi
tou nephein;* 2.37, pp. 216-17). The Greek sage was firmly opposed
to immoderate activity of any sort, and decided that he himself
would have none of drinking and sex, although he did not demand
that his disciples follow his example, unless the spirit moved them.
In the next chapter, 38, Apollonius' cult of the sun is discussed,
and Pound's Greek words *hymnon* and *hemeran* (meaning "hymn"
and "day") can be related to this; the two words appear side by side
in the text (3.14, p. 256).

In Book Three, Apollonius travels to the Ganges River, where
he meets the Brahman sages, especially Iarchas (Pound writes his
name in Greek letters on page 637). The sages teach him that
"living [is] . . . the universe . . . for it engenders all living things"
(*zoon . . . ton kosmon . . . gar zoogonei panta;* 3.34, p. 308).
Pound's next Greek words, *erota ischei . . . kai synistesin,* occur in
the same place, and are rendered a bit more completely in Conybeare's translation as follows: the universe "*is possessed by a love*
for itself more intense than any separate being has for its fellow, a
passion which *knits it together* into harmony." This idea of a universe that lives in all of its parts and is sustained by love is one of
the finest expressions not only of pantheistic philosophy but also of
the pagan metamorphic vision of creation. Pound himself was
always close to pantheism, as were Scotus Erigena, Anselm, and
most of the medieval mystics who abjured the "sin and guilt" ethic

of Judeo-Christianity; yet, like his medieval forebears, Pound did not want to cross over and join the Hindus, with their adoration of animals. At this pont in *The Cantos*, Apollonius is brought into an ideogram with Richard of St. Victor, Swedenborg, and Iarchas.

But if Apollonius is a mystic, he is also a rational natural explorer, such as Von Humboldt, Agassiz, and others in the Later Cantos. He learns about the various species of natural life in India, especially about "gold which the griffins dig up" in rocks that are "spotted with drops of gold" (3.48, p. 333). He also hears about the Egyptian phoenix, which "sings funeral strains for itself" (*propempterious hymnous hauto adein:* 3.49, pp. 334-35), an act that "is also done by the swans." After three lines which repeat elements mentioned above, Apollonius' departure is detailed. One sees him moving, like Odysseus and Hanno of Carthage, by periplum,[5] "keeping the Ganges on his right hand" for ten days (3.50, p. 335), until he arrives at the Red (Erythran) Sea, which is linked through its name to a man, Erythras (p. 337), not to the color "red," which in Greek is roughly the same word. This insistence on learning the eponymous tradition in places shows Apollonius once again uniting mankind with nature in an atmosphere of curiosity and love. On leaving Iarchas, Apollonius bids him adieu in this way: "I came to you on foot, and yet *you presented me with the sea . . . Farewell!*" (*hymas dedokate* [1970 ed., *dedokato*] *ten thalattan . . . errosthe;* 3.51, pp. 336-37).

Eventually, Apollonius and Damis arrive at Balara, "which is an emporium full of myrtles and date palms; and there they also saw laurels, and the place was well watered by springs" (3.56, p. 341). They then sail on the Red Sea, whose waters are so full of animals that the ships must "carry bells at the bow and at the stern, the sound of which frightens away these creatures" (3.57, p. 343). Pound uses the word "seals" to describe these animals, while Conybeare has "sharks" and "whales." The Greek word *ketos* can refer to any sea beast of some size. Retracing his steps through Babylon and Nineveh, Apollonius arrives at Ionia, where he excites no little esteem "among all lovers of wisdom" (*para tois ten sophian timosin;* 3.58, pp. 344-45).

Book Four recounts the triumphal progress of Apollonius through Greece to Rome. When he arrives at Smyrna, he says simply: "O ye Muses, grant that *we may also like one another*" (*kai *erasthenai allelon;* 4.1, pp. 350-51). The city of Ephesus fills him with disgust because of its pipers, "effeminate rascals" (so Conybeare; Pound has "buggars"), and noise (4.2, p. 351). After performing many wonders and issuing a number of true prognostications, Apollonius warns the men of Smyrna not to put their faith in ivory images (Pound's "set stone"), but to be like Homer and to envision their gods "under many shapes" *(pollais ideais;* 4.7, pp. 358-59). He further tells them that a good society is one in which "each man should do . . . what he best can do" *(to prattein hekaston . . . ho* [Pound has *hoi*] *ti dynatai;* 4.8, pp. 360-61). Apollonius is thus like Confucius, who, in Canto 13, saw every man acting ideally in accordance with his own given nature.

At Troy, Apollonius spends an entire night on a mound in company with the ghost of Achilles (one is reminded of Canto 1), while his companions go "on board ship, for it was already evening" *(epi ten naun hesperas ede;* 4.11, pp. 368-69). After this experience, Apollonius' followers regard him as "master of the tempest and of fire" (4.13, p. 371). Apollonius immediately raises up a neglected statue to the hero Palamedes in Aeolis, and also builds a shrine around it. Philostratus says that "I myself saw" the shrine, and he adds that it "was large enough for ten persons at once to sit and drink and keep good cheer in" (4.13, p. 373).

When his companions later demand to know what Achilles told him on the mound, Apollonius retorts that the restoration of this shrine to the youthful warrior-poet "in Aeolis close to Methymna" (4.16, p. 383) was one of his major suggestions. Achilles' ghost vanished "with a flash of summer lightning, for indeed the cocks were already beginning their chant" (p. 385). When his friends ask how he summoned Achilles' ghost to speak with him, Apollonius remarks wryly that "it was not by digging a ditch like Odysseus, nor by tempting souls with the blood of sheep . . . but I offered up the prayer which the Indians say they use in approaching their heroes" (p. 377). Pound obviously makes much of this incident, because *The Cantos* open in a similar vein, and indeed the entire form of the poem is an extended dialogue with the dead.

Apollonius next arrives at mainland Greece, where he is hailed on all sides. He visits shrines, corrects the rituals (resembling Confucius at work on the *Odes*), and educates the young.

Three of Pound's most beautiful lines occur here:

So that walking here under the larches of Paradise
the stream was exceedingly clear
      & almost level its margin

There is no exact parallel for these lines in Philostratus. For one
thing, "laurels" are usually mentioned rather than "larches," and
"Paradise" can only be a metaphoric concept. This is an amalga-
mated picture drawn from the visits of Apollonius to the shrines of
Dodona, Pythia, Helicon, and other places (4.24). It is meant to be
compared with the picture of Confucius walking with his disciples
and discoursing in a natural setting in Canto 13. For it is very clear
that Pound is constantly bringing Apollonius and the sage of China
together.

During his travels in Greece, Apollonius fearlessly speaks out
against the tyrant Nero, and, ignoring the advice of his friends,
even decides to visit Rome. There under pressure from Nero's
henchman, Tigellinus, all of Apollonius' thirty-four disciples save
eight desert him. Instead of being disheartened, Apollonius declares that the calamity is a touchstone (*gar basanos;* 4.37, pp. 434-
35) sent to him to help "test these young men." When the consul
Telesinus interviews him and asks why he is wearing linen,
Apollonius replies that his garment is "pure . . . made from no
dead matter" (*katharon . . . kai ap' oudenos thnetou;* 4.40, pp.
444-45). Despite the fact that he is harassed and even arrested by
Tigellinus, Apollonius courageously denounces the imperial
government. Refusing to undergo a passive martyrdom, he
ridicules Nero's public singing to Tigellinus' face and manages to
get away with it. He then discreetly departs from Rome when
Nero outlaws the practice of philosophy there.

Book Five continues his travels to the Pillars of Hercules in
Spain back through the Mediterranean islands to Rhodes, and
finally to Alexandria, where Apollonius confronts Vespasian. In
Chapter 1, the Straits of Gibraltar are mentioned in terms of the
mythology of Hercules. In geographic terms, Libyan Africa is
placed on the left (a country full of lions: Pound's Latin phrase
"Hic sunt leones") and the promontory of Europe, known as
Calpis, is put on the right. This extends to the ancient city of

Gadeira, where Geryon and his cows lived. Near Gadeira (modern Cadiz) are the fabulous trees of Geryon, which drip blood from their bark "as gold does from the Heliad[s'] poplar" (p. 473). The mentions of Hercules' Twelve Labors and the very word Heliad from *Helios* (Sun) enforce once again the solar background of the Hercules-Odysseus-Apollonius travels. Pound says that the pillars at Cadiz had "sumerian capitals," but Apollonius merely states that no one knows where they came from (p. 473). Pound probably guesses a Phoenician base because he is leading us to recall that other voyager to Spain, Hanno the Carthaginian, who was given so much space in Canto 40. Both Hanno and Apollonius are adventurers of the human spirit, sailing through instinct by periplum and native wit.

The philosopher and his company then arrive at Mount Etna in Sicily, where they admire the volcano. Apollonius offers a rational explanation of eruptive power, and then remarks that "the whole earth affords secure ground for the doers of holiness" (*de tois hosia prattousi gen men pasan asphale;* (5.17, pp. 500-3). He adds that "the sea is safely traversed not only by people in ships but even by people attempting to swim." On returning to Athens, he meets a friend, Demetrius, who praises their philosopher colleague Musonius, who was forced to dig the Corinth Canal as a slave laborer by Nero, but who said defiantly in the spirit of Apollonius: "You are distressed, Demetrius, to see me digging through the Isthmus for Greece; but if you saw me playing the harp like Nero, what would you feel then?" (5.19, p. 505). Pound admires Musonius, who, like himself, had the courage to stand up to the Establishment.

Moving on to Rhodes, Apollonius meets a *nouveau riche* with a fine house who is intent on "getting rich," as the Chinese characters *fa$^{1-5}$ ts'ai^2* tell. Apollonius replies with characteristic humor: "My good boy, it seems to me that it is not you that own the house, but the house that owns you" (5.22, p. 513). He enforces his talk about a mean (the Chinese character *chung^1*; 5.29, p. 529), when he urges Vespasian to overthrow Nero. Apollonius says: "For I was never the slave of wealth that I know of, even in my youth; and in the matter of the magistracies and honours in the gift of the Roman sovereign, I bore myself with so much soberness and moderation as to avoid being thought either overbearing or, on the other hand,

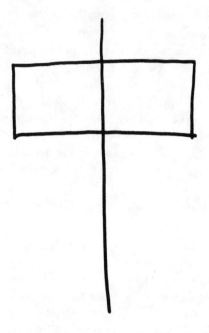

CHUNG¹
THE MEAN

craven and cowardly." These words neatly sum up the Hellenic
mean, which Pound aligns with Confucian moderation. Vespasian
listened to Apollonius, overthrew the government, and did effect
some important reforms, but, as Pound says, "did not show good
sense in Greece," and thus Apollonius abandoned him after sending him a series of brisk notes that are quoted later (Chapter 41).

In his words with Vespasian (Chapter 35), Apollonius stresses
the importance to an emperor of "the devoted service of his own
children" *(ton heautou* [not *eautou* as in Pound] *paidon;* pp.
548-49). Apollonius says: "I care little about constitutions (Pound's
"theoretical organizations"), for he says that he is "under the
gods," as I would render *hypo tois theois.* The Chinese characters
i¹ jin² (one man) are aligned with the following words: "For just as a

single man pre-eminent in virtue transforms a democracy into the guise of a government of a single man who is the best; so the government of one man, if it provides all round for the welfare of the community, is popular government" (p. 549). In the first case here, one may think of Adams, Jefferson, and Van Buren; in the second, of the Chinese emperors and (in Pound's mind) Mussolini. In any case, the emphasis is upon a monarchic dynasty, although a strong democracy led by a single man is also considered valuable.

Apollonius comes close to defining a philosopher when he says to Vespasian: "it is enough that he should say what he really thinks" (*epi noun elthon* [*eleon*, 1970 ed.] *eiresetai*; 5.35, pp. 550-51). In defining the role of a ruler, Apollonius begins by saying: "If

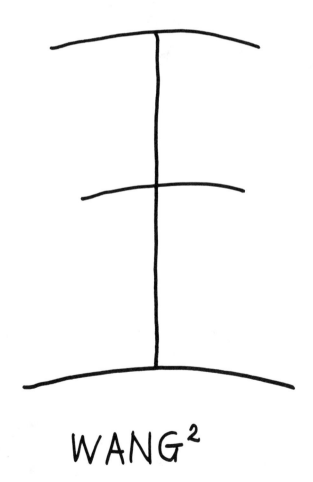

WANG²

you were the tenant of my breast" (*ei ten psychen . . . ten emen okeis;* 5.36, pp. 552-53), and goes on to implore him against amassing wealth or "hogging the harvest," as Pound often puts it. Paraphrasing Aristotle, Apollonius says: "Mow not down the loftier stalks"—meaning, don't destroy the intellectuals and the men of political capacity. Pound then names Antoninus and Severus, both men of significant political action, who were Vespasian's worthy successors in the Roman dynasty. The Chinese character *wang²* then appears twice, and is translated by Pound on page 641 as "the king shd/ be king." This statement accords with Apollonius' belief that "In what appertains to your prerogative, act as a sovereign" (p. 555). The words *hellenizontas men Hellenikon* ("over Hellenes should be set men who can speak Greek"; 5.36, pp. 556-57) stress Apollonius' and Pound's belief that every people has its native genius, and they should not be tampered with by outsiders. In his dealings with Vespasian, Apollonius was opposed by the jealous Euphrates and supported by his friend Dion. When Dion's philosophic style became too inflated, Apollonius said: "You should use a pipe and a lyre, if you want to tickle men's senses, and not speech" (5.40, p. 565), which is essentially what Pound himself had told the Edwardians.

The next five lines on page 640 of *The Cantos* tell of Apollonius' journey with ten followers up the Nile River (5.43, p. 573). There they encounter a lion which had the soul of Amasis inside, a former Egyptian king. Apollonius sees that the lion is hungry, and suggests that he be sent to Leontopolis (Lion City), where he can be cared for properly. The priests "conveyed him up country into Egypt with pipings, hymns and songs composed in his honour" (5.42, p. 571); Pound has "singing for him" (*ep' auto adontes*).

Book Six tells how Apollonius lands in Antioch after his journey into Ethiopia. In Chapter 2, as Pound notes, Apollonius condemns the Greeks for not being happy "unless one penny begets another" (*me obolos obolon teke;* vol. 2, p. 7):

"Which is all nuts" said Apollonius,
"The Africans have more sense than the Greeks."

Like the Africans, Apollonius worships the gold of the sun, not in coins. He makes sacrifices to Memnon of the Dawn (*Eoo Memnoni;* 6.4, p. 16) and to "the Sun of Ethiopia" (p. 17). The priests

explain that the name Ethiopia is "derived from the words signify-
ing 'to burn and be warm.'" Conybeare enforces this etymology in
a note by saying that *Aithiops* (Ethiopian) derives from *aitho*, "I
burn." Thus, once again the Logos and the land are yoked through
a ritual of nature adoration.

On page 641 of *The Cantos*, Pound presents Apollonius want-
ing to travel upriver to the Cataracts of the Nile "and hear the
water-roarings," as one might translate *kai keladoun[t]os akousai*
(6.17, pp. 74-75). But before they depart, Apollonius launches into
a long discussion with the Naked Sages of Egypt, in which he defends his Indian heritage through Iarchas, against theirs, and is
especially critical of their brutish representations of the gods.
When the Gymnosophs claim that they follow imitation in representing their ideals, Apollonius calls "Imagination . . . wiser than
imitation" *(phantasia . . . sophotera mimeseos;* 6.19, pp. 78-79),
because "imitation is often baffled by terror, but imagination by
nothing." Then, in discussing politics, Apollonius praises Sparta
because of its "desire to keep the institutions . . . in their original
purity by preventing outsiders *from mingling* in her life" *(me
enomilounton;* 6.20, p. 85). This is still another reference to the
melting-pot or pseudo-international concept that Pound finds
treacherous in politics.

In arguing about the nature of justice, the Egyptians point out
that the Athenian Aristides established a just tribute for the islands
to pay his native city, and when Athens "exceeded his valuations
and imposed heavier tributes . . . their naval supremacy at once
went to pieces" (6.21, p. 97). On page 640 of *The Cantos*, there is
still another mention of justice, a virtue that was as important to
Apollonius as it was to Pound. It occurs in the only line taken from
Book Eight, for Pound jumps over Book Seven to Chapter 31 of
Book Eight. He thus cuts out the magic element, in which
Apollonius is described as vanishing after a successful confrontation with the tyrannical Emperor Domitian.[6] The line about justice
is actually an amalgamation of three separate quotations, which
may be broken into the following three parts, all of which come
from the text facing page 405 of Conybeare's translation:

psyche athanatos: "The soul is immortal" (also on p. 402)
e ti meta zooisin eon: "So why, as long as thou art among living
    beings, dost thou explore these mysteries?"

timeteon: "to be honored"; actually this word does not occur in
   this form, but the notion is firmly there: "And his shrine at
   Tyana is singled out and *honoured* with royal officers: for
   neither have the Emperors denied to him the *honours* of which
   they themselves were held worthy."

These lines sum up Apollonius' achievements after his peaceful
death at an advanced age. The lines stress that Apollonius confined
himself to what he knew, deeming idle talk about mysteries inappropriate. He was honored by his people in the same way that
the Chinese honor their great and noble forebears.

   Two questions must now be asked:

1. Is Pound's use of snippets from Philostratus justified? Does he
   create an aesthetic whole?
2. Why should Apollonius be given so much space?

The first question necessarily involves matters of taste. Anti-
Poundians will resent the presence of the Greek language and say
that these short quotations do not create a full-blown picture of the
sage. However, Greek *was* Apollonius' language, and just as the
sage mastered the language of birds to converse with them, Pound
believes that one must encounter the Greek language to get the
full flavor of the man. Otherwise, one has only Conybeare's precious prose, in which castration is called "mutilating" and having
intercourse is called "knowing." The spirit of Apollonius was
suppressed, and if he is to speak to the world again, he must speak
in part in his native tongue.

   Furthermore, Pound's taglines are usually judiciously selected. They convey the nexus of certain ideas or the flavor of certain encounters. Everything except Apollonius' final address to
Domitian (which he was not allowed by the tyrant to deliver) is
covered. And finally, it is not Pound's intention to present a full
portrait of the sage. Pound supplies bits and pieces—sometimes
tantalizing in their incompleteness—but is history not always
incomplete? We get fast-moving flashes of animals, people, places,
as if we were retraversing the far-wandering sage's life in an encap-
sulated moment. The effect is to stress both vastness yet closeness
in the natural universe.[7] Even a reader who knows no Greek at all
leaves the canto with the feeling that this was a man who had

traveled far, had known many other men (like Odysseus), and had devoted a great deal of time to thought.

As for the second question, one may say in brief that Apollonius is to the European world what Confucius is to the Oriental: a sensible sage who acknowledged a cosmos of ideals, but who also stressed the relevance of the here and now. One cannot, of course, avoid a comparison with Jesus. Without belaboring the matter, one might say that the Apollonius portrayed by Pound is a much more nature-conscious, political-conscious man than was his Christian counterpart. His love of animals reminds one more of St. Francis of Assisi than of Christ. Apollonius shows in his words to Vespasian and to Domitian that he would never make a distinction between what is rendered to Caesar and what is rendered to God. He had a vital interest in politics, and was firmly committed to the workings of reason; miracles came spontaneously or as a last resort. He preferred to be called a philosopher than to be known as a worker of wonders. Apollonius was passionately committed to life, and would not passively accept a martyrdom; he fought with reason, courage, and wit. When asked why he considered himself a god, he replied tersely: "because I was good." In fact, of all the sages, Apollonius had by far the finest sense of humor—at times caustic and at other times gentle. As the Egyptian seer Kati said: "A man's paradise is his good nature" (93/623).

As Pound suggested, it is time for Apollonius to re-emerge from the shadows. As a world-traveler, sage, and worshiper of nature, he takes his place in *The Cantos* with many of the men cited in the foregoing explication, ranging from Confucius to Agassiz, and finally, of course, rhyming with Pound himself, who fought hard with reason and wit, while clinging constantly to his beliefs. Like the Greek, Pound in a sense went down at the hands of the powers that battled against him, but, also like Apollonius, he never once surrendered the quintessence of what he believed.

Chapter Eight

The Deacon and His Lombards: From Barbarism to Civilization

A Christian deacon fascinated by a race of pagans—both in turn capturing the imagination of Ezra Pound. The deacon is Paulus Diaconus, a Lombard historian (c. 725-799?) who was probably educated in Pavia, Italy, a city known in his writings by the Latin name of Ticinum. He undoubtedly lived for some time at Charlemagne's court, where he enjoyed imperial patronage. Paul the Deacon wrote two major histories: one was a central portion of the *Historia Miscella* (Mixed History), which continued Eutropius' history (Books 1 to 11) from the time of Emperor Valentinian to Justinian I (Books 12 to 16); it was in turn continued by Landulphus Sagax to the year 816. The other work was the more famous *Historia Langobardorum*, the *History of the Lombards.*[i]

Pound uses both of these works in the first half of Canto 96, where he builds a background for the city of Byzantium-Constantinople. Why should he use a Lombard historian to tell Byzantium's history, and why should he bother with Lombardy or Byzantium at all? For Pound, Byzantium is to the Occident what China is to the Orient, a civilized monolith that withstood the attacks of barbarians for centuries. Having established The City as his western pole, Pound finds that he must also deal with the rest of western Europe. The prime rival to Byzantium's glory was undoubtedly the Frankish Empire of Charlemagne. Between Aachen and Constantinople lies Italy, which languished in decline during much of the Middle Ages. Rome, for example, was a minor city overrun by cows and Vandals. Still, the Germanic invaders had to be accounted for, and, of all these, the Lombards, who settled in northern Italy, were the ones who offered the widest field for fruitful study. This is the intellectual reason for their inclusion.

Pound also had an emotional reason. He had, from the start, loved France, the troubadour country, and he had always had a special veneration for Greece, of which Byzantium is perhaps the prime medieval offshoot. But of all the places on the globe he held dear, none meant more to him than northern Italy, where the Lombards settled after they came out of Yugoslavia. Pound felt this affection early in life, and he also felt it later. After his return to Italy on being released from St. Elizabeths, Pound lived with his daughter, Mary de Rachewiltz, in her castle, Brunnenburg, near Merano. Mary, who grew up in the Tyrol, had married Prince Boris de Rachewiltz, who had longstanding family roots in the mountain country. He is quoted in Mary's autobiography:

> "We are descended from Rothar, who married the daughter
> of Teodolinda, legitimate heir of the Longobard kings,
> despite the *lex salica*, through alliance, her brother
> having been dethroned. In the year 900 Sigifredo still
> governed Lombardy . . ."[2]

It should not be surprising, then, to find Pound interested in the territory which received him after his incarceration. To his long-expressed love of Venice, Verona, and Ravenna, he added the High Adige.

The Great City is the center of Canto 96, and the first half of the canto is an attempt to find it, to place it; in order to do this, the reader must survey history. Canto 96 opens with the Greek word *kredemnon*, "veil," the protective covering that the nymph Ino or Leucothea threw to envelop Odysseus as he was swimming home to Ithaca (see the close of Canto 95). Pound, returning to his second homeland, needs a veiling to protect him from his enemies. There are some bitter words in French about the fact that aestheticism resembles church politics, in that neither is a true religion. Here Pound is putting down a great deal of nineteenth-century thought of the kind perpetuated by Arnold, Pater, and Ruskin. Either one has religion or one does not. There is no in-between.

As the hearth sends up scents of cedar and juniper to bear Pound through these shadowy presences, suddenly some mystify-

ing events of "true history" unfold: "The air is raining coins"
(Aether pluit numismata) and "The Earth is vomiting up cadavers"
(Tellus vomit cadavera). These grotesque images occur in a poem
in honor of St. Benedict in Paulus' *History of the Lombards*
(column 473), when he opens his account of his people in their
Scandinavian place of origin.[3] Actually, most of this information is
transferred to Canto 97/681:

> Upsala, was the golden fane,
> Ministrat virtutem, Fricco, pacem. Voluptatem,
>   ingenti Priapo.
> Dea libertatis, Venus.
>   Agelmund son of Ayon, reigned 33 years.

All these facts stem from a note in columns 447 and 448 of the
Migne edition, with a leap in the last sentence to columns 452-53.
The original golden temple from which Lombard belief stemmed
was located in Upsala, Sweden. The people had three primary
gods: Thor, Wodan, and Fricco. Thor was in charge of the aerial
forces like the storm; Wodan-Wotan administered *virtutem*—not
moral virtue, but the courage of warriors. Fricco was in charge of
peace (pacem) and sexual pleasure (voluptatem); he was often
represented by an enormous phallic or priapic figure (ingenti
Priapo). His wife was Frea, for whom Friday or Freitag was
named, which corresponds with the name *venerdi,* or Venus-day,
in Roman countries. The "frei" root of her name is associated with
freedom, for she grants men liberty (libertatis) through sex as the
goddess (Dea) of love. These gods formed the rather crude but
highly efficient pantheon of the Lombard people when they mi-
grated southward into Yugoslavia, where the Byzantine Emperor,
Justinian I, permitted them to settle. There Agelmund served as
their first recorded king.

Moving to Canto 103/736, one sees Wodan mentioned again,
in charge of "virtutem," Frico (Pound varied the spellings of many
names in this canto, just as the medieval historians did) in charge
of "voluptatem," and King Agelmund again. The other Lombardic
citations in this canto can be explained by what will be said about
Canto 96, where the Lombards are leaving Yugoslavia in 568 and
moving into Italy. One of the first places that Paulus mentions in
his account of Italian geography is Tuscany (Thusca, Thuscia),

where Rome is said to be located (492). The Latin name for Tuscany is believed to have been derived from frankincense (a thure). Pound was fascinated by this kind of etymology, which stresses eponymous activities, linking name to land. Paul then runs through the other provinces, including the region of the Sabines (Piceni, 494), with their "crow" (picus) flag, as well as the cities of Verona and Pavia.[4] He notes that the Gallic chieftain Brennus came down into Italy simply because he liked the wine there (495-96). Meanwhile, the important cities of Bergamo, Brescia, Milan, and Ticino (Pavia) were founded by other Celts (496).

The first great Lombard king in Italy was Alboin, who settled in Pavia. He fashioned a goblet out of the skull of Cunimundus, the father of his wife, the lovely Rosemunda, and then compounded the injury by demanding that she drink from it (498). She did, but had him murdered afterward. Paulus says that he saw the cup himself, thus hoping to lend realism to accounts that otherwise hover between actuality and myth.

Soon after their settling in Italy, the Lombards had difficulties with the Byzantines, who controlled the so-called Exarchate, or Pentapolis, area centering at Ravenna. To provide a contrast, Pound cites a few key Byzantine figures of the period: Tiberius Constantine, who freely dispensed his grain to the people (509-11); a rather unimportant general named Justinian, whom Empress Sophia Augusta, wife of the dead Justin II, was trying to install as chief ruler; she and her dead husband were called the two "lights of the world" in a eulogy (lumina mundi, 517 note). The name of the Persian king, Chos[d]roes, is added for contrast.

The words *epikombia . . . ton laon* mean, as Pound indicates, "handouts for the people"; they were distributed by Emperor Mauricius when he took over the command (517 note). Here one has a mixed ideogram, contrasting the generosity of Tiberius Constantine and Mauricius with the outsider, Chosdroes I, and the ever-political but highly intelligent Sophia Augusta.

The narrative then swings back to northern Italy and the Lombards. From the year 586 ("more or less"), Authar had a "marvelous reign, without any violence" *(mirabile in regno . . . nulla erat violentia,* 517-18) and—touch of sarcastic whimsy—no passports, things that dogged Pound's days in Europe.[5] Next is mentioned the death of the blessed Vitalis, namesake of the famous Church of San Vitale in Ravenna that Pound had always admired (520). Another of his favorite basilicas, San Zeno in Verona, had floodwaters up to its windows (525). Rome had snakes in its granaries in the fifteenth year of Childebert's reign, with water flowing everywhere (525).

Despite these disasters, the Lombards were organizing themselves. Empress Theodolinda of Bavaria married King Authar, thus establishing diplomatic relations with other Germanic nations, while the later King Theodoric of the Franks was ruling his people with his grandmother, Brunhilda (545), who is often connected with the famous heroine of Germanic legend. Rome had organized itself sufficiently so that Pope Boniface III could declare it the "head of the Church" (caput esse omnium Ecclesiarum), while the Persians were still running rampant, entering Jerusalem (570). Then Paul indulges in some personal history, putting himself into his chronicle much in the way that Pound inserts himself into The Cantos. He tells how the violence of the Huns impelled his own great-great-grandfather to flee from the Pannonia district of Yugoslavia, using a wolf to guide him (574):

and my grand-dad got out of what is now Jugoslavia
with a bow, arrows and a wolf acting as guide
till it thought gramp looked too hungry,
                comes itineris

There is undoubtedly a pun in Pound's spelling of Jugoslavia, because Paulus says that his forebear was trying to escape the "yoke (jugum) of captivity." But when Lupicis (his own name resembles lupus, wolf) got too hungry, the animal became suspicious and fled. Paulus calls the wolf a comes itineris, "companion of the route," and he thus joins the Dante-Pound gallery of "companionable animals."

Next comes the first truly great Lombard king, Rothar, who set down the laws that the Lombards up to that time had merely kept inside their heads (581-82). His legal code had a prologue that contained a brief history of his people:

Rothar touched with the aryan heresy
put father, son, ghost in that order

whereas we catholics stand for equality,
    And here, 77 years, lombards had been in Ticino,
and Rothar got some laws written down
    and a prolog . . .

Pound also remarks elsewhere that Rothar is "touched with the aryan heresy" (103/737: "arianae haeresios").[6] However, no sooner does Rothar establish the law than Lombard society begins to show signs of decadence: dope is used (*talis potio,* 582); a snake cult is employed (585 note); and Chrothar "debauches (bacchatur) with concubines" (586). Things reach a nadir when an aristocrat is cut down brutally in the basilica of San Giovanni in Pavia (592).

In another Byzantine interlude, Emperor Constans Augustus is stripping the Church of St. Mary (formerly the Roman Pantheon) and sending the brass tiles back to Constantinople (602). This cad was soon struck down in his bath: *in balneo . . . exstinctus est* (603) in Syracuse. In northern Italy, in the period from 600 on, much building was taking place as the Lombards settled permanently into their new homes. A friend named Hieronymus Antonius Reyna tells the Migne editor, who calls himself by the Latin name of Fridericus Lindenbrogius, that the Lombards of this period cast statues of their heroes in the name and cult of St. Michael; the editor documents his case with evidence in a note in column 620 of volume 95 of Migne's *Latin Patrology,* where the text appears. This statement appeals to Pound, who is always looking for anthropological roots to anchor the Christian religion: such as setting the stone face of the statue of Aphrodite back to face the sea again at Terracina. It also demonstrates how closely Pound reads the notes in his texts. The fact that a Germanic editor would use a Romanized name continues the process whereby Germanic heroes were merged with a Christian angel-saint and a barbaric people were civilized.

Paulus goes on to say that an Anglo-Saxon named Cedwald (otherwise Cedoaldus) visited Rome for absolution and died there (632); thus England enters the scene, though remotely. He then mentions that the Merovingian kings have yielded their power to the "mayor of the palace," the so-called Architriclin or *majus domus* (majordomo, 634). As a result, the true French rule is now passing into the hands of the Carolingians, who will bring western

Europe to its highest point during the central Middle Ages. As
Greco-Roman titles pervade the aristocracy, the continuity with
the past is maintained, and gradually the old Germanic values are
being tinged with Christian-Romanic-Hellenic influence. Geo-
graphically, one can see Lombard Italy in a perspective, with
England and France on the left, and with Byzantium on the right.
This position will be clarified later.

Then comes a new hero, Cunibert or Cuningpert:

From the golden font, kings lie in order of generation
        Cuningpert elegant, and a warrior . . .

Paulus says that the man was indeed *elegans,* and that he was also a
"bold warrior" (*audaxque bellator,* 636).[7] Upon his death, an
epitaph was engraved on his sepulcher next to the basilica in Pavia;
it began with the line quoted in English above: *Aureo ex fonte
quiescunt in ordine reges.* This verse could be applied in a much
more general way to Paulus' whole history, to the first half of
Canto 96, or to the flowing procession of golden rulers and saints
in the mosaics in Ravenna, especially in the nave of the stunning
Church of Sant'Apollinare Nuovo.

But the heroes tend to yield to villains or to nobodies. A man
whose name isn't even mentioned by Pound (it was Ferdulfus)
comes into power as a duke; all that is said about him is that he
hailed from the region of Liguria (de partibus Liguriae) and that he
was slippery (lubricus, 639). Speaking of slipping, King Aripert
actually did sink into the Ticino River while he was trying to run
away from his enemies, weighted down with kingly gold (gravatus
auro, 646). This causes Pound to indulge in a whimsical two-line
snatch about the difficulty of telling one bird from another:

Who shall know throstle's note from banded thrush
by the wind in the holly bush

With these minor tragedies come disasters on a grand scale: a flood
struck Rome, and the waters reach from the Tiber River up to the
Via Lata (Broad Street), and from St. Peter's to the Milvian Bridge
(648).

The scene shifts back to France then, where the "mayor of the
palace," Pippin or Pepin, is beginning to gain control. One hears
about "Pippin and his wars and that Carolus (et quia Karolus) his

son succeeded him" (648). Becoming confused, Pound wonders if the Karolus mentioned is Charles Martel or the great Charlemagne. He looks down at a note in column 649, which is itself a bit puzzling, but which says that Pippin's sons by Plectrude were Drogo and Grimoald; from Alpaide they were Carolus and Childebrand. Pound then assumes that this Pippin is the father of Charlemagne, but that would be jumping things, for the next person in the chronicle is very clearly the earlier Charles Martel.[8] Pound himself acknowledges that this man was at home in Poitou (apud Pictavium, 659), Aquitaine, Narbonne, and Provence "in the 'thirties'"—the 730s. Therefore, the Charles is Martel, and his father is Pepin of Héristal (dead c. 714), not Pepin the Short (dead 768). Pound and the reader breathe a sigh of relief.

By the time one unravels the Pepins and the Charleses, one is not quite sure who that "bloke" is whom Pound remembers as being buried in an empty grave outside San Zeno, nor the other one in Milan. Time effaces names, epitaphs; all that remain are the great names, and suddenly they emerge from the confusion with clarity:

Charles Martel, who extended Frankish rule through southern France, driving the Moors back into Spain after a great victory at Poitiers-Tours in 732.

Charlemagne, his grandson, who unified western Europe by conquest and towers as its greatest medieval ruler.

Liutprand (dead 744), who brought the Lombard kingship to its highest level, uniting northern Italy under a strong Roman-based law and rule, and overcoming the dissident southern duchies of Spoleto and Benevento. He is to Italy what Charlemagne is to France. The fact that Charles Martel sends his own son to Liutprand for a tonsorial rite is quoted in column 659 of the Migne. He maintained friendly relations not only with the Franks (pro Carolus: "for Charles") but also with the more threatening and barbaric Avars (672).

Pound closes his portrait of Liutprand by citing some tablets, laws, and epigraphs. The ACTUM TICINI IN PALATIO was "a deed performed in the Palace of Pavia" whereby Liutprand raised Hildebrand, his assistant, as his equal in governing when old age overtook him in 744 (662); this demonstrates a peaceful passage of succession. The little phrase "et Arimnium" ("and Rimini" attests

to his victories) is lifted from a eulogy for Liutprand written in
Latin and celebrating his triumphs (670). There is also mention of
the sacred spear that was given to Lombard kings in their
coronation rites; the editor of Paul's text says that he saw this engraved on "a stone on the back part (ambon) of the altarpiece in the
basilica at Monza" (Pound mistakes the Latin name for the town,
and writes Modena). The information is contained in column 667,
and there are two large pictures of Lombard kings being crowned
in columns 663 to 666. The tribute ends with a Chinese character
placed on the right, which resembles a crown, and which is not in
the Mathews *Chinese-English Dictionary*. It means "splendid,"
and can be translated by the Latin words to the left, which mean
"splendid in word and in deed."

With the line "in the second year of Eirene," the scene has
switched back to Constantinople, where the Empress Irene has
sent an ambassador to Charlemagne to discuss a wedding proposal
involving her son. This might well have united the Frankish Kingdom and the Byzantine Empire, but it did not take place. At this
point, the source shifts to the *Historia Miscella,* partly written by
Paul, but largely assembled by Landulph. Even the first part of the
work by Eutropius is brought into play with the mention of the
Roman Emperor Diocletian. The reader might well ask why all
these references.

Pound is here pulling a variety of things together:

> The ROMAN EMPIRE has won the
> civilized Occidental world, but breaks
> into two as

> Emperor Constatine
> moves to Constantinople
> and founds the Byzantine
> (Eastern) part

while the Roman (Western)
part is overrun by Goths and
finally stabilized by Lombards.
THE ROMAN POPE is in constant conflict with THE GREEK PATRIARCH.
Lombards threaten the Papacy,
which calls on the Franks for
help, leading to the defeat of
the Lombards by Charlemagne,
who is crowned Emperor
of the West in 800.

The next four hundred years show Europe divided between the Frankish and the Byzantine spheres of influence. Venice then emerges out of the old Lombard Kingdom as the new economic power, and finally leading to Venetian destruction of Constantinople in the Fourth Crusade (1202-4), long before the Turks completed the job in 1453.

In this canto, western Europe has been shown emerging out of the barbarism that set in over the dissolution of the Roman Empire. The canto is hard to read because it is put together in pieces and snippets, some of them difficult to pin down, just as the history itself is jerky, inconsistent, and vague, marred by tragedies and violent acts of man and nature. Lombard law and Frankish control would eventually change most of this, but in comparison with the shiny city of Constantinople, Paul the Deacon presents us with the piecemeal tale of tribes fighting for peace and stability, at one remove from barbarism.

Liutprand is an excellent transitional figure because he tries to hold the West and the East together. But he cannot; he dies fighting the Byzantines, and his kingdom is swallowed up in Charlemagne's pan-European progress. Still, the ideogram that emerges from the end of Lombard history is one of pride: a crown, words of light, bits from memorial stones, elements of achievement. It was on Liutprand's base that the building of Romanesque Italy—always in close touch with Byzantium through the Exarchate, especially in Ravenna—took place; and ultimately, although Pound does not follow through on the details, this same northern Italy, by way of Venice and with some help from France, would lay the groundwork for the destruction of The City.

Therefore, in getting to Constantinople, one looks first at Rome, which created it. In the same volume is the early part of the *Historia Miscella,* and from it Pound abstracts a few bits about the great

DIOCLETIAN, 37th after Augustus, thought: more if we tax 'em
and don't annihilate. Haud procul Salonis
not far from Salo otio senuit, quietly aging,
and alleged Saturn started brass currency

Diocletian, like many sage Chinese rulers, believed that it was easier to tax enemies than to wipe them out; the reference to brass

coins underscores Theodor Mommsen's idea that Diocletian and
other emperors gave this tax-free money to the cities to circulate.
The picture is given of him as he "aged in leisure" (otio senuit) not
far from Salona, Yugoslavia (Haud procul Salonis), tying his
currency into a religious framework.[9] The idea of serenity (serenitas) continues with Vespasian and his "renewed cities" (urbes
renovatae; 871, 874); with peaceful Antoninus, under whom was
no war (nullo bello, 884); and with Septimius Severus, who died
"at York" in England (apud Eboricum; read *Eboracum*, 891).
Mention of Severus reminds Pound of the man's wife, Julia
Domna, who asked Philostratus to write the biography of Apollonius of Tyana (Canto 94). This ideogram of peace, beauty, and
tranquility comes to a head with the name Galla Placidia, the
lovely woman who died 1165 years after the founding of the city of
Rome (reckoned a.u.c.—*ab urbe condita*—in the old Roman
calendar system). She was buried in the beautiful mosaic-filled
tomb that sits next to the Church of San Vitale in Ravenna
(954-55). This woman, who moved from France to Italy to Constantinople, is herself a way of binding East and West together.

The two names of barbaric tribes that follow—Picts and Vandals—
are meant to be read as harsh undertones to the civilized roll-call
before them; these peoples were fought by Placidia's brother,
Honorius, a rather ineffective ruler who drove her to Constantinople and helped to hasten the decline of the Roman West at the
same time that the Byzantine East was on the uprise.

With the words "called Bosphorus from the bull tax," the
reader has at last arrived at the fated city. In typical fashion, Pound
will not let one enjoy Yeats' dolphin-torn, gong-tormented seas.
Pound says that the great metropolis grew on its site because the
Bos-phorus or Ox-Ford could extract a tax from the many people
shuffling back and forth from Asia to Europe. The modern visitor
who watches the boats plying night and day from the Sirkeci Station in Europe to the Haydarpasa Station in Asia feels this economic rationale beneath the sweep of the natural scenery. After a
brief recall of Lombard achievement in a treaty with Justinian I
(988), the expulsion of the Goths from northern Italy (989), and the
establishment of law in the Italian republic (989), mixed with
Pound's reminiscences of some unforgettable Lombard types, he
presents the reign of the great Justinian I (ruled 527-65).

The important Byzantine rulers can be listed as follows, since, as Pound acknowledges, Landulph's chronology is "seven years less than the accepted":

Justinian I, assumes rule in 527	Alboin; first Lombard
Justin II, in 565	king in Italy
Tiberius II, in 571	
Mauricius, in 577	
Phocas, in 595	
Heraclius, in 602	
Constans, in 634	
Constantinus, in 660	
Justinian II, in 678	

Pound stops here because of an important event to which he dedicates a sizable chunk from the pages of the Migne edition; but Landulph goes on to the ninth century, to the time of the Leos, one of whom (Leo VI, the Wise, ruled 886-912) dominates the latter half of the canto.

Perhaps because the *Code of Justinian* and the building of the Hagia or Santa Sophia Cathedral are referred to elsewhere in *The Cantos*,[10] Pound restricts his words about Justinian I to the death of his wife, Theodora (991), who is impressively portrayed in the gold mosaics in San Vitale, Ravenna. Pound also mentions Justinian's iron-hand control of money in the form of embargos to protect local businesses (990) and his careful discipline of the money-sellers (993). Pound contrasts Oriental frills and modesty with the achievements of the great emperor. Justinian himself was never modest, if we can believe legend; upon entering his great church for the first time, he is alleged to have exclaimed: "O Solomon! I have surpassed you!"

After another reference to the Englishman Caedual (earlier spelled Cedwald), mention is made of the Eparch's Book (EPARCHIKON BIBLION) or the *Edict of the Eparch,* written by Leo the Wise. This work furnishes the material for much of the rest of the canto. This is a book which was created by the Emperor to bring order among the crafts and guilds of The City. When another Englishman is mentioned, King Alfred or Aldfrid of

Northumbria (died 705), one might well ask why. Clearly, contrast
is again the answer. But chance also intervenes, for by accident the
editor of volume 95 of the Migne edition of the Latin Fathers
appends the work of the Venerable Bede's *Church History* (*Historia ecclesiastica*) to the histories of Paul and Landulph. Pound
returns to the front of the volume to see what the British were
doing. Aldfrid is mentioned as a fairly good ruler in column 258,
and Bishop Aldhelm is described in columns 260 and 261 as having
written a number of works, some poetic and some scholarly, such
as: *De Virginitate . . . versibus hexametris* (On Virginity in
hexameters), *De Metaplasmo* (On the Remolding), and *De Sinalimpha* (On Unclean Waters). So, slowly culture is coming to
Britain; but, in the main, talk is about ecclesiastical tonsure rites
(285, 288), comets facing the north (282), and mere fads.

Returning to Landulph and the events described in column
994, Pound begins with the third year of Justin II's reign, along
with his wife, Sophia Augusta. Before going mad, Justin waged an
all-out war on usurers (994), restored money to the people, and
converted a synagogue into a church (996). These details, as a note
on columns 997-98 informs the reader, "follow Theophanes"
(Theophanem sequitur), author of the *Annals of the Greeks*.
Justin's successor, Tiberius (Constantine) II, was a terrible spend-
thrift (998-99)—Pound had praised his generosity earlier—but he
was followed by the brilliant general Mauricius, a rugged Cappa-
docian who overcame the Slavs in Thrace, the Lombards, and the
Avars (1000-1). In Persia, Mauricius defeated the enemy, who delighted in Roman calamities (1004: calamitatibus delectabantur),
but he could not stem the flow of Lombards into the Exarchate
(1005). He did indeed make the city splendid again (urbem splen-
didam reddidit) with his *commerciis* (business dealings) and his
"equestribus speculationibus," which can be rendered "dealings in
horses"—an activity that was important in Hippodrome-centered,
horse-loving Constantinople (1005). Pound emphasizes Mauricius'
"local control of local purchasing power," but the Emperor may
have exercised that too strongly, for his own army eventually cast
him out.

However, as Alexander del Mar stresses,[11] Mauricius and the
other emperors held a firm grip on coining. Mauricius is contrasted by Pound with the Asiatic Hormisda, who ruled with

typical barbaric "pleasure in blood, love of homicide, infidelity, vainglory, and violence" (Pound takes the Latin phrases from column 1006). Mauricius' praetor Priscus caught the barbarian Musaicus (*not* Musacius), totally drunk at his brother's funeral rite (1011). Mauricius was never guilty of too little control; ultimately, he erred by exerting too much, and thus caused "no absence of various great woes" (*non defuerunt imperio variae, ac ingentes aerumnae*, 1019), which led to his deposition. Pound ties his downfall in with the Fortune theme, which he associates with Canto 7 of Dante's *Inferno* (*e che permutasse:* "and who has thoroughly changed") and with the Chinese character *chen⁴*, "to tremble, to quake." Luck is an important but unforeseen element in human events. An essentially strong ruler like Mauricius may be overthrown, only to lead to power falling into the hands of a cad like Phocas.

But Heraclius, who was crowned in 602 according to the *Mixed History* (actually, in 610), at the same time that he was a bridegroom (imperator simul et sponsus, 1024), is an altogether admirable man from Pound's point of view. The poet devotes a great deal of space to Heraclius' activities, which can be listed as follows, in Pound's order:

1. Heraclius assumes power by coming to The City on castellated ships from Egypt that bore images of the Mother of God: *navibus castellatis . . . et imagines Dei matris* (1023).
2. He found the republic's business dis-solute ("unstuck"): *invenit dissoluta reip. negotia* (1024). He warred against the Avars, who had "made Europe a desert" (*Europam Avares reddidere desertam*), and the Persians, who had "exterminated all Asia" (*Asiam vero totam Persae exterminaverunt*, 1024), especially King Chosdroes II, who spurned an imperial message by saying: "I won't spare you until you deny the Crucified One, whom you profess to be God, and adore the Sun" (1025). Much as Pound himself adores the Sun, he does not ignore the Son or the human element in religion. Chosdroes gets off rather lightly by being called "pro sun," with the Chinese character *jih⁴* to enforce the solar element.
3. In order to defeat the Persians, Heraclius melts candles and sacred vessels for gold and silver coins: *nummos aureos et ar-*

genteos (1026), which in a footnote are called by their Greek names, *nomismata kai miliarisia.* Pound notes that this last word is not in *Liddell & Scott's Greek-English Lexicon.* Heraclius takes a sacred icon (Pound's Greek word *eikonos*), shaped like "the virile figure of God," and swears on it that he will fight to the death for his people; he states that he wants to base his authority on love, rather than on fear (1026).

4. Moving east to the Euphrates River, Heraclius creates a boat-bridge when a hempen one is burned (1032). While he winters at Sebastia, Chosdroes ruthlessly ransacks churches and robs private citizens to build an elite army called the Golden Spears (in Greek, *Chrysolochas*, 1033). Chosdroes tries to enlist the help of Bulgars, Gepids, and the "Hunnos" who are called Avars, as well as the "Turks called Cazars" (1033) to move against The City.[12] But with the superlaudable help of God's mother, a great hailstorm falls upon the army, killing many of them, and the Byzantines win. Finding great stores of animals in Persia, the Byzantine soldiers have a great feast (*populus epulantes*) and glorify God (1036).

5. Pressing on, the Byzantines find Chosdroes' great palace in Damastager deserted. There they see spices, such as pepper and ginger (*zinziber*), and huge live tigers (*tigrides mirae magnitudinis*), as well as antelopes and other beasts (1037). This is a froufrou Oriental delight, meant to be contrasted with the saner pleasures of The City, where horseracing was perhaps the greatest vice.

6. Heraclius finally defeats the Persians, and everything looks auspicious, but a giant swordlike sign stretches in the sky from Mesembra to the star Arcturus, announcing that the Arabs are on the way up, and soon most of the Middle East will belong to them (1045).

Moving then to the reign of Constans, Pound describes another natural calamity in the form of ashes from heaven: *cinis e coelo descendit,* 1049; but The City can withstand debacles of nature. It is the internal moral rot that Pound fears, as exemplified in the brutal and wanton destruction of the famous Colossus of Rhodes statue by Muhavis, who sold its parts to a dealer named Emesenus (1049). This destruction of an object of reverence and awe, with its overtone of shady dealings, is far more important than defeats by the Persians or Arabs:

and in the 11th of Constans ashes from heaven,
        in the 12th Muhavis broke the Colossus
that had stood thirteen sixty years,
        mille tre centos sexaginta, and   [1360]
sold 900 camel-loads, aere oneravit, of its brass   [brass-loaded]
    to a jew
(all this chronology seven years less than the accepted).

This brings the account to the Arab Habdimelich, who had won over most of the Middle East and was challenging Justinian II. At last they made peace (1058), and Abd-el-Melik, as his name may be spelled, promised to tender a tribute. But, flushed with victory over his rival Zubir (1059) and "devilishly instigated," the Arab first tried to break the peace and then offered to honor it, but by paying tribute with his own coins. Pound gives a long excerpt describing the event.

> In the sixth year of his rule Justinian (the second) out of folly dissolved the peace which he held with Habdimelich and unreasonably wanted the whole island of Cyprus and its people to transmigrate, and when he freshly looked at the stamp on the coin that had been sent from Habdimelich, he did not accept it . . . And when he heard this, Habdimelich, devilishly instigated, kept asking that the peace should not be dissolved, but that they should accept (sed susciperent) his coinage, since the Arabs would not accept the cut of the Romans on his coins. Indeed, giving the weight of the gold, he said: "There won't be any loss to the Romans if the Arabs are allowed to mint new . . . "[13]

Justinian stood firm in his demand of payment in Byzantine coins. To fully grasp the importance of this episode, one must read Alexander del Mar's *History of Monetary Systems*, where Pound learned of this event, which eventually led to the conception of the entire canto.[14] Justinian knew that if he lost his imperial right to coin, he would then lose everything. It is on Justinian's strong imperial base, with its recourse to law and to order, that Mustafa Kemal, more familiarly known as Ataturk, could build his modern Turkish nation in the 1920s.

Pound ends his geographic and historic placing of Con-

stantinople by rounding out Justinian II's life, telling how he was
expelled and "came back thru the aquaduct [*sic*]" (*per aquae-
ductum ingressus,* 1065). In that same year of his return to power,
Habdimelich died. Earlier Justinian had persuaded a leader of the
Slavs to support him with *viginti millibus Sclavorum,* which Pound
apparently thinks are 20,000 sclavons or coins:

bags, baskets full of, presumably, coinage,
and lured twenty thousand sclavons.

But they are most certainly troops of Slavs. With one last mention
of France and England (Watling St.), Pound is at last ready to
plunge into the *Edict of the Eparch* of Leo the Wise. He and the
reader have finally found The City.

It is appropriate now to reconsider Pound's methodology and
his whole attitude toward history, which are important in any
evaluation of this canto. As stated earlier, the canto divides into
two parts. The first section is the historical and geographical quest
for a city. The second section is an examination of how the
organism works. The first part takes the form of unraveling a
history that is full of tangles and twists, a history that is shifty and
never fully reliable. The second part is the application of order
stemming from laws that can be examined closely. One reads the
first part swiftly, glancing at the names of men and tribes and
places and battles, overcome by the difficulty of establishing anything permanent out of the welter of time passing. One reads the
second part slowly, savoring the mechanics of law and right that
made the machine, once it was assembled, work.

Pound as a historian is as liable to errors of judgment as were
Bede, Paulus, and Landulphus—or Toynbee, Mommsen, and
Rostovtzeff. No man can perfectly handle history, for the capitalist's hero is the communist's villain. Everything that Pound says
here by way of emphasis is anathema to one who is strongly pro-
Arabic or pro-Persian or pro-Slav. Pound would be the first to
agree. Thus, in assessing history, each man must cling to what he
respects: Pound respects the rules of Authar, the laws of Rothar,
the edict of Leo, the building of Justinian, the courage of Heraclius. Pound ignores or plays down the Avars-Gepids-Bulgars
who roll (the verb is used advisedly) off the pages of *Thrones.* To
him these people do not, in the end, matter at all. They are like

the bloke who is *not* buried in a grave that bears his name outside of San Zeno. They are *not* Justinian the Great.

Emerson doubted that history existed, except in the form of biography. Pound, I think, doubts that anyone's history except his own (and possibly Del Mar's) exists. But Pound is a poet, a craftsman of words, who ultimately doesn't care about exact dates (seven years off-kilter in Landulph) or niceties of truth, except insofar as they lead to IDEAS, which he can then free into dramatic or lyric activity. The first half of Canto 96 is a long, stumbling preamble appended to a picture of a droning honeycomb; it is a tale told by many idiots with half-remembered, half-pieced-together details— all of them suspect. But the search, the quest, dark and questionable as it may be, is important because it leads to the City of Light.

Chapter Nine

Byzantium: The Sacred Symbol of Yeats, the Well-run Metropolis of Pound

The latter half of Canto 96 concerns the building of an imperial city, one that Wyndham Lewis referred to as Constantinople, William Butler Yeats as Byzantium, the Turks as Istanbul, and many people simply as The City:

"Constantinople" said Wyndham "our star,"
Mr. Yeats called it Byzantium   (661)

The first half of the canto provides the historical foundation for the event (see Chapter Eight). The second half supplies the reader with the details of its organization, lifted largely from the pages of the *Edict of the Eparch* of Leo the Wise.[1]

The passage dealing with the *Edict* follows the long Latin citation on page 658 of Pound's text. The poet was especially interested in this proclamation because Leo, who ruled from 886 to 912 (Pound uses 911), employed it to implement the laws in order to maintain a strong and healthy government; he was most successful. The *Edict*, which was enforced by an "eparch," or local administrator, of Constantinople, contained twenty-two chapters, each dealing with a profession or craft important to the realm. The entire decree is meant to be balanced with the *Sacred Edict* of K'ang Hsi, which appears in Cantos 98 and 99. Clearly, in this part of his poem, Pound is again pulling East and West together.

One of the problems facing the reader of Leo's *Edict* is the obscurity of its technically precise language. Pound grapples with this from the very start. Pages 658-59 contain a variety of isolated words that puzzle not only Pound but also the best editor of the work, Professor Jules Nicole of the University of Geneva. Beginning with the Latin word "Hyacinthinis," one may turn to the notes on pages 92 and 93 of Nicole's text, where he is attempting to translate the Greek word *megalozelon* (literally, "big emulation or blessedness"), which is used to describe the differences in the magnificent robes in Chapter 4, the book of the Vestment-Makers (pp. 26-28). Pound somewhat facetiously suggests "fake purple" as a translation, though the staid Swiss professor settles for "d'un grand modèle" (of a great model) in his notes. The Latin word, which usually means blood-red, is mentioned because Nicole, not knowing how to render the Greek word that he is translating, has to ponder in search of precision; he notes that there were two types of purple used for imperial robes—one a blood-red (see the Chinese character *chu¹* nearby) and the other a purple-red (see the character *tsu³*). Pound obviously wants the reader to note that the Chinese characters are far more precise than their Occidental counterparts.

Continuing with definitions, Pound employs the phrase "chastised and brought into the house (coom ben)" to translate Nicole's Latin "verberator et bonis mulc[t]ator," which in turn is translating the Greek *paideuestho kai eiskomizestho* (p. 27). Here Pound is showing the difficulty of getting at an original text through a translator and one or two intermediary languages; yet the struggle, he lets one know, is worth the effort required. The phrase states the punishments meted out for irregularities in the Vestment-Maker profession; these are set down in very exact terms that delight Pound. His "coom ben" is a slang rendition of the Latin *cum benis*: culprits among the garment men will be hauled into court "with the goods"! The next two lines from page 27 (and the notes on 97 ff.) tell the Vestment-Makers to "register all silk purchases over ten aurei," with two Greek words for the sum, *deka nomismaton,* followed by another tricky noun, *ta blattia,* which Nicole renders as "purple vestments" (purpureas vestes).

If the reader is troubled by all this, so is the present writer, and so was Nicole, and so was Pound. But how else can one ever get to the truth without some consideration of the individual word? Pound is here dramatizing the whole act of unraveling history, of working from words to concepts, from the Logos to its actualization. Any attempt to conceal the *difficulty* of the process would be a mere sham. And so Pound goes on, preparing the blocks to erect his canto; for only when the individual pieces are in order can the whole organism hum. Most of the rest of page 659 offers other words from Chapter 7 (the Raw-Silk Dressers, pp. 34- 35), who are always "at free will . . . raising and lowering the price": *anaidos . . . me auxanontes e elattountes ten timen.* Pound tells the Doctor that *anaidos* is much stronger than his weak translation; it should be rendered as "recklessly," for these guilds- men are destroying the entire social fabric by destroying just prices. How long can a society survive when a suit costs the same as an egg?

Then comes a catalogue of Greek words, with some Chinese to the right that says in descending order: PURPLE—ARRIVE AT—SNATCH—RED; or, more smoothly, "purple succeeds in passing red."[2] These characters deal with the previous distinctions in the colors of robes, distinctions that are important for the Vestment-Makers; they are also important for Pound, who always insisted on verbal precision and was fond of Chinese words for colors.[3] The Greek words are defined as follows by the *Liddell &* *Scott Greek-English Lexicon:*[4]

alogistous	"silly, unreasoning"
kapeleuon	"to hawk, palm off"[5]
stomulos	as Pound says, "mouthy"; from *stoma*
agoraios	Pound's "forensic"; from the *agora* or *forum;* hence, vulgar, hucksterish
lalos	Pound's "babbler"; gossiper
tarachodes	troublesome, pesky[6]

All these words occur in a single passage describing vulgar mer- chants, who are to be penalized: "Anyone caught palming off the retail silk . . . or who is garrulous or pushy or obstreporous or annoying . . . shall be thrown out of the guild" (p. 35). The Em- peror and the Eparch do indeed speak to the point.

Only a few more blocks are needed before one can begin to form larger units. Pound insists that one can appreciate "a refine- ment of language" in a beautifully worded imperial decree as easily as one can in a poem by Wallace Stevens. After his list, he drops a few more Greek phrases that are all taken from Chapter 11, the Candle-Makers, warning them not to fool around with just weights and measures: "If a scale is found to be tampered with, crooked" (*stater . . . kampanon nenotheumenon*) "and not stamped with the Eparch's seal" (*me te tou eparchou esphragismenon . . . boulle*, p. 45), then the merchant is liable to punishment. According to both the Eparch and Pound—now the same person—an exact definition of weights, measures, and prices is obligatory for the preservation of a nation's well-being, and violators must be dutifully prosecuted. The lexicographer Charles du Cange is cited by the word *stater*, a Greek word that refers both to a weight and to a scale; it is related to the Latin *statera*, a scale.[7] If one wants equity, one must, to cite the Old Testament, show "justice in meteyard and measure."

Next comes an italicized statement that lies at the heart of Pound's poetic theory, and in his own answer to the often-made charge of obscurantism:

> If we never write anything save what is already understood, the field of undertanding [*sic*] will never be extended. One demands the right, now and again, to write for a few people with special interests and whose curiosity reaches into greater detail.

Having answered this charge, Pound is ready to serve up larger blocks. First come four lines about the Grocers, who are not supposed to file off or polish coins (*e kai nomismata xeei*), nor to increase an agreed price (*pactum pretium augens;* chap. 13, p. 48). These are absolute Poundian doctrines concerning the control of currency, promoted to no small degree by the works of Alexander del Mar. They are followed by a "few words about hoarding," telling the Grocers that they should not "store up wealth for a time of need" (*kairon endeias apothesaurize*). There are some further words about "raising house rents" (*auxon enoikion*), or as Nicole more widely expresses it, "raising the price."[8]

After a brief mention of the French author Jean de Bosschère, who lived in a society that reversed priorities by using leather to line carriages rather than to make shoes,[9] the Eparch tells the Pig-Sellers (Choiremporoi; Pound's Xoirempers) not to traffick in sheep or to hide pigs in "the house of an arkhon" (*oikon archonti-kon*).[10] The Eparch does not want one trader to usurp the calling of another, thereby killing small businesses. Then Pound is ready to present a large block concerning the Bakers. They are admonished to use government-approved, stamped staters, and are warned to keep the weights and worths of their bread in accordance with the selling price of grain (*kata ten exonesin*).[11] They must pay one gold coin (*nomismatos henos*) as a tax on grain bought, for which they are allowed to charge one keration as their own profit and two miliarisia for the price of the laborers. In this way, there can be no price-rigging or feigned shortages. Pound makes the rather curious observation that Professor Nicole puts a grave slanting on the word *henos*, which is perfectly correct in the context; the only mistake in the vicinity is Pound's editor's allowing the word "bankers" to appear instead of "bakers." With eparchlike "epis-kepsis" (looking over), Pound is watching Nicole's every step.

Bakers are so important to the imperial state that they are called for "no public service or charge" (*medemia leitourgia*). The word *leitourgia* is interesting; it is the source of Pound's amusing translation "liturgy," but here, of course, the word has no eccle-siastical overtone (the Eparch refers to military service); yet since Pound's notion of the Earthly Paradise constantly blends with the metaphysical, the word-play is cogent. The state depends on bread, and the bakers, and even their beasts, are exempt from onerous duties. They are cautioned to guard their ovens against fires.

Pound then offers a long stretch dealing with the Taverners (chap. 19, pp. 55-56). The Greek name for a taverner is *kapelos*, which Pound rather playfully connects with the Latin word *capellanus* or "chaplain"—wince who will! He calls them "chap-lains of cabarets" on page 663. With his Confucian-Protestant ethic in the background, Pound retains these people (what great city can exist without night life?), but he wants control over "the management . . . whereby . . . they sell" (*oikonomia . . . hopos . . . pipraskesthai*); there will be no unfair competition if there is "analogous ezonesis [exonesis]," that is, equal selling.

The Taverners' measures have to be supervised: a *stathmos* is a cask containing thirty litres; *aggeia* (Pound's "aggaia") are measuring vessels; a *mina* holds only three litres. Next, the hours of operation are posted: taverns are to be closed on Sundays (*kyriakais*); they should open at the second hour (*deuteras horas*) and close at the second hour of evening. Pound wonders precisely what the second hours are, and on page 666, he decides that they are 8 A.M. and 8 P.M. (two hours after dawn and vespers, traditional measuring times of the Middle Ages). In locking up for the night (*asphalizein*), the Taverners are urged to extinguish their cauldron fires (*sbennuein ta lebetia*) and to toss out those who are "full of wine" (*tou oinou emphoroumenoi*), making sure that these do not hurtle back to "instigate (*katakremnizontai*) fights or injuries (*bias*) or brawls (*diaphoras*)." Pound uses rather tame alternatives for these words in his listing of them. If a taverner does not heed the Eparch, he is to be "chased away" (*ekdiokesthosan*) from the "sunthema" (mistake for *systema*, the guild).

Next comes Chapter 20, titled "On Legates" (PERI LEGATORIOU; pp. 56-57), who, Pound guesses, are foreign importers, since their visits in The City are restricted. But Pound is wrong; they are actually the Eparch's deputies, who are to guard against foreigners taking over businesses and flooding the market with cheap goods. French wine bothers the Eparch in the way that Japanese automobiles might annoy his modern counterpart. Pound transmits this feeling in his statement that "No yugo-slav to propose to a girl/ until he has planted trees, 50 olives." These deputies blend with the men in Chapter 21 "of the BOTHRON," whose name is supposed to be apparent: *"The art of the 'bothorum' by its very name is given meaning"* (the last word in Greek is Pound's *diasemainetai*). The word *bothros* means "a pit," and Pound, after trying the similar *boter* (herd), decides that these are Cattlemen. Actually, they are Assessors (of Animals), whose duties keep them out in Amastriani Square, where the smell of their job won't offend the Emperor. One of their prime tasks is to point out the "defects of the animals" (*ton zoon tas aitias*) to prospective buyers, for as Pound humorously remarks: "some animals are imperfect."

Next comes a list of Contractors (*ergolaboi*), who round out the final Chapter 22 (pp. 60-63). The first ones mentioned are those involved with the "askothyrarion," who, as Pound explains, are connected with an "askos," a leather bag. One assumes that they would be Leather-Makers, but Nicole calls them in Latin *claustrarii,* either Door-Makers or Interior Decorators. The work of the LEPTOURGON (Fine Craftsmen) involves Plasterers, Stonemasons, Painters, and others. These are the real builders of The City. With a cunning use of words (*stomulia*), they lift up their earnings (*auxei tous misthous*), since they are often motivated by *aplestia* (cupidity) and *kakourgia* (malice), rather than by a desire to better a society or to beautify a city. Pound puts the average guildsman on as low a level as he does Pope Gregory the Great, who drove out the beautiful Mozarabic chant and Gallican song to promote his own watered-down taste. Pound implies that The City may easily fall because of their "awkward use of words" (*skaioteti ton logon*), a favorite ploy of the small businessman, who often charges double for his work after a vague assessment of a job.

Next follows a rundown of architectural words that are all defined in Pound's poem: *tholos, kamara, asphaleian, empeirian, themelios, sathros.* There is also the remark by Professor Norman Holmes Pearson of Yale that this is all "vurry . . . in'erestin'." Pearson's Yankee drawl (as rendered by Pound) blends into the colloquial feel of the entire canto, where the people are working together to create a place of beauty. One is not sure that Pearson did find it interesting that a contractor should not make "a foundation slanty" (*me to ktizomenon loxon*), but the words apply metaphorically to any undertaking.

Then comes a list of scholars (Morrison, Salmasius, Reitz) who had a hand across the ages in Professor Nicole's preparation of the text (pp. 67-75). These people are just as important to Pound's creation of the canto as the Contractors are to the rearing of the city. The name Julien d'Askalon (Ascalon) comes up because this Byzantine wrote what has come to be called a *Collection of Extracts,* which was appended to the Geneva manuscript that Nicole was editing. Julien was much concerned with the perfection of city life, and his paragraphs were classified under four rubrics: precautions against fire (*pyros*); the airing (*aeros*) and care of furniture and equipment; the uses of water (*hydatos;* not *hodatos,* as Pound prints it); and the laws of ownership of land (*ges*)—in other words, the four elements. These are brought into play with the crowded conditions of urban life, presenting the city of Constantinople in a context of nature. Indeed, modern Istanbul is remarkable for the way that it blends into its natural setting.

Next Pound writes an amusing line: "the old men on the sway-ing trapeeeeeezion," if I may tamper with the last word. A *trape-zion* is a bank or counter on which a banker leaned, and from which he got his name: in modern Greek, *trapezites*. Pound allies the word with the circus. But the state of the Empire's health de-pended very much on whether the bench or the bank swayed. Then comes a list of words that fascinated Pound, and are all de-fined in the text except for *byrsopoioi* (Leather-Makers).[12] Fiscal duplicity returns with the mention that the tetarteron coin, which was debased by Emperor Nicephoras Phocas, who ruled from 963 to 969 (p. 91). Earlier, the currency had been supervised by "epis-keptiks" (with the accent on skepticism), and the interest rate was not allowed to go over 12 percent per annum (p. 98)—far lower than in many Chinese periods (Canto 98/685). In his note on the tetarteron coin on page 91, Dr. Nicole says that John Tzetzes wrote a letter in which he accused a certain Siligudes of reducing the value of the currency. Tzetzes calls this otherwise unknown man an *andrarion agoraion kai banauson,* which Pound translates succinctly as an "s. o. b.," but which a more fastidious translator might render as a "vulgar, hucksterish Untermensch."

Talk of the decline of the value of money leads Pound to think of the decline of the Byzantine culture as a whole. He launches into a little threnody, a hail and farewell to the Sun (*Chaire ho Helios*), to "brightness" (clarore).[13] The Greek words above the lament, drawn from the Butchers in Chapter 15 (pp. 50-51), stress what these men should be working for—and the message applies to all men:

kata ten poioteta	[for the quality]
(ton zoon)	[of the animals]
acc. the quality	[accentuate]

The Butchers are to concern themselves with the quality of their product, just as every guildsman is to concern himself with the ex-cellence of his craft, his *techne*. When a society puts greed before the general welfare, it is on the way down. Hence, a goodbye to the Sun.

Then comes an abbreviated translation of the Latin passage that had occurred on page 658. This excerpt relates how the Arab

Habdimelich (Abd-el-Melik) tried to wrest the right of coinage
from Justinian II, but "Justinian's boy" would have none of it.[14] He
stood firm on his right to coin, a privilege that Pound and Del Mar
see as the prime function of any government. When a nation yields
this right to individuals, companies, or groups of banks—as it has
in most capitalist countries—financial chicanery is bound to result.

The passage from history excites some philosophical thoughts
from Cicero's *De Officiis* ("justice . . . nothing more ancient"),
from Dante on Cato's honesty (*Purgatorio* 1.42),[15] and from
Catullus' reproach to Julius Caesar: "I don't care whether you're
black or white" ("An ater, an albus"; reversed in *Carmen* 93). All
three of these men stood up in the name of justice against established authority, and all three were in some way put down.
Catullus' end has always been shrouded with a certain amount of
mystery. Pound's mind then swings away from these sad details to
the blue water at Catullus' villa at Sirmio (the eye of Verona,
Ocelle Veronensis), and to the other beautiful bodies of water in
Italy near Capri and Peschiera.

By a complicated thought process related to water, these
memories lead him to Constantinople again—through a word and a
verbal picture. The visual connection of religion in northern Italy
with water had been voiced earlier in *The Cantos*: the Doge
marrying the sea at Venice or the water-babies cut into marble in
the Malatesta Temple of Rimini—and the roots of these traditions
can be traced in part to the Byzantine Empire. Even today the
Greek Orthodox Church has rituals in which crosses and sacred
icons are thrown into the sea and retrieved. Furthermore, modern
Istanbul straddles the Bosphorus in a way that links the bustling
city directly to an aquatic world.

The word that triggers the association is the colorful Greek
adjective *galenotes*, meaning tranquil; it is a word that is often
applied to the sea. It occurs in the dedication of the work to
galenoteta ta rhethesomena, which Nicole translates into Latin as
"Nostrae Serenitati," Our Beloved Serenity. These words follow
the shortened title, *Eparch's Book*, written in Greek capitals.
Nicole notes that in the Parisinus Manuscript Greek 1351 in the
Bibliothèque Nationale, a much longer title is given, and Pound
excerpts four words from it below: PERI *POLITIKON SOMA-
TEION* DIATAXEON TOU *BASILEOS* KYRIOU *LEONTOS*

(On the *Political Bodies* Arranged by the *King*, Lord *Leo*). The word "bodies" and the statement that the aim of the work is "to stop trampling by one on another" affirm that Leo's concept of the state is corporate, just as a Confucian would see it.

Professor Nicole is then annoyed because of the difficulties of the language dealing with the Drapers (chap. 9, pp. 39-41), where peculiar words like the Greek *bambakinon* are rendered by Pound as "bombazine," and the Greek *arrhabon* (earnest-money, caution-money) comes through as the French "les arrhes." Nicole has a whole subsection at the end of the text dealing with problems related to words of clothing and other lexical matters.

The section extending to page 666 contains some large blocks that are, for the most part, self-explanatory. Having warmed to his subject and cleared away stumbling-blocks, Pound is now ready to embark on poetic flights. First come the Notaries, who must have some sense of "general culture" (*enkyklios paideusis* on the preceding page of Pound's text; from chap. 1, p. 14). Then come the Silversmiths (chap. 2, pp. 22-24), who are not allowed to buy copper or linen textiles (ni cuivre ni tissus de lin). Finally there is a long section describing the Perfumers (chap. 10, pp. 41-43):

> Not hoard 'em and hold for a rise,
>   any perfumer
> who wangles to get another's rent hoisted
>   *kata dolon epauxon*   [cheatily increasing]
> shall be shaved, whipped and chucked out . . .
> Perfumers not to buy groceries,
>   but nard, aloe-wood, cinnamon,
>   stick to what's sold on a two pan balance, not a "romaine"

After the Candle-Makers, who have to have their own workshops (chap. 11, p. 43), and the always necessary Grocers, whose profits have to be kept in check (Chap. 13, p. 47), come the Bakers for a second time around:

> No baker or mill beast shall be subject to other service,
>   bread must go on,
> No ovens in anyone's cellar
> and that they go to the Prefect when the grain price
>   rises or falls
>   to find the right bread price,

Whoso tries any monkey-shines
     shall be put on a jackass and led through the streets quite slowly,
flogged, shaved, and put out

After another brief go-round with the Taverners and the Contractors, Pound settles on the groups which interest him the most:
the Tabularies or Notaries, the Silversmiths and Goldsmiths, and
the Bankers. The reason for this preference is simple: the Notaries
handle the law and education, the Word; the Smiths and the Bankers control the money. If these groups perform their services well,
as they did for more than a millennium, the Empire stands.

Besides having an all-around education, the Notary must be
schooled in the *Book of Law*, the *Manualis Legis* or, as the 1972
Cantos spell it, the "Manuale." He must also know the *Basilika*
(*Basiliques;* Pound's "Basiliks"), which are a modernization of the
Code of Justinian, the cornerstone of Byzantine law. Notaries
must also have proper handwriting (German *Handschrift*), and
their personal habits must be excellent; in fact, one could shift to
the following chapter, which covers K'ang Hsi's edict to his
people, and see the same kind of character delineated for public
officials. The only Greek in this section, *thymiama enopion
Kyriou*, means "incense in the presence of the Lord," and tells
Notaries that the straightness of their lives should imitate the
steady rising of the perfumes off their altars. The Greek word for
the incense resembles the Latin word *thus*, frankincense, which
was linked to the name Tuscany and opened the canto. The pre-
scriptions read:

To be tabulary, must know the Manuale
    to recite it, and the Basiliks, 60 books
and draw up an act in the presence, and be sponsored
by the primicier and his colleagues
      and have a clear Handschrift
and be neither babbler nor insolent, nor sloppy in habits
and have a style. Without perfect style
    might not notice punctuation and phrases
        that alter the sense,
    and if he writes down a variant
     his sponsors will be responsible.
Give him time to show what he's got.
And the smoke at his consecration,

incense *thymiama enopion Kyriou*
shows how his thought shd/ go. Upward, videlicet.
And be fined if he miss procession
    and the college shall go to his funeral.

Next Pound turns to the Smiths, who are allowed to handle
"no copper" (*ou men chalkon*) because of the constant fear of "Anyone practicing trickery with uncoined gold" (*Ho dolon poion eis
asemion*)—so great was the fear of counterfeiting. And "if anyone"
(*ei tis*) wants to sell jewelry, he must be reported by the Smiths to
the Prefect. The penalty for tampering with the Emperor's gold is
severe: *cheirokopeistho* ("let him lose a hand"). The Goldsmiths
are to work in shops on *tes Meses*, which Pound playfully calls
"Main St." Following Nicole, he describes this major thoroughfare
as moving in a large half-circle from the Imperial Palace to the
seven-towered Castle overlooking the Sea of Marmara.

Then Pound indulges in an argument with the Swiss professor
concerning the following sentence on page 24 of the text: "they
should not cast silver without the awareness or notice of the
Eparch" (*me de aneu eideseos tou eparchou chrysochoon pro-
balesthai*). Pound thinks that Nicole is looking at Greek *aneu*
(without) and seeing French *aveu* (notice), but Nicole's concept of
"notice" is coming from *eideseos*, and once again Pound errs in his
attempt to trip up the professor. However, the haggle itself is fun,
and if the world is to have a scholarship with integrity, there must
be challenges of older readings—particularly of that vast store of
manuscripts that was edited in the post-romantic period of the
nineteenth century, when preconceived ideas were bound to
influence readings. The passage reads:

and a goldsmith report purchase of any unmarked
        gold over one pound;
Work to be done *en . . . tes Meses* on Main St.
        Not in the goldsmith's home
And no one to be brought into the guild without notice
        (aveu du prefet) What was the greek for aveu
in this instance? *eideseos tou eparchou*
        rather nice use of *aveu*, Professor,
        though you were looking at *aneu*.
From the Palace, half-circle that street is,
        ending near the seven-towered castello.

The Bankers round out the picture of The City. Like the Smiths, they are forbidden to tamper with money or to employ underlings who might be used for nefarious purposes. The coin-measurer (*Katallaktes*) must guard against counterfeits (*kekomme-non*—there is a *para* written inside the brackets separating the two words, meaning that Nicole inserted the prefix, but Pound removes it). With control over the coin being once again asserted, Pound clarifies the basic ideogram in the final words of the canto:

a usurping coiner (Habdimelich);
an Emperor who builds and controls the currency (Justinian II);
and "peace," the final word.

In one sense, this Byzantium Canto rhymes with the Malatesta Cantos, but there is a big difference. The earlier cantos showed one solid block of achievement created by one man in the midst of chaos. This canto, by contrast, details the building not only of a great temple (Santa Sophia), but of a jeweled city, a Dioce on earth, and a thousand-year Imperium. The reader is presented with words as tools, just as the workers had their building blocks. The Logos here is united with the Thing.

Wyndham Lewis once said to Pound: "Constantinople is our star," although neither Pound nor Lewis could ever remember exactly where, when, or why.[16] In his later years, Pound recalled those words, and it was to Byzantium that he went to find a Western parallel for the monumental achievement of the Chinese dynasties. This was as close as he could get to a coherent Occidental heritage that he could fully admire. Unlike Yeats, who saw Byzantium as a beautiful symbol that cast up eternal images of dolphins and sent out sounds of ringing gongs,[17] Pound heard the rabble, the welter of voices, the STOMULIA of the Byzantines moving inside the beehive of their activities. He saw the great cathedral rising out of the hubbub, just as he himself envisioned the formation of the canto. Logos is to canto what brick is to Basilica. Unlike Baudelaire, Joyce, Eliot, Crane, and many other moderns who could see the city almost entirely as an evil jungle or a place of entrapment, Pound saw the single city and The Great City as sources of light. To Pound, the city is one of man's greatest achievements of the past and, despite its problems in the modern world, one of the only hopes for the future.

Chapter Ten

What Confucius Told K'ang Hsi to Tell the Modern World

Cantos 98 and 99 afford the reader a chance to observe Pound's poetic method in one of its most easily apprehensible forms. Canto 98 lays down certain principles that were established in a sacred Chinese edict, and 99 takes these principles and enlarges upon them in the ever-changing dramatic medium of Pound's mind. Pound, in effect, passes on the rules of a Chinese emperor, and then becomes the emperor himself. Even the reader who is ignorant of the language can appreciate what is happening.

The edict forming the base for the two cantos is the so-called *Sacred Edict*, or *Sheng U* (characters on 693), which consisted of sixteen maxims issued by the Emperor K'ang Hsi in 1670, with each of the statements being limited to seven characters. The edict was based on firm Confucian principles of government and morality, but the text was so terse that it was not always comprehensible for all the readers. Therefore, K'ang's son, Iong Cheng (whom Pound calls Yong Tching in Cantos 58-61), decided to reissue the sayings in a book with sixteen chapters, devoting a chapter to each maxim. His production, like his father's, was written in the elaborate *wen-li* style (Pound's "Uen-li," 690), and thus was again not fully comprehensible for the masses. As a result, the Commissioner of the Salt Works at Shensi, named Ouang-Iu-p'uh (685/688), undertook the final job of translating the courtly language of the Emperor to the common language (Dante's *volgar' eloquio*) of the people.

Occidental readers seem to have been fairly oblivious of the edict until 1892, when a missionary named Frederick William Baller (1852-1922) published his edition of it.[1] Like many Christians working for God in China, Baller had a certain condescension toward things Chinese. He says, for example, in his introduction: "Nothing but Divine motive power can raise fallen humanity" (p. v), thereby subscribing to both original sin and divine grace in one fell swoop in a way that is utterly alien to Confucian thought.

Of course, Baller was not totally deaf to Oriental beauty and refinement: "The Chinese think in quotations; and he who can quote their ready-made expressions, will add a vivacity to his style." But Pound notes the difficulty of doing this, since the standard dictionary of Mathews does not fully account for the colloquial language of Wang.[2] Baller does an excellent job of editing, but he concludes that the edict "exemplifies both the strength and weakness of mere morality. There is high thinking, but the outcome is low living. . . . However brilliant these 'Lights of Asia' may appear . . . the people of China who have followed them for generations are still enveloped in a darkness which may be felt." Pound treats Baller rather sympathetically in working toward the subject:

> and our debt here is to Baller
> and to *volgar'eloquio*.   [popular speech]
>   Despite Mathews this Wang was a stylist.
> Uen-li will not help you talk to them,   [formal language]
>   Iong-ching republished the edict
> But the salt-commis[s]ioner took it down to the people
>   who, in Baller's view, speak in quotations;
>   think in quotations:
> "Don't send someone else to pay it."
> Delcroix was for repetition.
>   Baller thought one needed religion.   (690)

Baller is contrasted here, not unkindly, with Carlo Delcroix, a Mussolini deputy who worked in very practical ways in the world.

Before examining the sixteen rules and Pound's versions of them, the underlying bases of Confucian thought must be reviewed, for the two cantos constantly refer to the Five Virtues and the Five Relationships that are fundamental to Confucian morality. The virtues are:

1. *jen*^{2}: humanitas; benevolence   (544)
2. *chih*^{4}: knowledge, wisdom   (544)
3. *i*^{4}: righteousness; justice   (689)

4. *li³*: etiquette; propriety; ritual conduct (Mathews 3886)
5. *hsin⁴*: truth; trust   (564)

The first four of these are called the Four TUAN, or "Foundations" (544), which were mentioned prominently in Chapter One.

The Five Relationships form the focus of social conduct, and are described by Baller on page 69 this way:

1. prince and minister
2. father and son
3. husband and wife
4. elder and brother
5. friend and friend

In addition, there is talk in both cantos about the Four Books, which Baller lists (p. 67):

1. *The Great Learning* (Pound's *Digest*)
2. *The Doctrine of the Mean* (Pound's *Unwobbling Pivot*)
3. *The Analects*
4. *The Works of Mangtzu (Mencius)*

To these may be added the Five Classics that were written or edited by Confucius:

1. *Shu¹ Ching¹* (King): *Book of History*
2. *I⁴ Ching¹*: *Book of Changes*
3. *Shih³ Ching¹*: *Book of Odes*
4. *Li³ Chi³*: *Record of the Rites*
5. *Ch'un¹ Ch'iu¹*: *Spring and Autumn Annals*

All these works are cited by the edict as essential for a good education.

The importance of the Confucian doctrines that underlie the proclamation can be stated rather simply: man and his society are seen as firmly anchored in and colored by nature; there is no metaphysical mist on the horizon. The society of man and the world at large conjoin. Far from being above or free from his environment, man is placed squarely in it, and the basic metaphor enforces this

notion: for example, in Chapter One, Section 2: "Duty to parents
is a self-evident principle of nature, and the root of virtuous conduct in man." This idea is echoed repeatedly in Pound's poetry:

The State is corporate
                    as with pulse in its body
& with Chou rite at the root of it
The root is thru all of it,
                    a tone in all public teaching: . . .
The whole tribe is from one man's body,
    what other way can you think of it?
The surname, and the 9 arts.
        The father's word is compassion;
        The son's, filiality.
        The brother's word: mutuality;
            The younger's word: deference.
Small birds sing in chorus,
Harmony is in the proportion of branches
            as clarity (chao^1)   (707)

or again:

Filiality and fraternity are the root,
Talents to be considered as branches.
Precise terminology is the first implement,
                    dish and container,
After that the 9 arts.
AND study the classic books,
            the straight history
                    all of it candid.   (710)

    The two characters which best express the root metaphor are
called *pen*^{3} and *yeh*^{4} (692). They are best translated "root occupa-
tion".
These occur with respect to Rule Ten, where Baller's second note
on page 110 explains their importance. Man's roots are not totally
unlike those of a plant; he should have a fixed environment, and
not be nomadic; agriculture and land development are the basic
preoccupations of the state. Like Apollonius of Tyana, who be-

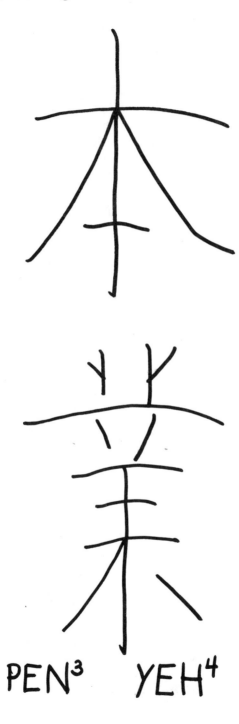

PEN³   YEH⁴

lieved in an organic, "zoogenic" universe, the Confucian believes
that:

The fu jen receives heaven, earth, middle   [blessed man]
                        and grows.   (712)

The first maxim of K'ang Hsi concerns duteousness and subordination: "Enforce duteousness and subordination, so as to emphasize social obligations." Pound mentions it when he settles
down to the edict on page 686, after the Chinese character *hsuan*[1]
(proclaim). As Yong Tching himself expresses the maxim: "Our Imperial Ancestor, the Benevolent Emperor, ruled the empire for
sixty-one years. Those he held in the highest esteem were his an-
cestors; consequently he exhorted everybody to duteousness and
subordination." Thus, Yong Tching, like a good son, follows the
steps of the father and acknowledges a filiality that is "very inclusive" (p. 6). It is based on the teachings of the Confucian philosopher, Tseng, who sat by Kung's door (Pound's *men*[3], meaning
"door" or "gate," should be in the second tone; 691).
        In his analysis of his father's words, Yong Tching says, and
Pound follows Baller's translation: "Parents naturally hope their
sons will be gentlemen" (691). The Chinese characters that express
the word "gentleman" are printed below Pound's English: *cheng*[4]
ching[1] (Pound follows Baller and prints "king" for the second character; p. 5). An upright (*cheng*[4]) man will follow the Orthodox
Classics, which is what the two characters may also denote (Baller,
p. 65). From the writing of *The Spirit of Romance* to *The ABC of
Reading,* Pound's veneration for the written tradition was unchanging. His addition of the characters for "land" and "money"
mirrors the words that fill out Section 8 of this rule: "All the squab-
bles that arise among brethren in the present day are on account of
property" (p. 11), with specific mention of Pound's two characters
among two others.
        Rule Two deals with clan relationships, and shows that the
entire state is, as Pound says, "one body" (707).[3] The rule is stated
by Baller thus: "Give due weight to kinship with a view to the dis-
play of concord." Pound's version on page 691 is far more literal,
relying on a character that Baller calls *ie,* that is used in Imperial
contexts and means "Lord of 10,000 years" (p. 1). The stress here

is upon social as well as family concord. Rules One and Two work together, as in these memorable lines:

The Sage Emperor's heart is our heart,
His government is our government . . .
The Venerated Emperor
                watched things grow with affection,
His thought was not dry on a shelf
Not exhaustible, on sale in a (kuei⁴) shop.
That job was the swan's flight (hung² yeh⁴⁻⁵)
To trace out and to bind together
From sonship this goes to clan   (695)

The Latin word for "bind together" is *re-ligio.* To Pound as to Yong Tching—and in spite of Baller—true religion must rely on a man's close family and social ties; these take precedence over the I-Thou relationship between God and man established by St. Augustine and other Christians.

Rule Three is stated by Baller in this way: "Pacify the Local Communities in order to put an end to Litigation." Pound extemporizes on this theme on page 696:

Rats' gnaws, and bird's pecks: litigations,
pine rat and oak cat, squirrel to you,
sparrow, hemp-bird, rats' gnaws and tit-horns
                rush to law without cause;
tie knots into ruin of property
fei (four), waste time, flounder in business,
The organization is functional
and to maintain a liquidity . . .
                begin at the precinct level . . .

A corollary with this point mentioned under Section 4 is the fact that a man should accept low interest from a poor man and be freely willing to absolve anyone from longstanding debts. On pages 32 and 33, *The Sacred Edict* states that 36 percent was not uncommon as a percentage of interest. Since this figure is much higher than the 12 percent deemed equitable by Antoninus of Rome or Leo the Wise of Byzantium (688), Pound cannot resist saying that:

In Byzantium 12% for a millennium
    The Manchu at 36 legal, their Edict
    the next pass.   (684)

Or again on page 710:

not for a quick buck at high interest
the legal rate does not exhaust things
        (Byzance did better) . . .
           The rate in Byzance was lower . . .

     Rule Four is concerned, as Pound notes on 696, with the fact
that "There are functions." Baller's version of this wording is:
"Attach Importance to Farming and Mulberry Culture, that there
may be sufficient Food and Clothing," or, as Pound says lacon-
ically: "Food is the root./ Feed the people" (695). This stress upon
husbandry leads to Rule Five, which is stated by Baller: "Set Store
by Economy, as a Means to the Careful Use of Property." A sound
economy depends on carefully nurtured husbandry. You cannot
have a sound monetary system without a sufficient means of
production of basic goods. Pound combines the two rules on page
692:

IV. Without grain you will not eat or tend silkworms,
      Imperial paradigm was by ploughing.
V.   and then waste not,
      Nor scrape iron off the point of a needle.

     Improvising later on this theme that a society is rooted in the
productivity of its land, Pound says:

To sprout in season
         and have trees for your silk-worms,
One big chap not plow,
           one female not weave
Can mean shortage,
From of old the sovereign likes plowing
& the Empress tends trees with reverence   (709)

The plowing emperor "rhymes" with the Roman Cincinnatus and
the American Nathaniel Macon of Canto 88—figures dear to

Pound's Yankee-rooted heart. *The Sacred Edict* goes on to give precise stipulations for the growing of rice or millet, as well as the care of silk-worms, stressing that:

There is worship in plowing
           and equity in the weeding hoe,
A field marshal can be literate.
          Might we see it again in our day!   (711)

Rule Six concerns education: "Attach Importance to Academies, in order to improve the Habits of Scholars." It mentions the Four Tuan, as well as truth. This is, of course, a subject again dear to Pound's heart, for, from the time he left Wabash College, he maintained a love-hate relationship with the academic profession. Following pages 67 and 68 of Baller, Pound says:

Uen Ogn [Wen Wong] of Han-time built schools,
        rode circuit,
          selected
And even now you can't *buy* office in Fourstreams
        ·tuan^1 [good]
          cheng^4 [life]

                                                 (699)

Then, assuming even more of the intonations of Uncle Ez, Pound ties this principle in with Rule Seven, which states, "Extirpate Heresy and so exalt Orthodoxy":

SEVEN: Get rid of flimsy foundations.
          Our ancestors thought that closed minds
               do no good to the Empire . . .   (700)

The defense of the Classics in education goes hand in hand with a rejection of outsiders, especially Buddhists and Taoists:

"and that Buddha abandoned such splendours,
          is it likely!" said Yong Tching . . .
"Who has seen Taoist priests fly up in broad daylight?
They destroy the 5 human relations . . ."   (687)

and just below that:

And as for these Bhud-foés,
        they provide no mental means for
Running an empire, nor do taoists
with their internal and external pills

The reference here is to page 75 of the text, which talks about the
Taoists' gold pills for immortality: "Taoism . . . speaks of plans for
asceticism, (such as) grasping mercury in lead; the dragon moan-
ing; the tiger screaming; the internal and the external pill."
Buddhism is also guilty of leading to foolish luxury and pomp:
dragon verandahs and a "feng-ko" (long leo feng koh: abodes of
royalty, p. 78), with a Phoenix Hall and other Oriental frou-frou.
Their God sits up in a heaven and seems to demand a roof, or at
least clay or gilded models, craven images (pp. 79, 86). Perhaps
the greatest trouble with Buddhism is that it "does not concern itself with anything in the four corners of the universe, but simply
with the heart" (p. 75), which Pound expresses this way:

Bhud: Man by negation.
But their First Classic: that the heart shd/ be straight,
The phallos perceive its aim . . .
But as Chu said, nowt to do with taking hold of anything
    in the four coigns of the universe   (702)

In this section, the edict speaks of the "princely man" (kuin-tsi)
created by Confucianism, as opposed to the hsiao jin [ren] or
"little man" that is produced by Buddhism (the latter two characters appear on page 688 of Pound). In other words, Buddhism
creates the selfish, pusillanimous man, while Confucianism creates
the kingly man who is clearly a gentleman (691).

    The eighth rule is so Poundian that it does not need explica-
tion: "State the laws in clear language," or, as Baller said: "Explain the Law, to warn the Foolish and Wayward." Pound's playing with words, his examination of their meanings, demonstrates
the principle thoroughly. Besides, his imagist writings in the early
part of the century established the same principle as a canon for
writing poetry. He states the idea on page 698:

VIII. Let the laws be made clear,
        Illumine the words of procedure

Rule Nine says, "Elucidate Courteousness, with a view to improving the Manners and Customs." Pound prints a very cryptic form of this rule on page 692: "Iu-an tied the stray cow and fed it." This refers to an anecdote about a farmer named Kuan Iu-an (p. 108) who found another man's cow eating his grain; instead of being vexed and causing trouble, he merely tied the cow up and brought it grass to eat. This act of patience and friendliness was praised throughout his community. General civility is, as Pound stresses, important to any state, and it should be found even—or especially—in men of the soil.

Pound expresses this rule in lovely poetic language that is adapted from the words of the scholars of the Han dynasty (pp. 99 ff.):

The sages of Han had a saying:
> Manners are from earth and from water
> They arise out of hills and streams
> The spirit of air is of the country . . .
Kung said: are classic of heaven,
They bind thru the earth
> and flow
With recurrence,
> action, humitas, equity   (698)

The direct placing of man by his "natural colour" is one of the most beautiful parts of the *Sheng U*. It equates a man's courteousness with his breath, and the customs of an entire society with *tso feng suh* or "breath of nature" (689; Baller, p. 99). The *su(h)*[2] (common or local preference) character consists of a man and a valley, for, as Baller says: "The Chinese attach great importance to the influence of climate and locality on character."[4]

Rule Ten states the PEN YEH principle discussed before: "Let the People attend to their Proper Callings, that they may have Settled Determination." Pound renders the abstract quality a bit more imagistically: "a developed skill from persistence," bringing the Greek word TECHNE (craft) into play with the Chinese.[5] Rule Eleven returns to education: "Instruct the Rising Generation, with a view to prevent Evil Doing." Pound states this most effectively on page 704, when he matches his Uncle Ez accent with that of the Commissioner of the Salt Works:

SU(H)²

XI Teach kids to keep out of mischief,
          Sow to the very corner,
Most people have sons or brothers,
Study the ancient King Sages
          as compass and T-square
To have masters in village schools
To teach 'em classics not hog-wash
&
that the Kiang Sheng[6] is to be read once a month

This is one of the finest translations in either canto, showing the point where improvisation on a significant model can lead to a fine, original production.

The subject of education, always dear to Pound's heart, is expatiated upon in another section where the Yankee straightforwardness approximates the Chinese precision in just the right way:

And if your kids don't study, that's your fault.
Tell 'em. Don't kid yourself, and don't lie.
In statement, answer; in conversation
          not with sissified fussiness (chiao[1])
          always want your own way.

Let 'em ask before taking action;
That there be no slovenly sloppiness
                    between goodman & wife.
Gt. is gt. Little is little;   [Great]
With friends one is one
                    2 is 2
Not to lie out of heedlessness
                    let alone out of trickery
Fitting the tone to their words
                    as water goes over the mill-wheel.
Dress 'em in folderols
                    and feed 'em with dainties,
In the end they will sell out the homestead.   (705)

   Rule Twelve says: "Prevent False Accusations, and so shield
the Law-abiding." This accounts for Pound's exclamation on page
693: "As for those who lie in a law-court!" and also for his emphasis on "Deliberate converse" a bit later. On Page 697 he states the
principle at greater length:

Laws must be for the general good,
                    for the people's uprightness,
                    their moral uprightness.

   Rule Thirteen says: "Prohibit giving Shelter to Deserters, in
order to prevent others from sharing their Fate." This is conspicuously absent from Pound's listing in Canto 98, and is certainly
not dwelled upon in Canto 99. Does the word "deserter" sound
unpleasant? Is the idea of giving refuge to someone in flight really
so repugnant? The reader must remember that, when Italy fell,
Pound was forced to flee from Rome, and he owed his life to the
many kind people who helped him along the way. Therefore, he
here seems to make an exception.
   Rules Fourteen and Fifteen go together: "Pay Taxes, and so
avoid being pressed for Payment" and "Unite the Tithings in order
to suppress Crime." This sharing of the responsibility for running a
state is a thing that Pound always insisted upon, especially since he
felt that the richest men were the most clever at dodging their part
of the general upkeep. On page 692, he connects tithing or percentage payment, as opposed to fixed-charge taxation, with

Mencius (Mang Tzu),[7] and on page 707, he enlarges upon the theme:

& there have been taxes in kind, and by (liang^2) measure
This is important
        as to the scope of such taxes
all Courts have levied them
            the right pattern of levy is yang^4 cheng^1
                        id est: for use
not a fountain of folderols
for top poppinjays.

Here he offers very pithy Americanisms to render precise, colloquial Chinese. Uncle Ez was never sharper.

The last rule says: "Make up Quarrels, and so respect the Person and Life." Pound seems to have taken these words to heart, almost as if they had been addressed to him personally: "Yield not to anger" (692). Reviewing his own tempestuous career, with its many periods of choleric indignation, he could well see some wisdom in the old Chinese proverb that he in turn rendered this way:

don't pester scholars,
nor lose life for bad temper.   (698)

These words, in turn, can be tied in with those of the Egyptian Kati (Khaty): "A man's paradise is his good nature" (699).

Good nature may, indeed, be the key to both of the K'ang Hsi Cantos. It is the tone that pervades the happy picture of an ideal society dreamed of through Confucian laws and recreated in the imagination of Ezra Pound. It is a society for all, based on the abundance of nature, which is, in turn, controlled, as Jefferson dreamed of it, by all. This was the dream of Pound's whole life— one that he fought for, risked for, suffered for, but never abandoned. When the nameless "gnomes of Zurich" and the anonymous socializers of the "sociétés anonymes" lie buried in their forgotten graves, these lines will endure like some faded but haunting Chinese print, summoning all to sup at the Utopian feast south of Fourstreams, prepared by the ghosts of Confucius and K'ang Hsi, and mediated through the voices of Wang and Uncle Ez:

"Each year in the Elder Spring, that is the first month of it,
The herald shall invite your compliance.
There are six rites for the festival
      and that all should converge!
And not to lose life for bad temper.   (693)

Chapter Eleven
Napoleon: The Lesson of Meaningless Revolution

Canto 101 opens with the mention of Monsieur de Rémusat, and a substantial section of the canto derives from the *Memoires de Madame de Rémusat* (1802-08), which has been published in several editions, such as the English version of Mrs. Cashel Hoey and John Lillie.[1] To understand the significance of the numerous references to her memoirs, one must first know something of Madame de Rémusat's role in history.

Claire Elizabeth Jeanne Gravier de Vergennes, Comtesse de Rémusat (1780-1821), is known not only for her writing but also because she was a lady-in-waiting to the Empress Josephine, and was thus a leading social figure during the Napoleonic era. Her husband, Augustin de Rémusat, was one of Napoleon's closest and most trusted advisors, along with the more famous Talleyrand. Her son Charles was an equally prominent political figure who found the time to write a series of important books on Abelard, Francis Bacon, English philosopher Lord Herbert de Cherbury, Saint Anselm, and the theologian and writer William Ellery Channing. He is mentioned conspicuously in Canto 100/720.

Erigena,
Anselm,
Cherbury,
Rémusat,
Thiers was against income-tax

and again in 109/774:

Erigena, Anselm,
   the fight thru Herbert and Rémusat

Charles is especially important to Pound because he stressed the role of the natural philosopher, combining an interest in natural science with an interest in economics. He (and Pound) could view Erigena's universal salvation and Thiers' desire to spread wealth among the people with Cherbury's wide concern for flora and fauna.

Charles's son, Paul, expanded this frame of interest by writing two more important books: *A. Thiers* (1889), an account of the French politician's life, and *Les Sciences naturelles* (1857), which carries on the work of his father. Still another Rémusat, Jean Pierre Abel (1788-1832), was a specialist in Chinese studies. This family, then, presents a dynasty of talent, and "rhymes" with the Adams family of America: old John, John Quincy, Brooks, Henry, and Charles Francis. The Rémusats can also be related to the Talleyrand family, for Charles Maurice de Talleyrand, Augustin's friend, was a direct descendant of a friend of the troubadour Bertran de Born, whom Pound refers to often (sometimes by the spelling "Dalleyrand," to indicate a dialect).[2] The old family of Périgord was thrown into close contact with the Rémusats as Napoleon rose to power.

The Rémusat family thus brings to focus a variety of interests that are of central concern in *The Cantos:*

NAPOLEON (the leader)

PROVENCE   NATURAL SCIENCE,
FRANCE   PHILOSOPHY

MYSTICISM
MIDDLE AGES

It is clear that they, along with Talleyrand and Thiers, are the French approximation of Adams and Jefferson. If they failed to effect a strong democratic state, it was because they were dealing with a Napoleon rather than a George Washington.

A look at Madame de Rémusat's *Mémoires* provides some idea of Bonaparte. Her observations are helpful because throughout *The Cantos* the Napoleonic dream is mentioned. Madame is frank to the point of being sardonic in her assessments of the general. She quotes him as saying violently egotistical things and being constantly melodramatic: "'Frankly, I am base, essentially base'"

(6). In fact, many of her negative assessments of the man accord with the reservations that John Adams and Thomas Jefferson had of him.[3] Claire speaks of his being bent on "interminable conquests; for he felt we must be occupied at all hazards" (57); she mentions the fact that "man in the abstract interested him but little" (103); and she reveals his basic cynicism about most human feelings: "'For what is love? A passion which sets all the universe on one side, and on the other the beloved object'" (94). How different these remarks are from those describing Adams! In the one case, one has an idealistic builder; in the other, a wandering destroyer.

However, the picture painted by Claire de Rémusat is not entirely negative. She cites Madame d'Houdetot saying of Bonaparte: "He diminishes history and enlarges imagination'" (511). She captures a great deal of the sweep of the man and ends with the statement that he "perfectly knew and always contended with his epoch" (547). If he failed to effect his dreams, ultimately one must blame Fate or Fortune; as Pound himself put it in Canto 50/249:

> 'Not'
> said Napoleon 'because of that league of lice
> but for opposing the Zeitgeist! That was my ruin,
> That I ran against my own time, turning backward'

Having established the focus of the canto, some of the details can be discussed. It begins with some words that are close to those occurring on page 301 of the *Mémoires:* "M. de Talleyrand, finding scarcely any one but M. de Rémusat who could understand him . . ." If Pound is actually using this translation, he simply changes the "but" to "save" and prints "anyone" as one word. From the start, then, Talleyrand is joined with Augustin de Rémusat. With the mention of Talleyrand comes a revery about France, especially the lovely towns of Chalais and Aubeterre in the southwestern section, where the Talleyrand family was extremely powerful— the region of Périgord, including the territory of Bertran de Born; earlier Pound has written:

> But to set here the roads of France,
>   of Cahors, of Chalus,
>   the inn low by the river's edge,

the poplars; to set here the roads of France
Aubeterre, the quarried stone beyond Poitiers . . .   (76/455)

In this canto, the references to France are blended with references
to Tibet and China:

Finding scarcely anyone save Monsieur de Rémusat
               who could understand him
(junipers, south side) M. Talleyrand
               spruce and fir take the North
Chalais, Aubeterre,
               snow-flakes at a hand's breadth, and rain.
Trees line the banks, mostly willows. Kublai,
Te Te of Ch'eng, called Timur, 1247, came hither
Forest thru ice into emerald

This is, in part, the world of the botanist Joseph Rock, who studied
the remote Na-khi tribes of southwestern China, and recorded
their ancient tribal rites, the oldest extant in the world as literature; his work will be discussed further in the Epilogue, for it relates closely with the Fragments. After this paradisal picture—
interrupted only with the names of two nomads, Kublai Khan and
Tamburlaine (Timur), who invaded the remote Na-khi world but
left no imprint—Pound returns to the French with the line
"Talleyrand, Thiers, tried to get sense into princes." This statement is clearly demonstrated in Paul de Rémusat's book, *A.
Thiers*, where the statesman is shown holding France together
with his sanity after a variety of debacles. Thiers opposed war in
1870 (pp. 167-68), was the guiding genius of the Third Republic
(pp. 200 ff.), was an excellent rhetorical stylist, and was also, in
Paul's mind, a great financier (p. 211). Talleyrand's role in
stopping Napoleon after the battle of Austerlitz is established in
the *Mémoires* (307). His intercession in financial matters is mentioned repeatedly (321, 345), as Pound himself points out:

Marbois and then Mollien at the Treasury
               and then Gaudin   (724)

François de Barbé-Marbois was replaced by Nicolas Mollien,
whom Claire calls a "skilled financier" (345). he was in turn fol-

lowed by Martin Gaudin, "whose perfect integrity and sound knowledge sustained credit and improved the system of taxation" (345) by taxing luxuries and those people who were conquered in Napoleon's battles: Tax 'em, don't exterminate 'em—a familiar Poundian echo.

After five lines dealing with the Na-khi culture of China,[4] Pound presents a series of short observations: the nomad as opposed to the productive, fixed agricultural man; the "squalor of taxes," unfairly assessed ones; a remark about trying to divine undivinable mysteries; a repetition of the leitmotif of Renan about the general stupidity of human beings; and then an economic observation that the prices of things are often far out of keeping with their actual values—a statement that has particular relevance to modern America.

With the line "Talleyrand, Austerlitz, Mme Rémusat," Pound offers an extended section that is based upon the *Mémoires.* Madame notes that, despite Napoleon's triumphs, near the Christmas of 1805: "Money had become still more scarce; in fact . . . I had to pay ninety francs merely for obtaining gold for a thousand-franc bank-note" (321). It is clear that the rhythm of this canto is disjointed, unlike the smooth flow of the Adams Cantos, which progress toward the building of America. There is an important deed (Austerlitz), and then inflation or usurious charges for moneychanging. The truncated rhythm continues. Jean Jacques de Cambacérès, who was a consul with Napoleon, is described as a silly old man who abdicated his consulship quickly but retained a false sense of pride (228; also, 53 f.). Christmas Day of 1805 is described as the zenith of Napoleon's power, with control over a maximum number of territories (320). The fact that a "new constitution was sent to the Italian legislature" (264) undoubtedly has to be classified as an achievement, from Pound's point of view. The line "that intelligent men can believe" refers either to this, or to Napoleon's general attitude whereby he "habitually ridiculed everything connected with religion in familiar conversation" (391).

Then follows a list of positive goals attained: the economic changes discussed above; the building of roads in the Mt. Cenis and Simplon tunnel areas (345); and the preservation of studies at Jena, despite the war (481). But these activities have to be balanced with Napoleon's constant striving for glory in battle, a thing that Madame de Rémusat deplored in one of her letters (455). Also, his attitude toward personal freedom was highly questionable: "Liberty . . . is needed by a small and privileged class, who are gifted by nature " (506) with more ability than the rest of mankind. Pound may agree with Napoleon's statement, since he emphasizes "a necessity," but Claire does not, for she sees the growth of the tyrant here. Next comes the name (Jacques de) Neuflize, who may be connected with the Neuflize & Co. Bank. The mention of Nessus, the poisoning satyr, indicates that the bank behind Neuflize is not to be trusted. By contrast, there again occurs the name Gaudin, whose achievement is now clarified: he would not pay interest on government credit, thereby avoiding the terrible deficits that the modern American government has incurred.

The section ends with Mme. Elizabeth d'Houdetot's inability to see evil anywhere. One is not quite sure whether Pound regards this as a virtue, although Claire de Rémusat calls her a "delightful old lady" (67) and treats her with respect. Madame d'Houdetot's connection with Jean Jacques Rousseau would not necessarily put her in a good light in Pound's eyes—and besides, her remark stands in direct contrast with the more often quoted line by the priest to Yeats that a kind of ignorance is constantly being disseminated from our schools. Blindness to scales and gradations is not something that Pound looked kindly upon.

The last part of the canto is devoted primarily to a continuation of the prelude, with pines and junipers reappearing, and with the Na-khi tribes of Tibetan China appearing not only in the mention of rituals (the Seng-ge or Sengper ga-mu rite of sacrifice to the Mountain Lion Goddess) and objects (rope bridges; the Chinese character *tso* for "rope"), but also with several significant landscape details: "Li Chiang, the snow range," Kuanon "With the sun and moon on her shoulders," the exorcist's face, the Snow Range, and so on (see note 4). Finally, the canto ends much like Canto 97, with the mention of a horse figure:

"His horse's mane flowing
    His body and soul are at peace."

But whereas Canto 97 has the violence of the horse-sacrificial rites in ancient Rome and China, this canto is far more tranquil, like the highly civilized rites of the Na-khi tribes.[5] In its framing, it resembles one of the poems from *Cathay*, a landscape that is crystal-cut in its natural, serene brilliance.

Even the other people mentioned in the latter part of the canto contribute to this subdued feeling:

Apollonius, Porph[y]ry, Anselm: three nature philosophers
Plotinus: an idealist; although he "had one vision only"
      and tended to see antelopes (misspelled in text) on the stars rather than
      on the mountains, where the Na-khi saw them
Hs'uan Tsung painting kittens
Joey (an acquaintance) admiring realistic portraits in the Mellon Gallery
Henry James saying that if his characters didn't really
      exist, then we ought to pretend for the good of
      the human race that they did exist
Rossoni and Delcroix, Mussolini's advisors,
      trying to create an equitable state

But does the canto hang together? Can one relate the nature passages meaningfully to the Napoleonic ones? I believe that one can, although this canto as a whole does not have the dramatic driving force or the pastoral serenity of many of the other Later Cantos. In fact, there is something pathetic about it. Canto 101 is a canto of losers, of people who did not quite succeed in one way or another. Napoleon is the prime failure, but Mussolini stands closely behind Delcroix and Rossoni, and even Henry James and Plotinus had their flaws (Plotinus had his famous belly-ache). The bright flash of Napoleon's victory at Marengo (333) seems like a mere flash-in-the-pan when compared to the true splendor of a distant star. The mint on the Snow Range in China lingers longer in the mind than do the roads that Bonaparte built—not to enjoy nature, but for military expediency. Napoleon is the key to the failure, although his society has to take some of the blame:

"Were in France" (Mme de Rémusat) "wholly ignorant
    of what was then passing outside."

Madame's concise but genteel style cuts the swashbuckling General down to size. Names like Gaudin, Marbois, and Mollien all tend to run into one another. Of course one remembers a significant deed—a man will not pay interest on public money to private individuals—but in the main the achievements dim when they are compared with the placidly beautiful frame of nature that encloses them.

Napoleon's deeds are gone—a mere whisper on the wind. They are worth recalling perhaps only insofar as they illuminate the more solid deeds of his American counterparts, who are given much more space in *The Cantos*. The nomad, the sweeping invader, moves on, yielding to the builder; but even he, the canto seems to say, is insignificant when viewed in the midst of the splendid panorama of nature, a thing so grand that it can encompass and dim "la bêtise humaine."[6]

Chapter Twelve

In Praise of Anselm and a Vital Christian Humanism

Saint Anselm dominates Canto 105, where his name appears early, and the middle section is devoted almost entirely to citations from his writings. Before asking how Pound employs Anselm, one should ask why. There is a primary reason for the saint's appeal. Philosophically, he and Scotus Erigena have been hailed by such Poundian favorites as the historians Francesco Fiorentino and Charles de Rémusat as the true fathers of a sensible Scholasticism, which was carried to an extreme by Thomas Aquinas.[1] Anselm is especially remembered today for his ontological proof of God, which can be stated simply: "if something can be thought of, it necessarily must be."[2] His theology stresses rationality, as is shown in a popular alternate title of the *Proslogion: Fides quaerens intellectum* or "Faith seeking intellect." Both Anselm and Scotus affirm the nobility of reason, but they stop far short of syllogistic hair-splitting. Anselm's famous definition of God is: that than which there is nothing greater. Both men affirm the glory of the visible world of matter, thus parting company with the hair-shirt ascetics, as well as the Hindu pantheists, who do not acknowledge gradations and values.

Pound's first citation from Anselm's *Monologion* concerns a definition of God, who exists "not huge in space, like a certain body" but "more worthily, as wisdom does"—that is, as an ideal form: "non *magnum* spatio, *ut est corpus aliquod; sed . . . dignius, ut est* sapientia" (chap. 2, columns 146-7). Thus, God or the Highest Nature, as Anselm prefers to call Him, is not a physical entity; it is known by knowing, not by direct confrontation. The other two members of the Trinity, the Son and the Holy Spirit, flow from this Highest Nature and are a part of it, as is everything: *in omnibus est, et per omnia, et ex qua, et per quem, et in qua* (chap. 14, col. 161).

However, the Persons are not all alike, for they show a dissimilarity (*dissimilitudinem*) in the way in which we apprehend them. The Father is the source of Memory and thus the fount of all Knowledge; His primary means of extending cognition is through the Son, who is also the Word; these two members know each other perfectly. Together they breathe forth the Holy Spirit, which Anselm often calls simply Love. The three Persons work ineffably together, but the Father is the source and is supreme, for, as Anselm says, the male principle predominates: *prima et principalis causa prolis semper est in patre* (chap. 42, col. 194), "the first and principal cause of progeny is always in the Father."

Pound's statement in mixed English-Latin that the natures of things "are not equal in dignity" is a paraphrase of the idea that "every created nature (*creatam naturam*) takes its place in a higher grade (*gradu*) of the worth (*dignitatis;* dignity) of essence, the more it seems to approach there" (chap. 56, col. 203). That is, all things are not beautiful or equal; differences exist, and they are important. *The Cantos*, with their many judgments and statements of value, depend on this basic assumption.

However, Anselm's world is not a rigid or a severe one. It exists in a medium of Love, which "proceeds from the Highest Nature ineffably, not in separating from it, but in existing out of it, perhaps in a way that can only be likened to breathing": *a se ineffabiliter procedentem, non discedendo ab illa, sed existendo ex illa, forsitan non alio modo videtur posse dici aptius ex se emittere quam spirando* (chap. 57, col. 204). Pound uses the non-existent word *discendendo* instead of *discedendo* from the Migne text, perhaps reading the Italian word for "descending" in place of the Latin for "withdrawing or moving apart from." Despite the mistake or reshaping, the same effect is achieved, for the departure of the Holy Spirit from the Highest Nature must to its creatures look like a descent, although any negative Fall aspects of the creation of Matter are not stressed here. Anselm is no Manichean or Puritan.

The first part of Pound's line, which cites Chapter 57 of the

Monologion, contains the words "non genitus." This chapter says that the "Father and likewise the Son do not make nor do they give birth to (*gignunt*) the spirit of Love." To find Pound's phrase, one has to return to Chapter 56, col. 203, where one learns that Love is not a progeny of the other two members, for it is "not inborn, nor, properly speaking, born" (*nec . . . ingenitus; nec ita proprie . . . genitus*). The point is this: Love is the natural condition of the created world, the emanative force of the Highest Nature (this semi-pantheistic word is not inappropriate because of the way that Anselm speaks of Love as divine breath); Love is an integral part of Godhead, not a mere product.

The fact that Anselm keeps using the term *Summa Natura* for God stresses the female principle because the word *Natura* is feminine in Latin. The subtitle of the *Monologion, De divinitatis essentia* (On the Essence of Divinity), does the same thing. In fact, whole passages, as in Chapter 67, col. 214, which describes the love of a creature for the highest essence (*summa essentia*), throw all the pronouns relating to the object into the feminine gender, and thus these could be read in terms of a lover and his beloved. Pound says with respect to this phenomenon:

                     but had a clear line on the Trinity, and
By sheer grammar: Essentia
                     feminine
                          Immaculata   [immaculate]
Immaculabile.   [unstainable]

The last word, "unstainable," neatly sums up Anselm's attitude toward created matter and could also describe his own style. This passage was discussed in Chapter Two because of its fervent indication of the female force.

However, Love cannot do the whole job. The Father is Memory, which is perceived through the Son, the Word. Thus the route to God lies through the use of reason:

"rationalem"
              said Anselm.
                     Guido: "intenzione."

Pound's citation of the first word, "rational" in English, probably refers to Chapter 68, col. 214, of the *Monologion,* which says: "to a rational nature 'being rational' (*esse rationalem*) is nothing else than distinguishing the just from the unjust." Again, this is what *The Cantos* are doing. But how does this reasoning process take place? Anselm says: "What is clearer than that the rational mind, the more eagerly it aims (*intendit*; likened by Pound to Guido Cavalcanti's Italian word for "intention") to know itself, the more efficiently it ascends to the cognition of [the Highest Nature]? Otherwise, it goes down (*descendit*)" (chap. 66, col. 213). This passage, which again insists on a scale of values in an atmosphere of love, may explain Pound's hybrid word *discendendo* above. Anselm goes on to say that "the mind itself is a mirror of [the Highest Nature], and its image": *mens ipsa speculum ejus, et imago ejus* (chap. 67, col. 213). Pound adds the word *vera,* "true," as the saint does elsewhere in the chapter.

Anselm then says that the rational creature should study nothing except "this image impressed by natural forces upon it" (*hanc imaginem sibi per naturalem potentiam impressam;* chap. 68, col. 214). Thus, there is a clear correlation with Guido Cavalcanti, whose epistemology, as stated in his *Donna mi prega* (first part of Canto 36), stressed the importance of the formation of "the trace in the mind." Like Guido, Anselm does not suggest the possibility of human perfection in knowledge. We see darkly, more in the moonlight than in the sun:

Ratio,   [reason]
      luna,   [moon]

but our mirror-minds do at least let us see those divine images, and we do indeed live by them—if we are rational creatures.

Anselm himself is always charismatic, accepting nature in the broadest way. One sees this stressed in two of the following lines:

Sapor, the flavour,
          pulchritudo   [beauty]

This little analogy is lifted out of the *Proslogion,* Chapters 17 and 18 (*Patrologia Latina,* vol. 158, columns 223-42 for the entire tract), which tell in memorable language adapted from St. Augustine about the ignorant nature of the non-knower, who "looks around him and doesn't see beauty (*pulchritudinem*)" and "tastes, yet doesn't know Your savor (*saporem*; Pound's sapor)." Pound plays on the pun inherent in the Latin word *sapio*, which can mean "I taste," or by extension, "I know"—a wide but still inclusive range of meanings. Like Anselm, Pound aligns the material possibility with the idealistic; one should not separate the two, as Pound's "ne divisibilis intellectu" (nor divisible by the intellect) indicates, for if one does, he will end up—to paraphrase Yeats—by bruising either the body or the soul at the other's expense. Sensual taste and intellectual knowledge are connected, as the story of the eating of the apple in Eden indicates. Anselm has balance, a fine awareness of opposite ends that owes nothing to syllogization or to the cutting of the all-embracing Trinity into separate parts.[3]

Like Erigena, Anselm was not often understood in his own age. The monk Gaunilo attacked his ontological proof of God by asking: "If I can imagine a beautiful island just as you imagine your God, does that mean that my island exists too?" Pound's phrase "(insulis fortunatis)/fertur" (he is borne to the Blessed Isles) reflects Gaunilo's words from Chapter 6 of his retort to the *Proslogion*, his *Liber pro insipiente* (Book for the Ignorant Man), which is included in the Migne edition after Anselm's work. Savoring the idea of Sapience as Sapor, Pound is then wafted away like the bees to the Blessed Isles (*insulis fortunatis*), wearing "light as an armycloak." This revery anticipates the vision of Charles of the Swabians, who is mentioned at the end of the canto.

Having discussed Anselm's world-view, we can now speak of his historical importance. To arrive at this, Pound examined the *Vita*, or biography, written by Anselm's friend, Eadmer, which serves as an introduction to volume 158 of the Migne edition. There he found some details that accorded perfectly with Anselm's philosophy. The saint loved nature. This is made clear in two anecdotes that Pound partially retells on page 748:

Canterbury well, above Capua
      by Anselm's direction,
           he said: dig there.
Puteus Cantauriensis
      nine miles approx east of Capua

And he said: ". . . eh . . .
> I might eat a partridge."
> So we scuttled all day
>> and no partridge
> Till the stable boy met a martin
>> that had caught one.

First, while visiting Italy, Anselm retired to the little town of Sclavia (Liberi), near Capua, to write his *Cur Deus Homo* (Why Did God Become Man?). When a local monk informed him of the desperate scarcity of water, Anselm went with him to a rocky place, told him to dig, and "behold! a living fountain!" (chap. 4, col. 101). Eadmer adds that it was called the "well of the Archbishop of Canterbury" (*puteus Cantauriensis archiepiscopi*) by the natives.

In the other anecdote, Anselm fell sick and said: "Perhaps I'd eat some partridge if I had it" (*Forse, ait, de perdice comederem si haberem;* chap. 7, col. 112). His monastic friends tried to find him a bird and failed; but then one of the servants, passing through some bushes, saw a *martyram* (marten; but Pound translates by the bird-name "martin") with a partridge in its mouth; he scared the weasel-like beast, making it drop its prey, and then took the partridge to Anselm, who was suddenly and quite miraculously cured. There is a charming Ovidian quality to these stories that links them to the mention of lion-founts at Ovid's Sulmona, Frederick II's hawks, Mozart's bird-melodies, the sheep on the Rham plains, and the Bari sacristan's Cupid.[4]

The only blemish on Anselm's character is his slight antifeminism, which is pointed out on page 750 in lines that probably imitate a distich that occurs in Anselm's poem, *Carmen de Contemptu Mundi* (*Patrologia Latina*, vol. 158, columns 687 ff.):

If one has a terrible wife, he loathes and hates her;
If a pretty one, he anxiously fears adulterers.

This would seem to match Pound's "Ugly? a bore,/ Pretty, a whore!" But this feeling is insignificant when one weighs the spirit of the whole man. The "contempt for the world" tradition, like the tradition of calling one's work his trifles (see Catullus' *Carmen* 1.4 for the phrase *meas nugas*, "my little nothings"), really adds little

to our knowledge of Anselm as an individual, but one does learn
that the saint loved and wrote poetry.

Aside from his philosophy, Anselm was also important as one
of the great fighters for the Church in its struggles against the
State. He stood with popes like Urban II and Paschal II against the
tyrannical King William Rufus of England: Pound's "Anselm verus
[versus?] damn Rufus." In this sense, he followed the footsteps of
his friend and teacher, Lanfranc of Bec, who, as Archbishop of
Canterbury, had had to contend with William the Conqueror.
Rufus was a ruthless tyrant who, as Pound says, raised the rent on
the land and gouged money out of clerics and laymen alike.

Charles de Rémusat had taught Pound to regard Anselm as a
fearless fighter for liberty and intellectual integrity.[5] In both respects, the saint thus joins the list of Anglo-Saxon kings who lifted
England out of barbarism and transformed it into the highly civilized nation that produced the Magna Charta, a document that
Pound revered as a forerunner of the American Constitution. With
help from de Rémusat, Pound increasingly saw pre-Puritan
England as a great state that was surpassed only by China and
Byzantium in its time. Anselm's fight for the liberties or *consuetudines* (habitual local rights) of the Church and the people aided this
development immeasurably.[6] The people might be one in Christ
under the monarch and God ("Unitas Charitatis": unity of charity),
but they were diverse in their operations or customs ("consuetudo
diversa").[7] This is but another statement of Pound's basic belief
that local power should be put under local control, to prevent vast,
anonymous monopolies and cartels from taking over.

As a result of Anselm's importance in history, Pound prints a
roll-call of kings in Canto 105/749, taken largely from the pages of
William of Malmesbury's history, *The Deeds of the English Kings.*[8]
Below are some key dates to the left and William's chapter and
book numbers to the right; also given are the Latin sources for
Pound's list, with some Latin quotations that support Pound's
descriptions in English:

Reigned 924-40   Athelstan: 2.131 ff.
       716-757   Ethelbald: *"ut omnia monasteria . . .*
                    a publicis vectigalibus . . . absolvantur"
                    (that all monasteries be absolved from
                    public taxes); 1.84

r. 802-839   Egbert: 2.106
r. 1099-1118   Pope Paschal II: 5.415[9]
1071-1127   Guillaume de Poictiers: 5.439[10]
1068-1135   Henry I: *"fere ad centum millia libras; erant et vasa"* (almost a hundred thousand pounds; and there were vases); *Historia novella* 1.14.

The fact that Henry left a monetary record on the so-called Pipe Rolls indicates the king's awareness that he is part of a tradition, and must not use every available cent to rear mammoth pyramids or to create mosaics that will help him to "bust out of the kosmos," an "accensio" (kindling; but perhaps Pound meant *ascensio*, a lofty flight) that is anyway impossible since, according to Anselm, the cosmos includes not only us but all that is.

Picking up the reference to Ambrose, whose *De Tobia* (*Patrologia Latina*, vol. 14) commentary on the now-apocryphal *Book of Tobias* from the Bible was solidly for the general benefit of the people against usurious profit, Pound continues the roll-call of civilized Franks and Angles. These monarchs should be added to the Lombards and Byzantines of Canto 96 (see Chapter Eight); they anticipate the great English kings of Cantos 107 to 109. Omitting names mentioned before, they include:

To A.D. 425   Franks/Faramond, first king of All Gaul (Omnia Gallia); 1.68
754   Pepin the Short (crowned) over an altar to Zagreus (another name for Dionysus, the Greek God; Pepin's coronation place was the Church of St. Denis in Paris, and that saint, Dionysius, was traditionally linked by name and myth to a pagan Greek heritage); 1.68
c. 796   Charles the Great (Charlemagne) gave Offa a *baltheum* and a *gladium Huniscum;* 1.93
821   Poor Kenelm, later considered holy, was *a sorore Quendrida innocue caesus* (by his sister Quendrida blamelessly struck down); 1.95

839-888   Charles of the Suevi or Swabians (see
            below); 2.111
849-899?   Alfred: "instituted the tenth-parts called
            tithings" (*decimas quas thethingas vocant,
            instituit*); 2.122
c.810-880   Erigena: "stabbed with their pens by the
            boys whom he was teaching" (*a pueris
            quos docebat graphiis . . . perforatus*);
            2.122
After 925   Athelstan "began to found guilds"; from
            Layamon's *Brut*[11]
924   Ethelfled: "took care of education . . . by
            the great zeal of his aunt" (*educandum
            curaverat; ubi multo studio amitae*);
            2.131 ff.
c.995-1035 Canute: "away from all toll stations"
            (*absque omni angaria clausarum*); 2.183
r.999-1003 Gerbert (later Pope Sylvester II): "was
            triumphant over Ptolemy in the science
            of the astrolabe" (*vicit scientia Ptholo-
            maeum in astrolabis*); 2.167

These items mark a return to the time of Anselm, with the reader
passing "savages" and "maniacs" amd "swine . . . with their
panourgia" (lust). Anselm's love of the world and his clarity of expression are echoed in Cavalcanti and (less certainly, perhaps) in
Villon, who lived in the middle of the fifteenth century, when the
great medieval visions such as that of Dante were blurring.

   Speaking of visions, one must not forget the previously mentioned Charles of the Suevi (Swabians), who is also mentioned in
other cantos. Pound probably stumbled on this interesting man in
William of Malmesbury's history, when he was tracing the English
kings. The common name of this descendant of Charlemagne was
Charles the Fat (Charles le Gros in French), but Pound more
mercifully calls him "of the Suevi," because Charles inherited
Swabia upon the death of his father, Louis the German, in 876.
Charles was emperor from 881 to 887, until he witnessed a
miraculous vision that prompted him to surrender his vast posses-
sions from Italy to France and to retire from active political life
into a monastery.

In his dream, which William took with vague acknowledgment from Hariulf's *Chronicle*,[12] Charles recounts how he was awakened by a terrifying voice that commanded him to witness the judgments of God. In language that is both eerily mystical and strangely romantic, Charles says:

> Suddenly I was seized by my spirit, and that one who took control of me was most shiny, and he held in his hand a solid ball emitting the brightest ray of light, just as comets do when they appear, and he began to unwind it and said to me: "Take a thread of this brilliant light, and tie and knot it firmly around the thumb of your right hand, because you will be led by this through the labyrinthine punishments of Hell."[13]

Charles then recounts how he entered "the deepest, most fiery valleys" and saw "the priests of my father and my uncles." While he was viewing the righteous punishments for many sinners, some of them tried to grab him and pull him down into their sulphurous pits, but the spirit-guide "threw a thread of light upon my shoulders . . . and drew me along strongly behind him, so that we thus ascended the highest fiery mountains" (col. 1288). Finally, Charles saw his own father enduring purgatorial pain, and he went on to observe his predecessors, Lothair I and his son Louis II, sitting on a hill "redeemed from these pains and conducted into the joy of the paradise of God." Lothair, especially, was seated "on a rock of topaz of great magnitude, crowned with a precious diadem." Thus, Charles offers through this narration a *Divine Comedy* in brief, woven here into the fabric of *Thrones*. Charles is like Sordello, the guide of the Vale of Princes; even more so, he resembles Anselm or Dante, who both had a complete vision.

Looking at the canto as a whole, one can see a great deal of order ("ordine," p. 749) as opposed to "brute force": the Byzantine Emperor Alexius Comnenus pitted against the ruthless crusader Boamund. If this is not the "Anselm Canto," then it must be "The Canto of the Betrayed":

Talleyrand was betrayed by	France
Bismarck by	Germany
Mussolini by	Italy
Frederick II by	the Church
Mozart by	patronless Austria

| Lanfranc by | William I and England |
| Anselm by | William Rufus and England |

Are we not bid to add: Pound . . . by whom?

Yet, for all its blend of violence with order, it is far from being a canto of despair. The noose of light that led Charles the Fat to a vision of glory is as strong and binding as the vision of Love emanating from a cosmos of Knowledge that inspired Anselm. An underground conspiracy of intellect (that "persistent awareness") goes on, despite the morons and madmen. In a way, Talleyrand, the nineteenth-century French statesman who opens the canto, is as important as Anselm himself, for it was Talleyrand's close friend, Charles de Rémusat, who wrote one of the books on Anselm that most attracted Pound. Talleyrand's name recurs on page 749 in a dialect form as Pound relates the advisor of Napoleon to his early ancestor, who was a friend of the troubadour Bertran de Born; the little catch-word "en gatje" (up for pawn, mort*gage*) enforces the comparison.[14] The eight-hundred-year interval from troubadour friend to friend of Napoleon merely shows again the recurrent factor in a chain of civilization, just as the roll-call of good kings does. The light lives on, even if it is often carried by underdogs like Cavalcanti, Talleyrand, or Anselm himself.[15] Ultimately the haunting image of the incandescent ribbon unwound from the glowing ball is what we carry away, and that tenuous but cohering luminous file may be taken as a symbol of the thread of history or the thin, beelike but certain flight of the mind into the dark recesses of the unknown.

Epilogue
Those Haunting Shards, The Final Fragments

There is no formal ending to *The Cantos*. After Pound establishes the importance of Edward Coke and English law in the course of world history in Cantos 107 to 109, the poem closes with the *Drafts & Fragments of Cantos 110-17*. Shortly after the poet's death, another fragment was uncovered and was tipped into later editions as Canto 120.

As a result, there is a question about unity if one wants to assess *The Cantos* completely. Since the poem does not offer a logical conclusion, it is once again subject to the charge of incoherence. Pound himself abetted this adverse criticism to some extent by his moments of despair:

That I lost my center
              fighting the world.
The dreams clash
                and are shattered—
and that I tried to make a paradiso
                       terrestre.
                                    [on earth]
                              (117 et seq./802)

Yet at other times, Pound insisted that his vision had moments of perfection, even if it did not have a logical underpinning:

i.e. it coheres all right
              even if my notes do not cohere.
Many errors,
           a little rightness,
to excuse his hell
              and my paradiso.
                                (116/797)

The "his" refers to Dante. Obviously, Pound believed that the Italian's vision of cosmic order was far superior to his own—indeed, one would expect it to be, since the Middle Ages was almost by definition a time of syncretic visions. Yet Pound suggests by the comparison that his own concept of an Inferno, of what is wrong with the world, may well surpass that of his medieval forerunner (a cynic would say that twentieth-century man is indeed more qualified to write about Hell, since he inhabits one).

As to the charge of lack of unity, this is somewhat irrelevant when considering a poem that never attempted to follow a strict Aristotelian scheme of a beginning, a middle, and an end. As late as Canto 113/787, Pound shows that the poem's movement is constantly shifting and interweaving:

The hells move in cycles,
    No man can see his own end.
The Gods have not returned. "They have never left us."
    They have not returned.
Cloud's processional and the air moves with their living.

Furthermore, the idea that a work must rise to a pitched climax smacks of eighteenth-century surety, and is out of keeping with a vision of the twentieth century. For example, James Joyce's *Ulysses* trails off in the subconscious, disorganized thoughts of Molly Bloom, while *Finnegans Wake* returns to its beginning, with the insistence that what is past is prologue. Since the man Ezra Pound always was in *The Cantos*—indeed, his mind is the medium in which the poem operates—there is really no possible ending for the work except death. For even in his willfully silent old age, Pound's constantly moving intellect gave him both the comfort and the torment that bless and afflict every man who thinks:

  Out of dark, thou, Father Helios, leadest,
but the mind as Ixion, unstill, ever turning.   (113/790)

To the end, Pound clung to the haunting possibility of realizing a heaven on earth. With unrelenting fervor, he held to his belief that a straightening out of the political and economic machinations of men could produce a worldwide society in which all men could be nurtured and could flourish. In spite of moments of deep and pressing pessimism, he fought constantly for the vitality of this dream.

Canto 110, for example, opens with a beautiful scene drawn from a water-city, which is doubtlessly Venice:

Thy quiet house
The crozier's curve runs in the wall,
The harl, feather-white, as a dolphin on sea-brink . . .

But the picture assumes broader proportions, for if the Venetian painter Canaletto is mentioned, so is the Buddhist mercy divinity Kuanon (Kuan Yin):

And in thy mind beauty, O Artemis,
                    as of mountain lakes in the dawn,
Foam and silk are thy fingers,
                    Kuanon,
and the long suavity of her moving,
                    willow and olive reflected,
Brook-water idles,
                    topaz against pallor of under-leaf
The lake waves Canaletto'd
                    under blue paler than heaven . . .   (778)

The lines form a tranquil meditation by setting the neatly carved stone house against the natural beauty of water and the mountain lake. The lines move from the closely portrayed to the distantly imagined, from man to nature, from here to there, from the specific to the archetypal—without losing sight of either. In fact, the specific enlivens the universal, just as the universal gives weight to the specific.

Pound's technique is always assimilative. It is not *just* Venice that he is talking about or just *any* scene from nature. In fact, here one hears an echo of the wave pattern cut in the wall of the castle at Excideuil or the descriptions of the palaces lining the Grand Canal. Behind his verbal painting lies the imagistic precision of his youth, as well as his mature purpose of trying to bring East into a meaningful relationship with West. Thus the rocking, lulling joy of riding in a gondola is transposed over a scene from Japan, where one might envision a sky-blue lake and a Shinto shrine:

Hast'ou seen boat's wake on sea-wall,
                        how crests it?
What panache?
                        paw-flap, wave-tap,
                        that is gaiety,
Toba Sojo,
                toward limpidity,
                            that is exultance,
                here the crest runs on wall

In his later years, when Pound was trying "to write Paradise,"
he made one of those discoveries for which he was famous: he uncovered through his researches a little-known society of Chinese
people living in the southwestern mountains close to the border of
Tibet, known as the Na-khi tribes. These people possessed the
oldest known traditions of the Chinese, expressed in their native
Na-khi dialects and preserved for centuries through the memories
of shaman-priests. Their religion was a mixture of pre-Confucian
shamanism, or nature-worship, and the pre-Buddhist Bön religion
of Tibet.

The source for this new inquiry was Joseph F. Rock, a man
who published widely about botanical species in such places as the
Hawaiian Islands, where he taught for a time. Rock then moved on
to China to study the flora and fauna of the remote mountainous
hinterlands, and it was there that he discovered these strange,
interesting people. Like Frobenius, Rock was interested in *total
culture:* he did not divorce geography from linguistics from botany
from anthropology from art; he saw all things in a vast cultural
ideogram that in turn resembled Pound's own central ideogram.

Rock's masterpiece is a two-volume work titled *The Ancient
Na-khi Kingdom of Southwest China.*[1] In it he traces his journey
into the uplands, from town to town and valley to peak, giving a
richly poetic description of the countryside and its natural life: the
berberis bushes and scrub-oaks and junipers and "pinus armandi"
that occur constantly in the Later Cantos. In one section he moves
into the Li Chiang, or Snow Range area, where the Yü-lung Shan
(Jade Dragon Mountain) dominates the landscape (Plate 54; see
Canto 112). He also mentions the Här-lĕr-gkv, or Wind-Call Pass,
where the Wind Spirit and her six companions must be propitiated
in the wind-sway rite, which he transcribes as follows:[2]*Har-²la-*

*¹llü-³k̓ö** (Canto 110/777).² Rock's appreciation for the local mythology can be seen in places where he describes, for example, the Golden Dragon Bridge over the Yangtze River. This is an iron bridge that replaced a rope (*tso*) bridge (Canto 101/725) that had been built under the following circumstances:

> Chiang Tsung-han, eloping with a girl, reached
> the ferry and wished to cross the river. The
> ferryman, however . . . refused to take them over.
> Chiang then swore that, should he ever become wealthy,
> he would build a bridge across the river.　　　　(vol. 1, 246; Plate 110)

Pound was fascinated by these "primitive" people, who worshiped nature and whose land was so beautiful that it almost can be envisioned as a Paradise, or Shangri-La, on Earth. Pound devoted almost all of the fragmentary Canto 112 to describe their very important "heaven-sacrifice" (*²Muan-¹bpö*) rite,³ which employs such talismanic animals as the owl, the wagtail, and the fire-fox, along with a generous use of nectar:

. . . owl, and wagtail
and huo³-hu,² the fire-fox
Amrta, that is nectar
　　　　　　　white wind, white dew
Here from the beginning, we have been here
　　　　　　　　　from the beginning

The rite is directed toward the Celestial Female (*²La-²mun-³mi*) and also involves an earth-sacrifice rite known as the *²ndaw-¹bpö*, which requires generous offerings of juniper to stimulate the growth of crops. Pound works these words and ideas into his own poetry as follows:

From her breath were the goddesses
　　　　　²La ²muṇ ³mi
If we did not perform ²Ndaw ¹bpö,
　　　　　　　nothing is solid
without ²Muan ¹bpö
　　　　　　no reality
Agility, that is from the juniper.

---

*Like Chinese, the ancient Na-khi language, now no longer used, was pronounced in four tones, here marked before the words.

The ceremony to heaven usually takes place at the foot of the Hsiang Shan (Elephant Mountain) near the Dragon King (Lung Wang) Temple and the Jade River (Yu⁴ ho²):

By the pomegranate water,
                    in the clear air
                            over Li Chiang
The firm voice amid pine wood,
                    many springs are at the foot of
                            Hsiang Shan
By the temple pool, Lung Wang's
                    the clear discourse
                            as Jade Stream

There is a lovely picture of this river flowing through a town, appearing as Plate 53 in Rock's work. The plant artemisia is also employed in this rite, and arundinaria, a reedy substance, is used to build the cane-brake tray that is supposed to winnow fate or life. Pound pictures this tray at the end of Canto 112, likening it, no doubt, to the siftings of Lady Fortune and the Moon (luna), as sung by Dante and Cavalcanti.[4] In transcribing this ritual, Canto 112 portrays the kind of offering to Heaven and to Earth that was once a part of the Eleusinian Mysteries and other pre-Christian rites that time has effaced (Pound's use of artemisia is also meant to recall the goddess Artemis-Diana). If the Communists have not intervened, this ritual is still being practiced in the Chinese-Tibetan mountain country.

Another important Na-khi myth forms the central organizing pattern of Canto 110. This is the moving story of a girl named ²K'a-²mä-¹gyu-³mi-²gkyi, who loves a shepherd named ²Ndzi-²bö-¹yü-²lä-¹p'ër, but is forced to marry another man. Like many other thwarted Na-khi lovers, she moves up into the Snow Range and attempts suicide. She "went to the water to die" but "the surface of the water was a deep blue, her eyes were also a deep blue, my heart is faint."[5] She then tried to twist a new rope to hang herself upon a tree, but "the black tree was born dumb" and "did not invite her." She then wrote a letter to her lover, begging him to join her, saying that she yearned for him like a white stag that has drunk from a salt spring whose taste remains in his mouth. Her lover replied coldly that it was autumn (gentian-time), and he had to look after his sheep. As a result, she went up to Mount Shi-lo (called Sumeru by the Buddhists) and hanged herself upon an oak (*quercus* in Latin).

The girl's lover eventually went up into the mountains and stumbled upon her body swaying in the wind. He said to her: "If I give you turquoise and coral eyes, will you again be able to see? If I attach the roots of the pine and the oak, will you again be able to walk?"; and she replied sadly: "Even if you give me turquoise and coral eyes, I will not be able to see . . . if you add the roots of the pine and the oak, I will not again be able to walk."[6] The lover cut down her body to spare her from being ravaged by birds of prey, but he was fascinated by her sacrificial death-dress, which contained jewels. He was about to steal these robes when the ghost of the girl wrapped the swaying rope around his neck and strangled him. The tragic story is told in pictographs, or picture-writing, and the last one, in which the boy is shown dangling grotesquely from the limb of a tree (p. 114), is particularly unforgettable:

The nine fates and the seven,[7]
    and the black tree was born dumb,
The water is blue and not turquoise
When the stag drinks at the salt spring
     and sheep come down with the gentian sprout,
can you see with eyes of coral or turquoise
    or walk with the oak's root?

This love-death myth reminded Pound of Orpheus's search in Hell for Eurydice (779) and a number of Japanese parallels that he came upon in his translations of Noh plays:

Awoi no Uye (text in *Translations*, pp. 323 ff.): the story of a gracious lady who is attacked by a ferocious spirit that seeks to destroy her;

Sotoba Komachi and *Kayoi Kamachi* (text in *Translations*, pp. 223 ff.): which relate the activities of a dead woman and her lover (at the time that he was translating the piece, Pound likened the girl to the Greek nymph Echo);

and especially *Kakitsubata* (text in *Translations*, pp. 332 ff.): which relates the story of the maiden of the title, who is dead, but who appears as an iris apparition to a priest and a Chorus:

The iris Kakitsubata of the old days
Is planted anew.

This last reference is used by Pound on page 778 to unite the Japanese Kakitsubata with the Na-khi ²K'a. The Na-khi write names using pictographs that merely suggest the sound; thus ²K'a can be referred to by ¹ba, which means "flower," and which is represented by an iris-head with froth or pollen flowing from it. This water-grave motif undoubtedly harkens back to the opening lines of the canto, with its Venetian setting. This Italian line, lifted from Dante's *Inferno* V (che paion' si al vent': "who appear so light on the winds"), describes the circular movements of the tormented lovers Paolo and Francesca. Together, these references form a tragic *Liebestod* ideogram, with ²K'a, Kakitsubata, Eurydice, and the others.

The Chinese words appearing on page 778 may be translated as follows:

> yüeh⁴⁻⁵: moon (or flowing or iris leaf)
> ming²: bright
> mo⁴⁻⁵: dead (or froth)
> hsien¹: fairy, spirit
> p'eng²: wind

The general sense is: The moon is bright, and a dead spirit is in the wind, although the words may yield other interpretations.[8] These words could well spell out the love-death ideogram developed here, for the women are all linked to the moon (see Chapter Two for a fuller development), and they are all part of the dead spirit world that is still vitally a part of nature, as the wind is. This Na-khi love myth brings together the seemingly disparate elements of death and fertility, turning tragedy into romantic absolution. It is as if the Tristan and Isolde story were a workable part of Catholic belief (as Pound would like to have it), as if Catholic mysticism and romantic mystery had found a way to unite. Ovid linked myth and religion beautifully, and Pound is attempting to do the same, against incredible odds.

After citing Mount Sumeru and the tragic oak, Canto 110 then approaches the ²Muan-¹Bpö rite directly:

<pre>
        heaven   earth
            in the center
                 is
               juniper
</pre>
The purifications
      are snow, rain, artemisia,
      also dew, oak and the juniper

This rite is graphically depicted in Plate 65 of the first volume of Rock's work, where he notes that "Each clan, designated by a family name, has its own altar, at which to propitiate Heaven. On the altar are three treelets . . . an oak representing Heaven, a Juniper representing the Emperor and an oak representing Earth." The offerings are sometimes made to Sa-ddo, the Great God of the Mountains, who protects the Na-khi. Behind the Temple of Sa-ddo loom the Three Protecting Lords (parallel here with the San Ku of Canto 90), mountain peaks in the Gangkar Snow Range which bear the following names:

1. The Holder of the Thunderbolt
2. The God of Learning
3. The Goddess of Mercy, Kuan-Yin (Pound's Kuanon), whose shrine lies just below her peak (Plate 55).

The sudden appearance of Artemis, the Greek goddess of woodland and sacrifice, connected with artemisia, forces the reader to leap from Tibet to Greece, and to keep the East-West nature of the ideogram alive.

The canto goes on to mention some courageous Italians who excelled in war or road-building without destroying nature, as well as some American senators (including Uncle George Tinkham, Pound's friend), and then one encounters the name Khaty (Kati), the Egyptian lord cited at the start of Canto 93, and of whom Pound says now:

In love with Khaty
      now dead for 5000 years.

The lines stress the meaninglessness of time, just as the canto has already abolished the arbitrary differences of space; one recalls Confucius: "How is it far if you think of it?" Pound then brings the world of Greco-Roman myth directly into focus with the Oriental by alluding to Eurydice, who was doomed to death; Daphne, who was changed into a laurel tree; and Endymion, who had an amour with the moon:

Over water bluer than midnight
      where the winter olive is taken
Here are earth's breasts mirroured
                and all Euridices,
Laurel bark sheathing the fugitive,
           a day's wraith unrooted?
Neath this altar now Endymion lies

    Passing by a Greek word that may be used to describe divinities (*kalliastragolos:* beautiful-ankled) and the Chinese character *hsin*[1], that means "new, fresh" and relates to both spiritual and physical regeneration, Pound thinks about the many deaths in World War II, and the passing of great restaurants like La Tour and Dieudonné, the economic stultification of Byzance-Istanbul (compare the vitality in Chapter Nine), the splendid desuetude around the Tomb of Galla Placidia in Ravenna, and the lovely but by-passed island of Torcello near Venice; his depression is voiced in the simple statement: "war is the destruction of restaurants."

    When no bird in Italy or Virginia can give him consolation as he ponders the wanton destruction from jet planes, which destroyed the sculpted lions at Brescia in Italy, he voices an oft-stated thought: without reflective pauses (the hitching-post character: Chinese *chih*[3]), the mind cannot find its root, its base. Pessimism increases as he recalls his friends Basil Bunting and Alan Upward, who won no critical acclaim; but with the Chinese character representing the sun (*jih*[4-5]), one of Pound's favorite signs, comes a renewed feeling of hope. The poet remembers that Joseph Rock, whose magnificent study opened the doors of an Earthly Paradise to him, lost all of his work of many years when the ship carrying it to America was torpedoed by the Japanese:[9]

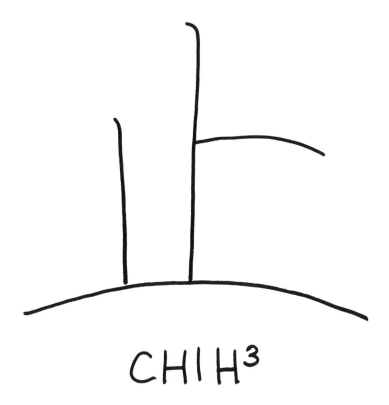

CHIH³

Mr Rock still hopes to climb at Mount Kinabalu
his fragments sunk (20 years)
13,455 ft. facing Jesselton, Borneo,
Falling spiders and scorpions!
Give light against falling poison, . . .

Almost in answer to his own imprecation, Pound thinks about his work and that of those who have been "blacked out," but who shine in the dark, like candles against a tempest, flickering but alive. The canto then gathers strength as it surges with the ritual force of prayer:

The marble form in the pine wood,
          The shrine seen and not seen

From the roots of sequoias
               pray   pray   [ching^4]
             There is power
Awoi or Komachi,
             the oval moon.

The tragic characters from the Noh plays are blended, like Cunizza da Romano in the *Pisan Cantos*, with their sister friends and the moon.

In the course of this canto, Pound has taken the reader from moments of tragic despair to scenes of vivid, eternal beauty. Nature, seen in the shapes of trees and mountains and bodies of water, supplies the ever-returning, regenerative medium that lifts the poet out of his depression into a feeling of triumph, and finally into a tone of quiet acceptance. Scenes from Europe and Asia are viewed in all of their splendor, particularly in the form of trees. As the reader sees the sequoias and junipers of the Himalayas being blended with the larches of Paradise that arched over Apollonius of Tyana (himself a visitor into the deepest mountains of Asia in search of wisdom), one realizes that Pound has indeed linked East with West in terms of myth and expectations, and has demonstrated the power that lies in prayer. Almost magically, the Na-khis have made him their shaman.

After the heavenly visions of Canto 110, one expects a falling off in the "Notes for 111." Although this section is clearly labeled as fragmentary, it holds together in a remarkable way. The "notes" begin with a comparison of two men, an I, who is Tze-Kung, and Hui (earlier editions have the name Yu), who are adapted from the Confucian *Analects*, Book 5, Section 8, which reads in Pound's rendition:

1. He asked Tze-Kung: who comprehends most, you or Hui?
2. The answer: No comparison, Hui hears one point and
   relates it to ten (understands its bearing on ten,
   I on one only); I hear one point and can only get to
   the next.
3. He said: Not the same, I agree you are not alike.

                                        (*Confucius*, p. 210)[10]

Clearly Hui, or Yu, is being upheld as the kind of man who thinks ideogrammically, while Tze-Kung is limited to mere plodding.

Next follows a sizable stretch that is related to French history, particularly to Napoleon and Talleyrand. In Chapter Eleven, Napoleon was said to be regarded in *The Cantos* primarily as a failure, a man who had dared much, risked all, and gained very little for himself or posterity, particularly when compared with his contemporaries, Adams and Jefferson. There is no reason to see a different development here. For even though the triumph at Austerlitz and the founding of the Bank of France are mentioned prominently, as well as the rational conduct of Talleyrand ("heart's field" by the Chinese words can mean "thought"), a negative judgment is also clearly intended:

Enlarged his empire
        diminished his forces,
Ten years a blessing,
           five a nuisance,
that was Napoleon

Tsar Alexander's quizzical question about the French and the description of the ministers at Vienna, who were constantly changing their words and their intentions, prepared the way for a twentieth-century sequel:

And 600 more dead at Quemoy—
        they call it political.

The botched situation in Viet Nam can be linked directly to the botched situation earlier in Europe. Pound himself would prefer adjectives like "moral" and "economic" to "political" here. As for his verdict on Napoleon's culture, Pound says:

Voltaire could not do it;
The french could not do it.
        they had not Magna Charta   (107/757)

With the phrase "A nice quiet paradise," the tone changes, however. The editor A.R. Orage, who worked constantly to try to establish saner ways of handling money, is cited for his basic pity, compassion, love (Amor).[11] Then, in another sudden shift, a continuous stretch of poetry runs from "Cold mermaid" (earlier

editions had "Gold mermaid") to "Serenitas" (Serenity). Pound has
a vision of a sea-creature lured from the depths, "but in splendour"; her brilliant form is contrasted with the dark water and the
grey sand being drawn back into the sea.[12] For a brief moment, the
poet compares the mermaid to the monster Geryon, especially
when he uses the line from Dante's *Inferno* 17.19: *come burchiello
in su la riva* (like a little boat upon a bank), which describes the
beast's tail as it dangles over a cliff above the depths of the Eighth
Circle, the round of Fraud. But then he hastily changes his interpretation. Instead, Pound sees the mermaid as "Veritas, by anti-
thesis" (truth coming out of its opposite): light issuing from
darkness, beauty from the terrifying unknown. For a moment he is
blinded by this troublesome vision, since no light is issuing from
the depths (ex profundis), but he stalwartly refuses to pretend that
it is anything other than what it is. In short, Pound refuses to "fake
it." Then suddenly, instead of seeing the female body emerging
from the water, he sees the flight of a soul into the air or the breeze
(aura), and he feels a sense of serenity.

If the notes ended here, the reader would feel that the movement was once again paradisal. But instead, the tone shifts once
more, as Pound closes the section with the following words:

Coin'd gold
            also bumped off 8000 Byzantines
Edictum prologo
            Rothar.

The reference is to the Lombard king who figured prominently in
Chapter Eight. Rothar was the famous lawgiver who issued an
"edict with prologue" (Edictum prologo), coined his own gold
(always to Pound the sign of a true ruler, since he exercised control over the currency), and, like a courageous warrior, protected
his people by fighting off the Byzantines.

This portrait echoes Tze's talk about Hui (Yu), for Rothar
is a man cut after the model of the latter, who could see things in
many directions. Both Hui and Rothar, in turn, are contrasted with
the pathetic general who tried to issue good laws in his Napoleonic
Code, tried to effect monetary reforms through the actions of the
Directory, but unfortunately enjoyed battlefields more than he

should have. The apparition of the mermaid can be related to all three men because she seems to represent economics (I prefer "gold" as her description), money—the secret force that lurks in the background, the relative power that must be understood if one is to stand strong like a Rothar and not collapse like the Little Corporal. The notes are thus preparations for a canto that would have been largely purgatorial. Even in its fragmentary form, it can stand with those others that emphasize the works and deeds of doers.

After these samples of Paradise and Purgatory, the reader may well ask what happened to Hell in the shifting context of the Fragments. The answer is: it is still there. Evil, in Pound's view, is a constant; in fact, it almost generates the necessity of creating a Paradise of the mind, for, like Tertullian, Pound believes "because it is impossible" (quia impossibile est; Canto 87/570). The great difference between the Fragments and the other cantos lies in the presentation, which is more muted and somewhat less particular. The young Pound responded to evil with great rage; the old Pound more often voiced a quiet despair. This difference can be seen dramatically in the first "Addendum for Canto 100" and in the lines "From Canto 115." The addendum is dated early, circa 1941 (before the *Pisan Cantos*), while the section from Canto 115 was written after Pound had been released from St. Elizabeths.

The Addendum for Canto 100 is a continuation of the famous Usury Canto, 45, and its sequel, 51. It works primarily by presenting images of disease and corruption and uses the Hebrew word *neschek* instead of the Latin word *usura* to describe monetary crimes, particularly usurious moneylending. Pound uses the Hebrew word specifically to show his awareness that the Jews themselves have a word that distinguishes between fair and unfair rates for moneylending. Moneylending *per se* is necessary for expansion; it is only wrong when it is handled unfairly:

The Evil is Usury, *neschek*
the serpent
neschek whose name is known, the defiler,
beyond race and against race
the defiler   (798)

By noting that the crime is "beyond race," Pound specifically shows that it is not limited to the Jews, who were forced in the Middle Ages to assume the profession of moneylender because they were denied the ownership of land. The double standard of using the Jews for a condemned service and then blaming them for performing that service did not escape Pound's keen sense of irony. Furthermore, Pound was always aware that the Christian bankers of America had long usurped the primary role of money-lender, although, through the Rothschilds, the Jews were still very powerful in Europe.

Much of the young, vitriolic Pound shows in the choleric tone of this poetry:

Here is the core of evil, the burning hell without let-up,
The canker corrupting all things, Fafnir the worm,
Syphilis of the State, of all kingdoms,
Wart of the common-weal,
Wenn-maker, corrupter of all things.

This is the same kind of rhetoric that appeared in Canto 45, without the names of great artists, who were used as contrasts. Here is the firm, even archaic, language of the King James Bible, especially the books of Leviticus and Deuteronomy. In fact, here, as in Canto 45, one hears the voice of Ezra the Prophet, almost as if Pound were weighing pounds (money units) or pounds (weights) as he pounds his message home. When Ezra was incarcerated in the camp at Pisa, and the Bible was one of the few books available to him, the poet rediscovered the strong, upright language of the Old Law that he himself had admired in his youth and then for-gotten.

In fact, the litany of evil gradually transforms itself into a frenzied prayer:

A thousand are dead in his folds,
                    in the eel-fisher's basket
          Chaire! O Dione! Chaire!   [Hail, Dione, hail!]
          pure Light, we beseech thee
     Crystal, we beseech thee
Clarity, we beseech thee

This prayer is not at all like the tranquil one contained in Canto 90. Aside from its frenzy, there is something schoolbookish about it: the poet has learned his lesson that Finland is nickel and Spain is mercury! He has also learned that someone whose name begins with an S is replacing the Rs (Rothschilds?) in the field of monetary evil. The poet goes on to state that allegorical or symbolic language is not to be preferred to direct statement and repeats that usury is the world's last great mystery. The fragment ends with the suggestion that most of the world ignores this mystery and quietly puffs on its opium out of Shanghai, living the lives of Lotus-Eaters (Lotophagoi).

All in all, when compared with the fragments around it, this is not a very interesting performance. Of course those who prize unity will see a repeat of theme here, but the repetition smacks more of *dejà vu* than dramatic restatement. In short, this is not really the Pound of the Later Cantos speaking at all. It is the voice of the man who had not yet endured the chastening experience of Pisa and St. Elizabeths. One must remember that for a great deal of his life, Pound had mistaken a symptom for a cause: he had put usury, the crime, before greed, the cause of the crime.[13] This brilliant perception by Pound of his own failing is alone reason enough to re-examine this kind of poetry at this point in the poem and to find it somewhat lacking. Canto 45 is brilliant where it occurs: an island of lucidity rising out of the surface of the Middle Cantos and clarifying the economic base of the poem. But here, toward the end of the work, one wants to learn more than the fact that Finland "is" nickel; one wants to—and can—learn about matters of the heart.

A more meaningful kind of presentation is apparent in the short excerpt "From Canto 115" on page 794. The selection begins with a comparison:

The scientists are in terror
        and the European mind stops
Wyndham Lewis chose blindness
        rather than have his mind stop.

Pound juxtaposes a Europe that he considers unthinking with the writer-artist Wyndham Lewis, who willingly went blind because he refused to stop reading in order to save his eyes.[14] This persistent dedication to intellect is contrasted with the "terror" of the scientists, who unshackled a world of technology that they can no longer control, and that threatens the very existence of the race. Then comes a lovely interlude:

Night under wind mid garofani   [amid carnations]
        the petals are almost still
Mozart, Linnaeus, Sulmona . . .   [Ovid's birthplace]

One feels that he is walking with three geniuses in a paradisal landscape (contrast Confucius walking with his disciples in Canto 13): the musician Mozart, the natural scientist Linnaeus, and Ovid, the nature and love poet from Sulmona. But the harmony here is suddenly disrupted by a jarring thought:

When one's friends hate each other
        how can there be peace in the world?
Their asperities diverted me in my green time.

The eternal bickering that causes wars on a grand scale and petty animosities on a smaller one fills the poet with a certain sense of despair. On the political scene, Pound had watched his native land battle his adopted one; in his own household during the war, he had watched his wife, Dorothy, hating his mistress, Olga. In Paris and London, he had been partially diverted by the petty animosities among the many artists whom he had supported, but that is no longer amusing.

For a moment Pound drops further into depression as he thinks of his impending death (he is a "blown husk"), but then he recalls the "song" of the light within him. This reaffirms not only his poetic powers but also that brilliant force of illumination that he had found again and again in Chinese characters ("The sun under it all": Canto 85/544) and in the most enduring words of the Christian Neoplatonics:

A blown husk that is finished
        but the light sings eternal
a pale flare over marshes
        where the salt hay whispers to tide's change

The poet's inner light is likened to the pale-fire over swamps near a seaside, where the endless changing of the tides is as much a comfort as a challenge. This perception brings him to a moment of stasis:

Time, space,
    neither life nor death is the answer.

But as soon as he forgets his own vantage point and thinks about humanity in general, Pound again becomes slightly depressed, as the fragment ends:

And of man seeking good,
    doing evil.
In meiner Heimat   [in my homeland]
        where the dead walked
            and the living were made of cardboard.

It is impossible to read these lines of quiet desperation without comparing them with the work of T.S. Eliot, which they in some ways resemble. One can sense here both the tranquility of *Four Quartets* and the sardonic comment of *The Waste Land*. The contemplation of nature resembles Eliot's late mystical poetry, while the direct condemnation of his fellow Americans for being made out of cardboard (Eliot's "hollow men") is frankly and openly stated. What is amazing is that *both* strains occur here in a single passage, whereas in Eliot they are separated in time and work. The later Pound's metaphysical yearning never let him forget particulars; he could not "get through hell in a hurry" (Canto 46/231) as Brother Eliot had done. His beliefs—in the dignity of man, the abundant beauty of nature, and (despite certain comments to the contrary) his own poetic powers—did not forbid him from commenting on mankind's errors to the last. Eliot abandoned satiric verse in the later phases of his life, and, in many people's eyes, he thereby abandoned his finest poetry. Pound never abandoned frank perception.

Canto 113, one of the most memorable of the Later Cantos, opens with what seems to be a proclamation of universal order in terms of the zodiac, with a weighing of opposites, and a picture of Father Sun turning around to enliven the cosmic scheme:

Thru the 12 Houses of Heaven
      seeing the just and the unjust,
      tasting the sweet and the sorry,
Pater Helios turning.

Then, with a quotation from Dante's *Inferno* 7.92 on the detach-
ment of Lady Fortune, the tone changes to threnody (Greek
THRENOS):

"Mortal praise has no sound in her ears"
                (Fortuna's)
threnos
And who no longer make gods out of beauty
threnos   this is a dying.

Pound is mourning the passing of an idealistic culture, where men
could "make gods out of beauty," and where they now make "art"
only out of soup cans and copper plates. But the notion of surrender is repugnant to the poet, and he summons his imagination
to project himself into an idyllic scene:

Yet to walk with Mozart, Agassiz and Linnaeus
      'neath overhanging air under sun-beat
Here take thy mind's space
And to this garden, Marcella, ever seeking by petal, by leaf-vein
      out of dark, and toward half-light

Louis Agassiz, the natural scientist who taught at Harvard, was
dear to Pound because of his anti-evolutionary teachings. Without becoming pedantic, one can say that the educated reader could
sense Agassiz' importance by the *tone* of the passage; in these
lyrical moments, one does not want an open encyclopedia at his
side. Similarly, even if one does not know that Marcella Spann
Booth collaborated with Pound on the anthology *Confucius to
Cummings,* one can sense that she was a lovely, gracious lady. The
same can be said for phrases like "old Pumpelly crossed Gobi,"
where the context makes the meaning clear.
    Pound moves from the garden to that brilliant world of the
Chinese-Tibetan mountains that was preserved in the courageous
and penetrating work of Joseph Rock:

And over Li Chiang, the snow range is turquoise
Rock's world that he saved us for memory
            a thin trace in high air

Rock's explorations remind Pound of a series of other "Men Against Death," and this leads to thoughts about the sun and serenity; Pound remembers that the poetess Hilda Doolittle used the Latin word "serenitas" with relation to a Sapphic poem about Atthis in a restaurant at a time long gone by.[15] The mention of this Greek girl loved by Sappho arouses a perception that will be repeated at the end of the canto: that life encompasses competing and paradoxical tensions, and it is ever-changing:

The long flank, the firm breast
            and to know beauty and death and despair
and to think that what has been shall be,
            flowing, ever unstill.

This mention of change arouses a revery that blends the movements of clouds with the procession of the gods and the cyclic movement of states of mind:

Pride, jealousy and possessiveness
            3 pains of hell
and a clear wind over garofani   [carnations]
            over Portofino 3 lights in triangulation
Or apples from Hesperides fall in their lap
            from phantom trees.

These triads, which unite the infernal (3 pains of hell) with the purgatorial or recurrent (3 lights) with the divine (golden apples from ghostly trees), "rhyme" with the loss of friends such as H. D. and good restaurants such as Dieudonné's, and lead to the thoughts of the loss of whole countries: Russian society collapsing under the Communists and Poland succumbing to its enemies, after vain promises from the British and the French.

Before the tone can become sentimental, Pound takes recourse to a natural beauty untouched by man:

And the road under apple-boughs
            mostly grass-covered

And the olives to windward
        Kalenda Maja.

This last is a rousing South French dance song (the music sur-
vives), attributed to the troubadour Raimbaut of Vaqueiras; it has
much of the joy and verve that Pound associates with the pagan
roots of Provençal song and the beautiful landscapes in Languedoc
and Spain.[16] The joy does not last, however, as the poet thinks of
the hauntingly sad Chinese poem Li Sao (On Encountering
Sorrow).[17]

    Yet once again Pound refuses to stay in any one state of mind,
especially one that is morose. He presses back to that force in
nature that he stubbornly called "intelligence" (others use "instinct") and describes a city of sensibility like Venice, which grew
into its natural setting on the lagoon without making the setting
conform to it:

        but there is something intelligent in the cherry-stone
Canals, bridges, and house walls
                        orange in sunlight
But to hitch sensibility to efficiency?
            grass versus granite,
For the little light and more harmony
Oh God of all men, none excluded

This leads the poet to recall his youthful optimistic days, when he
was feverishly backing various economic reforms like the Schwund-
geld system (couponed money that would decrease in value if not
spent). He balances just rates of interest (12 percent, the rate of
Byzantium) with unjust ones (104 percent). Equating justice with
mercy, Pound declares that religions were stronger when they
placed their emphasis on exacting justice from laws, as in the Old
Testament, rather than on demanding blind faith. He then praises
ancient Egyptian builders over the prefabricated constructors who
are ruining communities by boxing in the soul (critics looking for
anti-Semitic references in Pound might well note the opposite
here):

And the host of Egypt, the pyramid builder,
        waiting there to be born.

No more the pseudo-gothic sprawled house
                        out over the bride there
                                (Washington Bridge, N.Y.C.)
                        ,but everything boxed for economy.

The notion of man imprisoned in his self-made environment is then contrasted with Plotinus' idea that the soul envelops the body in an incandescent shroud that animates and nurtures it.[18] Yeats had observed this phenomenon in the Cathedral of Notre Dame:

That the body is inside the soul—
                        the lifting and folding brightness
                                the darkness shattered,
                                        the fragment.
That Yeats noted the symbol over that portico
                                (Paris).
And the bull by the force that is in him—
                not lord of it,
                        mastered.

Then come three waves of different valences, all reflecting the constant shifts of feeling within the poet: first, a restatement of the purgatorial struggle of usury opposing the "just price" (prezzo giusto), as the sacristan Luigi Cairoli had indicated in his book, *Il Prezzo giusto nel medio evo* (The Just Price in the Middle Ages); secondly, a paradisal painting of Rock's world of frozen emerald grass and saffron light; and finally, plunging back into a hellish despair, a statement that the educational system is constantly growing worse, that constitutions are being ignored, and that the doctrine of original sin obscures the beauty of religion, as signified by the goddess Artemis.

Yet despite these unpleasant thoughts, the poet does not sink into mere *malvagità* or grumpiness, grouchiness. The thought of the sea brings him to an awareness of the eternal female force and an assurance that "in every woman, somewhere in the snarl is a tenderness."

With this sense of woman as redeemer, the poet rises up from visions of decay and emptiness to one of his favorite maxims, taken from Mencius, that a tax can be considered a share and is always

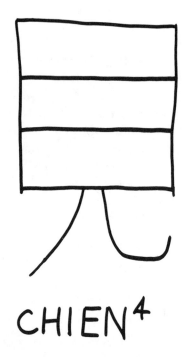

better than a fixed charge. The little phrase *scala altrui* (another man's staircase) is spoken by Dante's grandfather Cacciaguida to the Italian in his *Paradiso* 17.60 ("you will find how hard it is to climb another man's staircase"); it buttresses the idea of the poet's being forced to beg for his bread in someone else's house (not being part of a thriving, sharing community like the Siena under the Leopolds), and it also furthers the notion of an orderly rising (a staircase), which the reader is experiencing here in the verse.

Then occurs one of the most brilliant lines in *The Cantos:* "God's eye art 'ou, do not surrender perception."[19] Behind it lies Pound's study of the Chinese character *chien,*[4] which means "to see, to perceive, to be aware"; it is, in effect, a walking eye, and this human eye imagistically is but a mutation of the sun, which can be thought of as the eye of God:

A blue light under stars.

The ruined orchards, trees rotting. Empty frames at Limone.
And for a little magnanimity somewhere,

And to know the share from the charge
                    (scala altrui)
God's eye art 'ou, do not surrender perception.

Then comes Artemis again, goddess of untamed nature and purposeful slaughter, followed by Daphne, who is being changed into a tree. These rapid transformations are followed by another mention of Father Sun, who returns as the visible eye of the good in the universe, leading from darkness to illumination. However, the human mind, incapable of sustaining this magnificently detached movement of extralunary space, rolls in its own ceaseless motion from agony to serenity back to agony, like Ixion tortured on his wheel.

The poetics contained here are, of course, extraordinary. The reader comes back almost to the place where he began, with the sun and the light, but in the process he has moved through perception and pain. Pound lets us experience in this canto a true sensation of serenity and beauty that is a part of the ultimate contemplative vision. Yet one does not feel that Paradise, though perceptible, is fixed; indeed, why should it be? Even if this vision is not lasting, it is as close as any poet has come since Dante to a direct transmission of the beautiful and the good.

Canto 116, which seems to stand in its entirety, might appear to be a canto of despair. It contains lines like the following, which can be quoted out of context to show the general failure of Pound's poem:

I have brought the great ball of crystal;
                    who can lift it?
Can you enter the great acorn of light?
                    But the beauty is not the madness
Tho' my errors and wrecks lie about me.
And I am not a demigod,
I cannot make it cohere.

Despite the words about noncoherence, the lines do not say that Pound's mind is incoherent; they say that he cannot convert his senses or feelings into a rational mould; furthermore, they *do* say that he has delivered the ball of crystal, and thus, like all of

Pound's poetry—or, for that matter, poetry in general—they must be read *in context;* and they must also be balanced with differing statements elsewhere.

The canto does have its slow, sad, andante moments, but it opens with an allegro feeling, with the brisk leaps of dolphins, as in the Adriatic Sea off Venice or as caught by the gold craftsmen in the splendid mosaics of the Church of San Vitale in Ravenna:

Came Neptunus
         his mind leaping
             like dolphins,
These concepts the human mind has attained.
To make Cosmos—
To achieve the possible—

This is unquestionably one of the high points of enthusiasm in the Later Cantos. Here, as in his youth, Pound dreams of human perfectibility within a cosmic structure. At this point, the triumphant leaps forward seem to admit no limitations. But then Pound thinks of his real situation and of failure:

Muss., wrecked for an error,
But the record
         the palimpsest—
a little light
        in great darkness—
cuniculi—   [holes, dark passages]

The failure of Mussolini, who was ruined probably because he made a "mass" or mess "of laws" (Italian: *mucchio di leggi*) rather than a coherent form of government, is compared with a judgment by the poet of his own work, which is a palimpsest—that is, a manuscript that has been covered over many times with rewritings and erasures. Although Muss's work is gone, *The Cantos* affords a well-worn, well-hewn record that sheds "a little light"; the work offers glimpses of clarity out of the darkness, like the underground passages that issued from the tombs outside of Rome. In this sense, Pound is superior to Mussolini, who went down with his ill-fated production. Like Justinian, whose famous legal code was criticized for being too untidily inclusive ("Letters curing nothing": Litterae nihil sanantes), Mussolini left behind "a tangle of works unfinished." Pound, however, is moving through drafts and fragments toward an end.

For a time the poet thinks of unpleasantnesses: another old crank dead (it scarcely pays to wonder who); education burdening the young without inspiring them; and the Madonna shrouded by cigar smoke. Yet these things cannot depress the poet, who then proclaims his bearing forward of the light, and affirms:

How came beauty against this blackness,
Twice beauty under the elms—
        To be saved by squirrels and bluejays?
          "plus j'aime le chien"   [the more I like dogs]
Ariadne.

Once again, it is nature that redeems: the world of lovely creatures, including the beautiful Ariadne, who was abandoned by Theseus on Naxos, but was saved by the god Dionysus (Canto 2), who came to her in the company of leopards and other animals.

This affirmation of the natural world leads to a bold artistic preference, followed by a catalogue of writers and then a natural scientist who made definite, ascertainable achievements:

    Disney against the metaphysicals,
and Laforgue more than they thought in him,
Spire thanked me in proposito   [by design]
And I have learned more from Jules
          (Jules Laforgue) since then
deeps in him,
        and Linnaeus.

Pound prefers Walt Disney—either the Disney of childhood fantasy or of superb nature films—to a typical modern metaphysician, with his dry abstractions and total divorce from the physical world around him. Similarly, Jules Laforgue and André Spire were men who wrote in precise, memorable langue,[20] and Linnaeus has already been praised for his work in biological categorizing. This catalogue leads to a remarkable line from Dante's *Paradiso* 5.105, where the souls in the planet of Mercury exclaim: "Here is one *who will increase* our loves" (*Ecco chi* crescerà li nostri *amori*) as

Dante comes to join them.[21] The accent here is upon sharing—
upon welcoming more and more people into the brotherhood of
love and achievement—rather than upon selfishness or jealousy.

    This last paradisal thought, with all due thanks to Dante, leads
to a further involvement in the Italian's Paradise, as Pound dreams
of the third heaven (terzo cielo), the planetary round of Venus
(Venere), the spirit of love:

but about that terzo
          third heaven,
                    that Venere,
again is all "paradiso"
     a nice quiet paradise
                    over the shambles,
and some climbing
               before the take-off,
to "see again,"
the verb is "see," not "walk on"

At least two ideas seem to be on Pound's mind. In his reaching out
for the heaven of love, the poet realizes that he must try only to
envision it; he must not try to insist upon the idea as a reality, for
the"shambles" are all too present. Heaven to him is not a material
place to be walked on. Then, too, he may be thinking of the "walking eye" Chinese character, *chien*[4], which means "to know," and
which was discussed in relation to Canto 113. When Pound says "it
coheres all right," he is referring to his vision, his dream—not to
his notes, the logical build-up for his ideas, or to the real world in
Italy around him, where love is not in the house.

    The comparison with Dante continues as Pound excuses the
Italian's Hell and his own Heaven (see Chapter Four). Then, citing
the opening line of Dante's famous sestina, "With little daylight
and with a great circle of shade" (al poco giorno/ ed al gran cerchio
d'ombra),[22] Pound moves from the shadows upward:

But to affirm the gold thread in the pattern
                    (Torcello)
al Vicolo d'oro   [on the Lane of gold]
          (Tigullio).
To confess wrong without losing rightness:
Charity I have had sometimes,
               I cannot make it flow thru.

With the frankness that always marked his expression, Pound acknowledges that he has been wrong sometimes, but he does not grant complete error. He confesses that he has had "some" charity, but obviously, as he lamented in the *Pisan Cantos*, not enough at all times, and certainly not enough now to bathe his poetry with a final, all-accepting glow. Yet the idea of radiance never leaves him. He affirms the gold thread in the mosaic patterns on the island of Torcello north of Venice and on the "golden lane" near the Bay of Tigullio (possibly on the bay itself as the sunset trails its golden wake).

Then, in lines adapted from Dante, Pound asks for a quiet wish-fulfillment:

A little light, like a rushlight
　　　　to lead back to splendour.

These lines may be modeled from *Purgatorio* 1, where Dante gathers a rush or reed before beginning his ascent of Mount Purgatory in the golden glow of dawn. Or they may be related to *Inferno* 34.130, just before the incident, where he and Vergil ascend from the depths of the Underworld past the navel of Satan, along his lower body, and up through a little brook (*ruscelletto;* pronounced *roosh-eh-let-toh*) to view the Easter dawn. In either case, the hope is for light leading out of chaos or despair. The canto thus opens with dolphins leaping forward with intellective enthusiasm (the Christians of early times viewed dolphins as merciful, loving animals, full of vigorous hope), and it closes with the rush of humility and a vision, no matter how optative, of splendor. If this is not Paradise Gained, it is still not Paradise Lost; and it will never be Paradise Surrendered.

Even you were happy last Wednesday.
(Canto 92/621)

The Fragments trail away in the many moods of their maker: in joy, in sorrow, in hope, in despair, but not in passive acceptance or choleric indignation. The American edition closes with the compelling prayer and commitment to nature titled Canto 120. In a sense, these cantos show Pound accepting his mortality, asserting for the thousandth time the beauty and dignity of the cosmos, and muting his argumentations, but not surrendering his ideas. There is something haunting about an unfinished work, something that appeals to the imagination; in many ways, it is fitting that this most dogmatic of poets should have ended his life and his production quietly.

The second "Addendum for Canto 100," appearing on page 800 and dated "Circa 1941," shows the continuity of Pound's technique. It contains sharp images that recall the Pound of *Personae*: bamboo sticks striking olive branches; birds singing to the Renaissance composer Clement Jannequin; a bell-ringer from the little church of San Pantaleo in the Rapallo area playing a line from the famous aria of Verdi's *Rigoletto*—"one and two . . . that woman is fickle" (è mobile). Pound depicts a black head of hair bobbing through the white cherry branches on the sloping hill-path leading from Sant'Ambrogio down into town. This description is startlingly reminiscent of the two-line poem "In a Station of the Metro" that Pound wrote after he had visited Paris in 1911 and noted the blossomlike apparition of faces coming out of the dark subway tubing.[23] The gallery of pictures closes with an indelible scene from nature:

And a black head under white cherry boughs
    precedes us down the salita.
The water-bug's mittens show on the bright rock below him.

In March of 1941 Pound wrote these very lines from Rapallo to his Japanese friend Katue Kitasono, asking about the last one: "can you ideograph it; very like petals of blossom," and twice in the Later Cantos, he wove the exact image into his poetry.[24] The lines are classically lyric, showing that a man in his mid-fifties is fully capable of writing with the vigor and conciseness of youth.

The so-called "Notes for 117 et seq.," however, stem from a later period, when Pound had returned to Italy. Much of the love that Pound felt for nature is tinged here with sorrow concerning the inability of his friends and relatives to get along with one another. He was also drawn to two women, both of whom he loved, yet who did not like each other:

M'amour, m'amour   [my love, my love]
    what do I love and
        where are you?

Especially in the castle in the Tyrol, there were blue streaks of
wisdom and moments of blessedness, but there were also the
pangs of tragedy. The details are described by Princess de Rachewiltz in the closing pages of her biography, up to the time when
Pound finally uttered some lines from the Greek play *Electra* and
later left.[25] Pound describes this period in this way:

For the blue flash and the moments
        benedetta   [blessed]
the young for the old
      that is tragedy
And for one beautiful day there was peace.

The lines of this fragment are like a still-tense lightning rod quiver-
ing into stasis.

Taking refuge in an art that imitates and perfects nature,
Pound thinks of the sculptor Brancusi's lovely, rounded bird
nestling in the hollows of some real pines, and of snow frothing like
the foam of the sea, and—a favorite image that he also used elsewhere—a "Twilit sky leaded with elm boughs."[26] But the passion of
human commerce was so poignant that it constantly troubled him.
One can see the rationale for his last years of silence in the
following lines, where he moves from the Tarpeian Rock (from
which criminals were thrown in ancient Rome) to a prayer for the
construction of a church that will honor natural forces like Zagreus
(alternate name for Dionysus) and Semele (his mother, the bride of
God):

Under the Rupe Tarpeia
      weep out your jealousies—
To make a church
      or an altar to Zagreus   *Zagreus*
Son of Semele   *Semele*
Without jealousy
      like the double arch of a window
Or some great colonnade.

The voice of Pound as prophet, however, was never totally muted. His last advice to the tribe appears in the fragment on page 802. The first six lines (sestet) of this unrhymed sonnet have already been discussed in relation to the troubadours (see Chapter Three), for they contain two lines from Bernart de Ventadour's lark poem, mention of the rollercoaster roads of southern France, a scene of larks from Allègre, and a line about the bankruptcy (*faillite*) of François Bernouard, a publisher of magnificent editions of books.

After this evocation of human commitment to the beauties of art and nature—"The earth belongs to the living" (Thomas Jefferson)—Pound, like the Odysseus of Canto 1 come home, is ready to enter the spirit world, using two little mice and a delicate moth as his guide. The scene is somewhat reminiscent of Homer's *Odyssey*, with Odysseus equipped by Hermes with milkweed (*molü*) to face the temptress Circe in order to gain the means of entering the Underworld.[27] When this scene occurred in Canto 1, the Underworld was the past; now, at the end of the poem, it is death.

The depiction is also reminiscent of Dante's *Divine Comedy*, when the souls of departed kings assemble on the island of Mount Purgatory after their flight in an angelic chariot across the world from Rome (the other pole from the mountain); there they sleep, uneating, under the vigilant eye of Sordello. Dante can also be felt in the mention of the *farfalla*, or butterfly, which is gasping between two worlds—trying to slough off the earthly cocoon that enwraps him and to bob freely in the spiritual world of the afterlife.[28] But the poetry belongs neither to Homer nor to Dante; the poetry belongs to Ezra Pound. Here, at the close of his career, the poet exits with his precise collection of unforgettable words and images, and, before entering the outward stretches of the arcane, bequeaths a last word of hopeful warning to his fellow human beings:

Two mice and a moth my guides—
To have heard the farfalla gasping
    as toward a bridge over worlds.
That the kings meet in their island,
    where no food is after flight from the pole.
Milkweed the sustenance
    as to enter arcanum.

To be men not destroyers.

Author's Notes

INTRODUCTION: The Man Behind the Later Cantos

1. See *New York Times* (Nov. 2, 1972), p. 39.
2. For biographies, see Noel Stock, *The Life of Ezra Pound* (New York: Pantheon, 1970); Michael Reck, *Ezra Pound: A Close-Up* (New York: McGraw-Hill, 1967); and Charles Norman, *Ezra Pound*, rev. ed. (New York: Minerva, 1969).
3. *Letters of W. B. Yeats*, ed. Allan Wade (London: Hart-Davis, 1954), p. 543.
4. *Letters*, pp. 239, 247, 263.
5. See John P. Diggins, *Mussolini and Fascism: The View from America* (Princeton Univ. Press, 1972), pp. 240-69.
6. For an account by Pound's lawyer, see Julien Cornell, *The Trial of Ezra Pound* (New York: John Day, 1966).
7. See *Charles Olson and Ezra Pound: An Encounter at St. Elizabeths* (New York: Viking, 1975), which details the eventual rift between the two men.
8. Recounted in Harry M. Meacham's *The Caged Panther: Ezra Pound at St. Elizabeths* (New York: Twayne, 1967).
9. Mary de Rachewiltz, *Discretions* (1971), rpt. as *Ezra Pound: Father and Teacher* (New York: New Directions, 1975), p. 306.
10. Michael Reck, "A Conversation Between Ezra Pound and Allen Ginsberg," *Evergreen Review*, no. 55 (June 1968), pp. 27 ff. See also Allen Ginsberg, "Allen Verbatim," *Paideuma*, vol. 3, no. 2 (1974), pp. 253-73, esp. p. 266 for a defense of Pound's economic beliefs.
11. *Letters*, p. 294.
12. Archibald MacLeish, "The Venetian Grave," *Saturday Review* (Jan. 9, 1974), p. 29.
13. C. David Heymann, *Ezra Pound: The Last Rower* (New York: Viking, 1976), esp. pp. 279-92. Also, Alan Levy, "Ezra Pound's Voice of Silence," *The New York Times* (Jan. 9, 1972), Section 6 (magazine), pp. 14 ff.
14. Canto 120/803; the Faber edition does not contain this passage, because in the words of Peter du Sautoy, "we did not feel certain that these lines were what Pound intended to come at the end of the long poem" (*London Times Literary Supplement*, August 20, 1976, p. 1032). Despite the sudden, rather mysterious appearance of this final canto, there seems to be no question that Pound wrote it, and many readers feel that it is as fitting a close to the poem as one could wish.

199

CHAPTER ONE: The Central Ideogram of the Cantos

1. For Pound's own analyses, see *Confucius*, pp. 20-23; Canto 95/644.
2. See *ABC of Reading*, pp. 21-22; 101/723; 86/564.
3. *Guide to Kulchur*, p. 77.
4. E.g., George Dekker, *Sailing After Knowledge* (London: Routledge & Kegan Paul, 1963).
5. For details on characters, see *Annotated Index to "Cantos,"* ed. J.H. Edwards and W.W. Vasse (Berkeley: Univ. California, 1971). Pound freely renders last stanza of Sordello's *Atretan dei ben chantar* (Likewise I ought to sing well), ed. De Lollis, p. 180; Boni, p. 15.
6. See James J. Wilhelm, *Seven Troubadours* (University Park-London: Penn State, 1970), pp. 23-59.
7. For the added importance of the number five, see David Gordon, "The Sources of Canto LIII," *Paideuma*, vol. 5, no. 1 (1976), 129.
8. "Love of humanity," "righteousness," "reverence, propriety," "wisdom, prudence,"; see Chapter Ten.

CHAPTER TWO: The Three Changing Phases
of Woman and Gold

1. "She has won by lot the monuments of Cyprus"; the *orichalchi* is translated in the phrase that follows.
2. For identifications, see *Annotated Index to the "Cantos,"* ed. J.H. Edwards and W.W. Vasse (Berkeley: Univ. California, 1971).
3. *The Science of Money*, 2nd ed. rev. (New York: 1896; rpt. Burt Franklin, 1968), p. 3.
4. Cf. Cantos 77/468; 79/487. See Hugh Kenner, *The Pound Era*, p. 473, for picture, and p. 471.
5. See John Peck, "Pound's Lexical Mythography: King's Journey and Queen's Eye," *Paideuma*, vol. 1, no. 1 (1972), 3-36; also, Guy Davenport, "Persephone's Ezra," *New Approaches to Ezra Pound*, ed. Eva Hesse (Berkeley: Univ. California, 1969), pp. 145-73.
6. For Pound's uses of Egyptian material, see Boris de Rachewiltz, "Pagan and Magic Elements in Ezra Pound's Works," *New Approaches*, ed. Hesse, pp. 174-97.
7. Scotus, *De divisione naturae*, chaps. 20-23, in vol. 122 of *Patrologia Latina*, cols. 893-905; trans. in part by Myra L. Uhlfelder as *Periphyseon* (Indianapolis: Bobbs-Merrill, 1976).
8. Christine Brooke-Rose, *A ZBC of Ezra Pound* (Berkeley: California, 1971), pp. 183-207, has a masterly analysis.
9. Most professional philosophers will resent Pound's suggestion of pantheism here, as with Scotus, but the point is grammatical; alternate title of *Monologion* is *De divinitatis essentia* (On the Essence of Divinity) and that essence is rational *and* amatory: *Patrologia Latina*, vol. 158, esp. cols. 200 ff. Despite

Anselm's disclaimer that he is talking about essences and not substances, the Highest Nature is "through all and in all": *per omnia, et in omnibus* (chap. 14, col. 161).

10. Analyzed by Kenner, *Pound Era*, p. 544; Thomas Grieve, *Paideuma*, vol. 4, nos. 2-3 (1975), 390.

11. *History of Monetary Systems* (London, 1895; rpt. New York: Kelley, 1969), pp. 463-69 for Charles; 107-32 on gold.

12. Excellent treatment of this difficult part of poem by David Gordon, "The Azalea Is Grown," *Paideuma*, vol. 4, nos. 2-3 (1975), 223-99, esp. 291-92.

CHAPTER THREE: The Troubadours As Guides
                     to Poetry and Paradise

1. Stuart Y. McDougal, *Ezra Pound and the Troubadour Tradition* (Princeton Univ. Press, 1973).

2. *Personae*, pp. 28-29.

3. *ABC of Reading*, p. 52. See James J. Wilhelm, "Arnaut Daniel's Legacy to Dante and to Pound," *Italian Literature: Roots and Branches*, ed. G. Rimanelli and K.J. Atchity (New Haven: Yale, 1976), pp. 67-83.

4. *Essays*, pp. 94-108.

5. For text, see *Anthology of the Provençal Troubadours*, ed. R.T. Hill, T.G. Bergin, and others, 2nd ed. rev., 2 vols. (New Haven: Yale, 1973), vol. 1, no. 154.

6. Dante's description of Sordello "like a lion . . . when he crouches" (*a guisa de leon . . . quando si posa*) closes the canto.

7. Original text in Cesare de Lollis, *Vita e poesia di Sordello di Goito* (Halle: Niemeyer, 1896), p. 196, v. 1 and refrain.

8. Ed. De Lollis, p. 180, Canso 21, v. 17.

9. See Henry Bett, *Johannes Scotus Erigena: A Study in Medieval Philosophy* (rpt. New York: Russell & Russell, 1964); Peter Makin, "Ezra Pound and Scotus Erigena," *Comparative Literature Studies*, vol. 10, no. 1 (1973), 60-83; Walter B. Michaels, "Pound and Erigena," *Paideuma*, vol. 1, no. 1 (1972), 37-54.

10. See James J. Wilhelm, *Dante and Pound: The Epic of Judgement* (Orono: Univ. Maine, 1974), pp. 69-85.

11. *Lieder*, ed. C. Appel (Halle: Niemeyer, 1915), Canso 43, pp. 249-54.

12. *Translations*, pp. 19, 106-7.

13. Canso 41, vv. 23-24, ed. Appel, p. 235. The troubadour Folquet of Marseille is mentioned before, with an echo from Dante's *Paradiso* 9.112-13 ("nearby in this light").

14. Told in *Essays*, p. 139; 3rd ed. of dictionary (Heidelberg: Winter, 1961). Word occurs in Canso 13, v. 7, of *Er vei vermeils* (Now I see green).

15. Repeating words in *Lo ferm voler* (The firm will); see incomplete version in *Translations*, p. 425.

16. *Essays*, pp. 111, 137; *Translations*, p. 174, of Canso 12, v. 32.

17. For a picture of Excideuil's wave pattern and the news that the "real" Arnaut in this passage is T.S. Eliot, see Hugh Kenner, *The Pound Era* (Berkeley: Univ. California, 1971), pp. 336-37.

18. Hill-Bergin, *Anthology*, no. 80, v. 10.

19. Reprinted from James J. Wilhelm, *Medieval Song: An Anthology of Hymns and Lyrics* (New York: Dutton, 1971), p. 164.

20. Hill-Bergin, *Anthology*, no. 107; see Canto 113/788.

21. See Hendrik van der Werf, *Chansons of the Troubadours and the Trouvères* (Utrecht: Oosthoek, 1972), pp. 91-92; also, James J. Wilhelm's article in *Paideuma*, vol. 2, no. 2 (1973), 333-35.

22. Ed. Appel, Canso 44, vv. 45-48, p. 262.

23. For Bertran, see James J. Wilhelm, *Seven Troubadours* (University Park-London: Penn State, 1970), p. 156; for Cardinal, pp. 175 ff.

24. Identified as a town in the Haute-Loire department of France by Eva Hesse, *Letzte Texte* (Zurich: Arche, 1975), p. 81. For a relation of Pound's poetry to the geography of southern France, see Donald Davie, "The Cantos: Towards a Pedestrian Reading," *Paideuma*, vol. 1, no. 1 (1972), 55-62.

25. See Richard Sieburth, "Canto 119: François Bernouard," *Paideuma*, vol. 4, nos. 2-3 (1975), 329-32.

CHAPTER FOUR: Dante As a Cohering Voice
                  in the Later Cantos

1. Influence traced more widely in James J. Wilhelm, *Dante and Pound: The Epic of Judgement* (Orono: Univ. Maine, 1974).

2. Pound used the 1921 Società Dantesca ed. of *Divine Comedy;* I use the up-dated 1966-67 ed. of Giorgio Petrocchi, 4 vols. (Milan: Mondadori).

3. *Letters*, p. 331.

4. *Convivio*, ed. G. Busnelli and G. Vandelli, 2nd ed. A.E. Quaglio, 2 vols. (Florence: Le Monnier, 1964-68).

5. Francis Fergusson, *Dante* (New York: Macmillan, 1966), p. 37.

6. *Convivio* 4.8.2.

7. "The love that makes you beautiful": *Convivio* 3.13.9.

8. Hugh Kenner, *The Pound Era* (Berkeley: Univ. California, 1971), p. 448.

9. *Paradiso* 10, "in the Sun," Heaven of theologians, esp. vv. 40-43.

10. Pound says, "O Queen Venus,/ who moves the third heaven," adapting Dante's opening line of *Convivio*, First Canzone: "You (spirits) who by your intentions (*intendendo*) move the third heaven."

11. "What he (Love) dictates or says within" Dante writes down.

12. Entire passage is an amalgam of three cantos of *Paradiso: letizia,* 18.42; virtue, 18.60; *Buona . . . ,* 19.86; *Lume . . . ,* 19.64; gemmed light, 20.17; river over stones, 20.19-20; form from lute, 20.22-23.

CHAPTER FIVE: The Battle Against the Unholy
                      Marriage of Banking and Politics

1. All Benton references and quotations from vol. 1 of *Thirty Years' View,* 2 vols. (New York: Appleton, 1854-56; 2nd ed., 1861-62), pp. 70-221 *passim.*
2. H. J. Eckenrode, *The Randolphs: The Story of a Virginia Family* (New York: Bobbs-Merrill, 1946), p. 225.
3. Benton, p. 74.
4. St. George Tucker of Williamsburg, Va., edited Blackstone's work in 1804.
5. Pound here follows the work of the official U.S. Government statistician during the latter part of the nineteenth century, Alexander del Mar, *The History of Monetary Systems* (London, 1895; rpt. New York: Kelley, 1969), esp. pp. 107-32, 463-69.
6. Benton, p. 446.
7. See Pound, *Selected Prose,* pp. 309-11.
8. Benton, p. 87.
9. Details from Benton, respectively: pp. 104-5, 95, 112, 115, 123-24, 144, 167.
10. Benton, pp. 187 ff.
11. Benton, pp. 97-99.
12. Benton, p. 100; "Freeholds," pp. 102-4.
13. Benton, p. 106.
14. Benton, p. 111.
15. Benton, p. 112.
16. Benton, p. 119; cabinet, p. 120.
17. Benton, p. 122; West Indies trade, p. 124.
18. Benton, p. 133.
19. Benton, p. 187; preferred spelling; Pulteney.
20. Benton, pp. 191-93.
21. *Paideuma,* vol. 2, no. 1 (1973), 143.

CHAPTER SIX: Canto 90 As Incantation:
                The Poet As Priest of Nature

1. *Selected Prose,* pp. 71-72.
2. See Boris de Rachewiltz, "Pagan and Magic Elements in Ezra Pound's Work," *New Approaches to Ezra Pound,* ed. Eva Hesse (Berkeley: California, 1969), p. 190 *et passim.*
3. The San[1] Ku[1] are the "Three Officials" under the Emperor as stipulated in

the *Chou Kuan: Shao⁴-shih¹, Shao⁴-fu⁴*, and *Shao⁴-pao³*. See Mathews 5675a. Pound may also be thinking of the "Three Protecting Lords," peaks in the Gangkar Snow Range.

4. Cf. Part 7 of "Meditations in Time of Civil War" in *Collected Poems of W.B. Yeats* (New York: Macmillan, 1956), p. 203. See Leon Surette, "A Light from Eleusis," *Paideuma*, vol. 3, no. 2 (1974), 191-216.

5. Richard of St. Victor, *Benjamin Minor* 13; see *Paideuma*, vol. 2, no. 3 (1973), 501.

6. *Benjamin Minor* 20.65; *Paideuma*, vol. 2, no. 3 (1973), 500; a *per* should precede *quam*, and *similitudine* should read *similitudinis*.

7. See Chapter Five; also, Henry Adams, *John Randolph* (Boston: Houghton Mifflin, 1898), and William Cabell Bruce, *John Randolph of Roanoke*, 2 vols. (rpt. New York: Octagon, 1970), vol. 2, pp. 41, 49-60, for slaves.

8. Canto 104/741.

9. Inter alia: *Selected Prose*, p. 45.

10. *In avibus intellige studia spiritualia, in animalibus exercitia corporalia;* trans. in *Selected Prose*, p. 71.

11. The romantic sigh of *Purgatorio* 14.109: "the ladies and the cavaliers, the toils, the eases."

CHAPTER SEVEN: Under the Larches with Apollonius:
                     The Message of a Lost Messiah

1. Philostratus, *Life of Apollonius of Tyana*, 2 vols. (Cambridge: Harvard, 1969). All trans. by Conybeare unless indicated otherwise. Vol. 1 contains Books One to Five; vol. 2 has Six to Eight, with *Letters* and Eusebius' attacks. See also James Neault, "Apollonius of Tyana," *Paideuma*, vol. 4, no. 1 (1975), 3-36; also, Hugh Kenner, "Under the Larches of Paradise," *Gnomon: Essays on Contemporary Literature* (New York: McDowell, Obolensky, 1958), pp. 280-96. Greek transliterations follow Pound's excerpts, with only major errors noted.

2. Trans. C.P. Jones, ed. G.W. Bowersock (Baltimore: Penguin, 1970).

3. Pound derived his information about Julia from G.R.S. Mead, *Apollonius of Tyana* (1900; rpt. New Hyde Park; University Books, 1966), p. 55. Gerrit Lansing called my attention to the importance of Mead's work on Plotinus and mysticism for the Later Cantos, as well as Charles Olson's effect on Pound concerning Apollonius.

4. Cf. *The Great Digest* 10.12, 20, in *Confucius*, trans. E. Pound, pp. 75, 83. For King Hui (Huey), see *Mencius* 1.1-2; *Analects* 6.5-12.

5. Latin *periplum, periplus* derives from Greek *periplous*, "sailing around" by a feeling for the land in pre-compass days; it is free, instinctual, nonlogical.

6. 8.3, p. 277, is cited in Canto 91/616, when Apollonius is asked to strip on

appearing before Domitian, and replies: "Is this a bath-house? Or a Court House?"

7. Spatial effects conveyed in beautiful, lyric terms in Charles Olson's "Apollonius of Tyana," *Selected Writings*, ed. R. Creeley (New York: New Directions, 1966), pp. 133-56.

CHAPTER EIGHT: The Deacon and His Lombards: From Barbarism to Civilization

1. Both contained in *Patrologia Latina*, ed. J.P. Migne, vol. 95: *Ad Langobardicam Historiam*, cols. 419 ff.; *Historia Miscella*, cols. 739 ff. I italicize my own direct quotations from Latin, printing Pound's in Roman. Authorship of *Miscella* disputed. See Paul the Deacon, *History of the Lombards*, trans. W.D. Foulke, ed. E. Peters (1907; rpt. Philadelphia: Univ. Pennsylvania, 1974).

2. Mary de Rachewiltz, *Discretions* (1971), rpt. under title *Ezra Pound: Father and Teacher* (New York: New Directions, 1975), p. 269.

3. I find no exact sources; col. 448 mentions Thor presiding in bronze and quieting storms, while bodies (cadavera) are everywhere, as in II.4. All numbers in parentheses refer to column nos. in Migne edition.

4. "Woodpecker" or "magpie" is more exact for *picus*.

5. Latin says: *unusquisque quo libeat securus sine timore pergebat*. Passport troubles were involved in Pound's failure to leave Italy before World War II: Noel Stock, *Life of Ezra Pound* (New York: Pantheon, 1970), pp. 391 ff. Pound's date, 586, follows text.

6. See *The Lombard Laws*, trans. K.F. Drew, ed. E. Peters (Philadelphia: Univ. Pennsylvania, 1973), with "Rothair's Edict," pp. 39-130, followed by laws of Grimwald and Liutprand.

7. For details, see Canto 103/737, where his opponent Alchis or Alachi cries in Latin (and Pound translates) that he "would fill a well with priests' balls,/ heretics', naturally," based on col. 620.

8. "*Carolus cognomento Martellus post patrem*" (659).

9. Col. 903; the taxation phrase doesnot occur here; nor is the later reference Julia Domna in *Historia Miscella*. Pound would like Salonis to mean Salò, Italy, where Mussolini tried to piece together a republic, but the reference is to Yugoslavia.

10. Esp. Canto 97/682:

    Mirabile (read *mirabili*) brevitate correxit, says Landulph
    of Justinian's Code
    and built Sta Sophia, Sapientiae Dei

The fact that Justinian "corrected with marvelous brevity" is cited in cols. 467-68. Santa Sophia means "holy wisdom"; Sapientiae Dei, "for the wisdom of God."

11. The idea of "bronze to the cities" is from Mommsen: see Canto 89/594.

12. The Chinese phrase "Fu Lin" refers to the Prefect's City, here Constantinople; again linking East with West.

13. The rest of the quotation concerns the building of a temple.

14. Alexander del Mar, *History of Monetary Systems* (London, 1895; rpt. New York: Kelley, 1969), p. 115 *et passim;* even Pound's interest in Apollonius can be traced to p. 3.

CHAPTER NINE: Byzantium: The Sacred Symbol of Yeats,
                    the Well-run Metropolis of Pound

1. *Le Livre du préfet,* ou *L'Edit de l'Empereur Leon le Sage,* ed. Jules Nicole (Geneva: H. Georg, 1893) in *Institut nationale genevois,* vol. 1; repr. *Paideuma,* vol. 2, no. 2 (1973), 261-311, with commentary by Carroll F. Terrell, 223-42.

2. I use Terrell's rendition: pp. 236-37. Cf. David Gordon, *Paideuma,* vol. 2, no. 3 (1973), 503.

3. *ABC of Reading,* p. 22.

4. Pound used this dictionary, possibly in an abridged form, see p. 656. The first word, *alogistous,* literally means "untalking" or "not connected to the Logos"; hence, Pound's comment on its Utopian usage.

5. Obviously meant to be compared with $chih^1$, a word applied to crass go-getters.

6. Pound thinks of "the East bank from Beaucaire," which is the town of Tarascon across the Rhone River in southern France. Both cities were known as fair centers, and, probably like Marseille, founded by Greeks. More remotely, there is the suggestion of "beautiful Cairo" and its bazaar.

7. For a summary of Du Cange's activities, see Terrell, p. 237.

8. Technically, modern Greek *enoikion* is "rent," but Nicole's reading is possible, and even more plausible when dealing with a grocer; see his text, p. 55.

9. For De Bosschère, see Charles Norman, *Ezra Pound,* rev. ed. (New York: Minerva, 1969), pp. 114, 225; also, Nicole, chap. 14, p. 49, which pictures an ideal state, and has the leather going for the proper purpose.

10. Chapter 16, p. 52: the distinction from Sheep-Dealers is implicit in the precise delineation of the activities of both classes.

11. Same meaning in Latin *ad pretium empti,* chap. 18, pp. 53-55; repeated by Pound for emphasis.

12. The name for bakers (*mankipes*) is taken from their ovens (*mankipia*, p. 53); *four* is French (Nicole's language) for "oven."

13. The fact that the direct address form for *Helios* is not used stamps this as Pound's own creation.

14. Canto 97/668; Alexander del Mar, *History of Monetary Systems* (rpt. New York: Kelley, 1969), pp. 131, 107-32.

15. In *De Officiis* 2.89, chap. 25, Cato the Elder, when asked how to run an estate, replies, "Raise cattle well," and the second best way: "*Raise cattle well enough*" (*Satis* bene *pascere*); and when asked, "What about money-lending?" replies, "How about murder?" (*Quid . . . occidere?*) Cicero also says (2.71, chap. 20) that "all humble people are not dishonest" (*omnes non improbi humiles*). In *Purgatorio* 1.42, Dante describes Cato as moving like a proud, honest bird; see James J. Wilhelm, *Dante and Pound*, p. 148.

16. Unpublished letters in Cornell University Library: Nov. 19, 1954: "'Constantinople our Star' (just to annoy you by retrospect). You can't have KNOWN much"; and Feb. 3, 1957: "wish you cd/ remember what putt you onto CONstantinople our star. You thought it was central."

17. See *Collected Poems of W.B. Yeats* (New York: Macmillan, 1956); "Sailing to Byzantium," p. 191; "Byzantium," p. 243.

CHAPTER TEN: What Confucius Told K'ang Hsi
to Tell the Modern World

1. *The Sacred Edict*, ed. F.W. Baller (Shanghai: China Inland Mission, 1892), 6th ed. (1924) reprinted in part in *Paideuma*, vol. 2, no. 1 (1973), 83-112, preceded by Carroll F. Terrell's introduction, 69-81. Chinese characters examined in great detail by David Gordon, "Thought Built on Sagetrieb," *Paideuma*, vol. 3, no. 2 (1974), 169-90, and "Pound's Use of the Sacred Edict in Canto 98," vol. 4, no. 1 (1975), 121-68. For Thomas Grieve's "Annotations to the Chinese in *Section: Rock-Drill*," see *Paideuma*, vol. 4, nos. 2-3 (1975), 361-508.

2. *Mathews' Chinese-English Dictionary*, rev. ed. (Cambridge: Harvard, 1972). Baller also published *Analytical Chinese-English Dictionary* (Shanghai, 1925). Chinese characters are known by their Mathews numbers in consecutive order.

3. Baller, p. 20: "All these members of the same clan are like . . . the many branches and countless leaves of a tree; which all spring from the same root."

4. Baller, p. 99, note; see Mathews 5497. Adjacent characters align i^4 (justice) with $shen^1$ (profound); $t'ai^4p'ing^2$ means "very flat," and refers to the Earth and equilibrium. En^1 is "virtue"; $ch'ing^2$, "passion." $Feng^1$ is "wind" or "breath"; cf. Gordon, vol. 4, no. 1, 139-40.

5. See 98/687.

6. Baller, p. 119: *Kiang Sheng U* are "Laws of Government."

7. See Canto 88/580, citing *Mencius* 3.3 (Baltimore: Penguin, 1970), p. 98.

CHAPTER ELEVEN: Napoleon: The Lesson of
Meaningless Revolution

1. I use the 1880 ed. of the Hoey-Lillie trans. *Mémoirs of Madame de Rémusat*, 3 vols. (New York: Appleton), with consecutive page nos. This may have been Pound's source, since French is conspicuously absent in his citations.

2. Canto 105/749. See James J. Wilhelm, *Medieval Song* (New York: Dutton, 1971), p. 155; *Personae*, p. 152.

3. Cf. Canto 62/349; 70/409; 71/418.

4. See articles by John Peck and Jamila Ismail in *Agenda*, vol. 9, nos. 2-3 (1971), 26-69, 70-87.

5. Pound seems to be looking at a pictograph involved in the death rites of the Na-khi (see Epilogue): "The Na-khi ^{1}Hä^{2}zhi^{1}p'i" in *Bulletin de l'Ecole Française de l'Extrême-Orient*, vol. 37 (1937), 40-119; esp. 59, 94; on 103: "The soul and body of the deceased is now at peace." See Plate 27. Cf. Peck, p. 51, n. 13, based on Rock's *The ^{2}Zhi^3 Mä Funeral Ceremony* (Vienna: St. Gabriel's Mission, 1955), 197, n. 7.

6. Pound often cites the words of Ernest Renan: "*La bêtise humaine est la seule chose qui donne une idée de l'infini*" (*Selected Prose*, p. 424).

CHAPTER TWELVE: In Praise of Anselm and
a Vital Christian Humanism

1. *Compendio di storia della filosofia*, ed. A. Carlini, 2 vols. (Florence: Villacchi, 1921-24), vol. 1, pp. 238 ff.; *Saint Anselme de Cantorbéry* (Paris: Didier, 1856), pp. 459 ff.

2. *Liber apologeticus contra Gaunilonem*, chap. 1, col. 249: "*si vel cogitari potest esse, necesse est illud esse.*" All of Anselm's works cited here contained in vol. 158 of *Patrologia Latina* (abbreviated in notes *PL*), ed. J.P. Migne, with column numbers for pages.

3. In *Proslogion*, chap. 18, col. 237, he uses the phrase "*nullo intellectu divisibilis,*" and in *De fide Trinitatis*, chap. 3, col. 271: "*nec intellectu dissolvi posset.*"

4. At Bari, Anselm made his famous speech against the Greeks, who were trying to tamper with the Trinity by linking the Holy Spirit directly to the Father and thus bypassing the Son, the human Christ element.

5. *Saint Anselme*, p. 371.

6. For the use of *consuetudines* as legal rights, see Eadmer, *Historia novorum*, *PL*, vol. 159, cols. 352, 336, 337, 375, 383; for Pound's phrase *usu terrae*, col.

372. Related to Coke and English law by David Gordon, *Paideuma*, vol. 4, nos. 2-3 (1975), 223-99.

7. As corrollaries for Pound's political phrases, Anselm offers the metaphysical *"unitas essentiae"* and *"pluralitas personarum"*: *De processione spiritus sancti*. chap. 29, col. 324.

8. *Gesta regum Anglorum* in *PL*, vol. 179, as well as other eds.

9. For his letter to Anselm, see *PL*, vol. 163, Epistola 73, cols. 90-91, Epistola 85, cols. 105-06, esp. *"Unde Jesum . . . ,"* Pound's "byJayzus," p. 749.

10. Treated at length in James J. Wilhelm, *Seven Troubadours* (University Park-London: Penn State, 1970), pp. 37-38.

11. For an excellent analysis of phrase and role of Layamon, see Christine Brooke-Rose's "Lay me by Aurelie," in *New Approaches to Ezra Pound*, ed. Eva Hesse (Berkeley: Univ. California, 1969), pp. 242-79.

12. *Chronicon Centulense*, contained in *PL*, vol. 174, cols. 1211 ff.; *Visio Caroli* in 3.21, cols. 1287 ff.

13. *PL*, vol. 174, col. 1287.

14. See James J. Wilhelm, *Seven Troubadours*, pp. 154-55, for translation and relationship of Bertran to Pound.

15. The importance of the saint was not emphasized until Karl Barth, who popularized him; Barth stressed Anselm's faith rather than his reason—in direct contrast with Pound.

EPILOGUE: Those Haunting Shards,
the Final Fragments

1. Joseph F. Rock, *The Ancient Na-khi Kingdom of Southwest China*, 2 vols. (Cambridge: Harvard, 1947), Harvard-Yenching Institute Monograph Series, vols. 8-9. Excerpts and pictures by Carroll F. Terrell, *Paideuma*, vol. 3, no. 1 (1974), 90-122. Articles on Fragments by Hugh Kenner and Donald Davie in *Agenda*, vol. 8, nos. 3-4 (1970), 7-18, 19-26, resp. Also useful for explanations of allusions is Eva Hesse's German translation with notes: *Letzte Texte* (Zurich: Arche, 1975). I omit from discussion Canto 114, which I do not find poetically exciting.

2. Rock, "The Romance of ^{2}K'a-^{2}mä-^{1}gyu-^{3}mi-^{2}gkyi," *Bulletin de l'Ecole Fran-çaise d'Extrême-Orient*, vol. 39 (1939), 1-152; 5 ff.

3. Rock, "The ^{2}Muan ^{1}bpö Ceremony or the Sacrifice to Heaven as Practiced by the ^{1}Na-^{2}khi," *Monumenta Serica*, vol.13 (1948), 1-160. See Jamila Ismail, "'News of the Universe' . . . ," *Agenda*, vol. 9, nos. 2-3 (1971), 70-87.

4. See James J. Wilhelm, *Dante and Pound*, pp. 131-33.

5. "Romance," following quotations from pp. 41, 42, 50, 51, 67.

6. "Romance," pp. 89, 92.

7. The Na-khi believe that men have nine fates and women seven; they put this number of grains under the tongues of corpses to guarantee safe passage into the afterlife; "Romance," p. 5.

8. See the suppositions of John Peck, "Landscape as Ceremony in the Later *Cantos*," *Agenda*, vol. 9, nos. 2-3 (1971), 56-59; also, article in *Agenda*, vol. 8, nos. 3-4 (1970), 33.

9. "²Muan ¹bpö," Preface.

10. Cf. Canto 103/732.

11. *Selected Prose*, pp. 437-39.

12. Cf. Canto 90/607.

13. "re USURY:/ I was out of focus, taking a symptom for a cause./ The cause is AVARICE," signed 1972 (*Selected Prose*, p. 6).

14. See Hugh Kenner, *The Pound Era* (Berkeley: Univ. California, 1971), pp. 549, 551.

15. The reference is to Richard Aldington's translation of a Sappho poem titled by him "To Atthis"; see Kenner, *The Pound Era*, pp. 55-58; p. 185 for mention of Hilda Doolittle, Richard's wife.

16. Text in *Anthology of the Provençal Troubadours*, ed. R.T. Hill, T.G. Bergin, and others, 2nd ed. rev., 2 vols. (New Haven: Yale, 1973), vol. 1, no. 107.

17. See Jamila Ismail, "'News of the Universe' . . . ," *Agenda*, vol. 9, nos. 2-3 (1971), 75.

18. *Enneads* 4.23.

19. Cf. Canto 106/755.

20. For Laforgue, see *Literary Essays*, pp. 280-84; Spire, *Literary Essays*, pp. 285-89.

21. See also Cantos 89/590, 93/631.

22. *Dante's Lyric Poetry*, ed. K. Foster and P. Boyde (Oxford: Clarendon, 1967), pp. 162-65.

23. *Personae*, p. 109; *Selected Poems*, p. 35.

24. See *Letters*, p. 348, with note; cf. 87/574, 91/616.

25. *Discretions* or *Ezra Pound: Father and Teacher*, pp. 302-7.

26. Cf. Cantos 106/755, 107/761.

27. *Odyssey* 10.305; cf. Cantos 47/237, 53/263.

28. *Purgatorio* 10.125; cf. Canto 92/619.

Bibliography

Works of Ezra Pound in editions cited in text:

ABC of Reading. New York: New Directions (paper), 1971.
A Lume Spento and Other Early Poems. New York: New Directions, 1965.
The Cantos. New York: New Directions, 1972; London: Faber & Faber, 1968.
Confucius: The Great Digest, The Unwobbling Pivot, The Analects, New York: New Directions (paper), 1969.
Guide to Kulchur. New York: New Directions (paper), 1970.
Jefferson and/or Mussolini. New York: Liveright (paper), 1970.
Letters of Ezra Pound. Edited by D.D. Paige, New York: Harcourt, 1950; rpt. *Selected Letters (1907-41),* New Directions (paper), 1971.
Literary Essays. Edited by T.S. Eliot, New York: New Directions (paper), 1972.
Make It New. New Haven: Yale, 1935.
Pavannes and Divagations. New York: New Directions, 1958.
Personae: Collected Poems. Rev. ed. New York: New Directions, 1971.
Selected Poems. New York: New Directions (paper), 1957.
Selected Prose 1909-65. New York: New Directions, 1973.
Spirit of Romance. New York: New Directions (paper), 1968.
Translations of Ezra Pound. Introduction by Hugh Kenner, 2nd ed. New York: New Directions (paper), 1963.

Index of Allusions to Pound's Cantos

General Index